Step-by-step tutorials with tips and techniques for beautiful, modern celebration cakes

Pamela McCaffrey

First published in August 2022 by Squires Kitchen Publishing. The Packhouse, Blackmoor Estate, Blackmoor, Liss, Hampshire, GU33 6BP, UK.

Copyright: Pamela McCaffrey 2022

ISBN-13: 978-1-905113-62-0

Printed and bound in Turkey by Imago Publishing Limited.

Publisher: Squires Kitchen Publishing

Editor: Stephanie Roker

Creative Director: Sarah Ryan

Photography: Iain McCaffrey

SK Photography: Alister Thorpe

I would like to dedicate this book to the two loves of my life: my late husband John (Mac to everyone) and our son Iain.

First of all, I would like to say a general thank you to everyone at Squires, past and present, for creating such a warm and welcoming environment with which to be involved. More specifically I would like to thank Jenny Weaver (Royle) for putting my cakes in *Wedding Cakes: A Design Source* magazine and later including me in the book *Designer Cake Decorating*; Adele Harrison (Duthie) for asking and trusting me to create projects for *Cakes & Sugarcraft* magazine; Sarah Ryan for championing me and for her consistently fabulous design that showcases all of our work so flatteringly; and Stephanie Roker for her tireless editing and extreme patience as deadlines come roaring into view.

To Sarah and Stephanie in particular, huge thanks for their faith in me and for giving me this incredible opportunity to write and put this book together.

I must also thank Shikhita Singh and Jessica Wigg for convincing me that I was up to teaching and for the confidence that it gave me.

I have to thank the many people online who have favourited, liked and followed me from my first tentative steps right up to now. You have been so encouraging and supportive.

Finally, special thanks to my son Iain for taking such beautiful photography of all my cakes and step-by-step photos, and for his unfailing love and support. I couldn't do it without him.

Everyone has played an essential part in guiding me to this point. I have been very fortunate and am phenomenally grateful.

cakes
MADE WITH
LOVE

INTRODUCTION

I am amazed to find myself writing this. I had no intention of selling my cakes, of teaching, of doing tutorials or even of writing a book, and yet somehow I have accidentally wound up doing them all – and at a most unexpected time. For many, many years the only decorated cakes I made were the occasional ones for friends or family, until – suddenly – I caught the bug. As the cakes mounted up, my son suggested that I put them online and the response was incredibly generous and flattering.

While I do have a creative background (I trained in costume and design at Central Saint Martins), as a cake designer/maker I am completely self-taught and I did wonder if people were just being nice. But as requests came in and I was asked to teach in London, as well as being published in magazines in the UK, the United States, India and Australia, my confidence grew – maybe I was quite good at this!

I realise that I have been very lucky. I think that some of my luck has come from the fact that I was fortunate enough to start doing this with no thought of where it might take me but purely for the pleasure of it, the joy of it, the love of it.

I hope that this passion is something you can take from the book as you try things out and experiment. That the joy and love you put into a cake can not only be its own reward, but that it somehow translates when you make a cake for someone else. They'll be able to sense that pleasure and joy in a cake that has been made, for them, with love.

Approach To Decoration

Of course, it's not all sunshine and roses (well, there are quite a few roses!). All skills take practice and your first attempt is not likely to be your best. Sometimes there is more than one way of doing things; I don't always do things the same way, perhaps a result of being self-taught. So, where possible, I'd highly recommend trying different methods and figure out which one is the best fit for you.

It's easy with something like sugarcraft to get caught up in aiming for perfection, and while that is something I would generally support, it is important to realise when to step away from that path. If a cake in the book has a geometric element, then aim for as much precision as possible because errors in this will show. If it is an abstract or floral element, there is a point after which small things will not affect the cake as a whole.

This is particularly true when it comes to flowers and leaves. The organic world is messy; a bunch of flowers can look uniform and perfect from a distance, but get up close and they will all vary to some degree in size, shape, colour and condition. Your flowers don't have to look like they came off a production line. Variety is good and a broken petal is not the end of the world, in fact it may even add character!

Another aspect of flowers to consider is how realistic you wish them to be. My approach leans towards the essence of a flower rather than a botanical recreation, similar to an illustrator with a style versus a botanical artist. The instructions in this book broadly reflect this, but they will also give you a good foundation if you wish to move in the botanical direction.

An advantage of not restricting yourself to botanical accuracy is that it gives you creative freedom. You can modify flowers or even create fantasy flowers in sizes, shapes and colours that suit your design. It is important that all of a cake's components work together to give the final piece balance.

Thoughts On Design

Balance is key when it comes to the overall look of a cake. It relates not only to the whole cake, but also to local areas of it. A floral display should be balanced within itself, as well as with other components on the cake.

To be honest, I feel that balance, along with a lot of design, is an instinctive thing; a feeling that something is missing or that something is needed. However, if you are struggling with it, perhaps think of an element having a complimentary component, frequently in a diagonal direction. If a cake has only one decorative piece, the balance comes from the element itself and its placement on the cake in relation to the size, shape and number of tiers.

The aesthetics of a design is of course influenced by personal preference, and mine – which I hope shows from the cakes in this book – is for clean, elegant or pretty cakes. With this in mind, I think it's worth remembering when (hopefully) you design your own cakes, not to

do too much. When it comes to colour try not to use too many, as more than three or four plus white risks becoming muddled. An empty space does not have to be filled; sometimes things need room to breathe. Space can be a choice, as well as a consequence of a design. Lastly, just because you can do something doesn't mean you should. Throwing too many techniques at a cake makes it lose focus.

Moving Forward

I hope that the projects contained here give you the tools and confidence to enjoy cake design, and that you can take the cakes, techniques and approaches in this book and use them as inspiration and a starting point for your own designs, whether pursuing cake design as a hobby or with an eye to a business.

To finish with, a note of encouragement to all beginners. I mentioned at the start that my journey came "at a most unexpected time." So I want you to remember it is never too late to start yours. I didn't start on this path until I was 78, and that was 11 years ago – I'll let you do the maths!

In the meantime, I encourage all of you to carry on making cakes with love.

CONTENTS

104

Orange Blossom Beauty

116

Spring Wedding

126

Golden Anniversary

136

A Sign Of Summertime

148

Fresh As A Daisy

162

A Walk In The Woods

176

Fabulous Fondant Frills

190

Hello Autumn

204

Frosted Fantasy Flowers

216

Deck The Halls

EQUIPMENT, EDIBLES AND FOOD COLOURS

You will need the same basic edibles and equipment to decorate most of the designs in this book. If you make cakes regularly, it's worth investing in the items you don't already have.

Any specific requirements for edibles and equipment are listed at the beginning of each cake design tutorial, so you can make sure you have everything you need before you start.

All of the items are readily available from sugarcraft suppliers, see page 232.

EQUIPMENT

The possible list of cake decorating equipment is almost endless but it's not essential to have everything, especially when getting started. The equipment listed here will comfortably allow you to do most things. It's always good to look at your tools and think what else you can do with them above what they are each intended for – you may not always need to get a specialised tool.

1 Cake Boards And Drums

Use these as a base for all of your cakes. Thicker cake drums should be used to support the whole cake and thinner cake boards should be used underneath each cake tier. They come in an array of shapes, sizes and thicknesses.

2 Cake Leveller

A cake leveller helps you easily split cakes into level layers of equal depth. Having a consistent depth of layers keeps the filling evenly distributed and enhances the appearance of a cut slice of the finished cake.

3 Spirit Level

A spirit level is a vital tool for making sure your cakes are level, from assembling the cut layers of a tier to stacking multiple tiers together. Aesthetically it is important cakes are level, even just a singe tier, and it is technically essential when stacking cakes.

4 Turntable

A turntable that rotates and tilts will make it easier for you to work around the sides of a cake without handling it.

5 Palette Knives

Large cranked palette knives (spatulas) are ideal for smoothing cake fillings and coverings. Mini palette knives have a flexible blade you can use for sliding under thin petals and leaves, and for picking up tiny pieces of modelled sugar. The tip can also be used to cut rolled out pastes.

6 Cake Scrapers

Whether you're covering a cake with buttercream, ganache or royal icing, a scraper will ensure it has a smooth, even and professional finish. Simply apply a little pressure, then run the straight edge of the scraper around the side of the cake.

7 Non-stick Rolling Pins

Use a large non-stick rolling pin for rolling out sugarpaste to cover cakes. Use small rolling pins to roll out pastes for finer, more detailed work.

8 Non-stick Boards

These are essential for rolling out the pastes smoothly. Some boards have grooves within them to create ridges in the paste for wired petals and leaves. This type of board can also be turned over and used as a flat, non-stick surface.

9 Pastry Brush

A pastry brush has multiple uses, from brushing off crumbs and brushing on water to applying paint effects to a covered cake.

10 Smoothers

Cake smoothers are used to smooth sugarpaste-covered cakes to achieve a flawless finish. They are either solid or flexible plastic. Solid smoothers help give a flat, smooth finish to the sides and top, while flexible smoothers used in a combination of rounded and straight edges can be utilised to create perfectly crisp edges for a clean, polished and professional finish.

11 Dowels

Both solid and hollow cake dowels provide stability when inserted into stacked cakes. Dowels are typically plastic or wooden.

12 Sharp Knife

Always helpful to have in your tool kit when needing to trim away edges, cutting out sugarpaste strips or simply neatening things up.

13 Cornflour Duster

You can buy these dusting bags or make your own. They're ideal to use with flower paste, sugarpaste and modelling paste for lightly dusting work surfaces and prevent sticking.

14 Pizza Cutter

Not just for pizza, you can use this cutter to easily trim round drums, boards and cakes.

15 Spacers

Spacers can either be long strips that lay at the sides of the sugarpaste or rings that fit on your rolling pin. Use them whilst rolling out to achieve an even thickness.

16 Foam Pad

Work on a food-grade foam pad when using tools to shape a petal or leaf. If you use tools to shape flower paste on a hard surface like a non-stick board, it will damage the petal or leaf. Some foam pads have holes in which are useful for shaping flowers and calyces made using the Mexican hat technique.

17 Modelling Tools

Modelling tools are essential to have in your cake decorating arsenal, all of which can be used with flower paste, sugarpaste, modelling paste, marzipan and much more. Each tool has a purpose and is there to help you make stunning models and sugar flowers. You don't need to have every tool out there, but it would be helpful to start off with a few. I'd recommend a ball tool, dresden tool (also known as a petal & leaf shaper) and a veining tool, as these are most frequently used.

18 Cutters

Basic circle pastry cutters and other simple shapes can be used to create a whole array of decorations. There are also cutters available for most types of flowers and leaves, which make recreating the natural shapes quick and easy. If you are thinking of buying a metal cutter, choose one made of stainless steel with a solid structure so it will not warp or go rusty.

19 Veiners

Moulded veiners are the best way to recreate the natural lines found in petals and leaves, especially those with complex veins. Available in either one piece or as double-sided veiners, they are used to emboss the surface of the flower paste. You can find a wide range of specially designed veiners in sugarcraft shops; among them, double-sided veiners are the most effective ones for creating a realistic finish as they vein the front and back of the petal or leaf.

20 Acrylic Discs

Use acrylic discs to achieve a perfectly smooth, flawless finish on your cakes with buttercream or ganache. These acrylic discs are also sometimes called ganache plates.

21 Formers

Formers can be used for drying and shaping sugar work. Small polystyrene balls, bud shapes and egg shapes can be used as the bases for flowers and buds; these work well as they are lighter than flower paste. Food-grade foam drying trays, apple trays and polystyrene domes and balls in different sizes are useful for keeping petals and other shapes in a cupped form while they dry.

22 Paintbrushes

It is helpful to have a range of good quality, food-safe brushes in different sizes. For edible glue, use a small brush for precision. When dusting colour onto cake tiers, use a cosmetic brush reserved solely for sugarcraft as it has lots of fine hairs and holds more dust colour for better results. For dusting colour onto the edges of petals and leaves, use a flat brush held at a right angle to the edge. For painting, use a fine brush.

23 Floral Wires

Covered floral wires are used to give petals and leaves extra support. Usually, white wire is used for a petal and green wire for a leaf. The higher the gauge (width) number, the finer the wire.

24 Floral Tape

Floral tape is used to cover the wire stem of a sugar flower or leaf. It is also used to bind arrangements together. Floral tapes are available in a range of widths and colours.

25 Tape Splitter

This handy tool allows you to safely cut and shred floral tape evenly and easily.

26 Stamens

Flower stamens are used to create your sugar flowers. They come in bunches and are available in an array of different sizes and colours.

27 Piping Nozzles And Bags

Use small greaseproof paper bags to add decorative piping with royal icing or chocolate, and use large plastic bags (ideally reusable ones) to fill cakes with neat swirls of buttercream. Piping nozzles (tips) can be used in both types of piping bag to create a wide variety of patterns and borders, as well as petals and leaves.

28 Micro Scales

Useful to have on hand if you need to weigh out small quantities of pastes.

29 Ribbon Cutter

An adjustable ribbon cutter is an invaluable tool for creating sugarpaste or flower paste strips of an equal width. Strips can be cut from a couple of millimetres to a couple of inches wide. The strips can be used in various ways, such as stripes on a cake or shaped into ribbons.

30 Tweezers And Pliers

Pointed tweezers and fine nose pliers are essential tools for sugar flower arrangements. Use them to bend the wire stems; it can sometimes be hard to arrange them using just your hands without knocking the delicate sugar work.

31 Small, Sharp Scissors

Fine, pointed scissors are useful for making small cuts in sugar work. The finer the point of the blades, the easier they are to use.

32 Craft Knife

A craft knife is ideal for adding details and cutting out templates or small elements of a design. If you don't have a craft knife, a scalpel makes a good substitute.

33 Razor Blades

Perfect for making clean, neat cuts.

34 Rulers And Tape Measure

Useful for measuring the circumference of cakes or when cutting out specific heights and widths of paste.

35 Posy Picks

These are pushed into cakes and flowers and leaves are then inserted into them.

EDIBLES

Cake decorations are usually made from edible products to ensure they are safe to display on your cakes. However, make sure the recipient is aware that decorations, such as sugar flowers, shouldn't be consumed if they're made with any inedible items like stamens and wires. In the instance where inedible items are used for decoration, such as dried foliage, always remove them before cutting the cake.

Sugarpaste

Sugarpaste is used for covering cakes and cake drums. It sets firm but not hard, so it is still soft enough to be edible. Sugarpaste can be made to set harder if required by adding CMC, a cellulose gum. When colouring sugarpaste, it's best to leave it to sit for a few hours to allow it to settle and for the colour to fully develop.

Flower Paste

Flower paste is primarily used for making flowers and leaves. Unlike sugarpaste, it sets hard. This means it is important to keep it wrapped up when not in use. Stiff or slightly dried out flower paste can be softened to a degree by adding a bit of white vegetable fat. Flower paste and sugarpaste can be mixed together to make a paste that won't set fully hard but is firmer to work with.

Modelling Chocolate

Modelling chocolate – essentially a combination of chocolate and glucose syrup – is malleable like flower paste and holds a shape but stays soft enough to eat. Its smooth consistency makes it great for moulds, modelling and sculpting. It can also be combined with sugarpaste and used to cover cakes.

Royal Icing

Royal icing is made with icing sugar, egg whites, lemon juice and water, but it's also available in packets that just need to have water added. Depending on the consistency it can be used in various ways, including piping, flooding or for fixing items together. Stiff peak icing holds an upright peak and can be used to join items or to pipe dots and fine details. Soft peak icing is when the peak droops and is good for outlining on biscuits. Flood icing is used for filling in outlines: it does not leave a peak and will settle to flat in about eight seconds.

Edible Glue

Edible glue is used to stick together the components of sugar flowers and is one way to attach decorations to cakes.

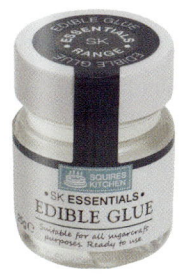

Confectioners' Glaze

Items can be brushed, dipped or sprayed with this edible glaze to give them a shine.

White Vegetable Fat

This can be used to attach decorative flower paste or sugarpaste elements to cakes or cake drums. It grips firmly but still allows the items to be repositioned. It also prevents edible pastes from sticking to your work surfaces, cutters, veiners and moulds.

Clear Alcohol

Edible dust food colours can be dissolved in clear alcohol, such as vodka or gin, to make a watercolour-like paint.

Wafer Paper

Wafer paper is an edible paper made from potato starch. It can be shaped into petals and leaves or any number of other shapes – organic and geometric. It can be coloured with edible food dusts, painted or printed on with an edible ink printer. Wafer paper can be used stiff or softened by steaming or with a mix of cooled, boiled water, glycerin and gelatine.

GUIDE TO FOOD COLOURS

There are many different types of food colouring, each suited to one or more of the various mediums that can be coloured. When it comes to colour, you usually get the best results by mixing your own colours rather than using them straight from the pot. You can achieve more subtlety and variety this way.

Dusts

Edible dust or powder colours are most often used to colour dried flower paste flowers and leaves, and is applied with a brush. Once the dust has been applied, it can be fixed in place by carefully holding the item in the steam of a steamer or a boiling kettle. Dusts can also be mixed with a little cooled, boiled water or clear alcohol to make a watercolour-like paint.

Pastes

Paste or gel food colours are primarily used to colour flower paste and sugarpaste. They are concentrated and therefore it is best to add tiny amounts of colour slowly until the desired shade is reached. Too much paste food colour in a modest amount of paste can soften its consistency. This is most likely to happen when trying to make a very strong or very deep colour from white paste; sometimes it is better to simply buy a pre-coloured paste and enhance that instead.

Liquids

Liquid food colours are generally used to colour buttercream, royal icing or cake batter. If they are being used to colour cake batter, look for them to be bake stable as this preserves the colour once baked. A downside of liquid colour is that too much can thin cake batter; to get stronger colours, use a gel food colour designed for baking instead.

Chocolate Colourings

Food colouring for chocolate or cocoa butter needs to be oil-based so that the chocolate does not split. It is best mixed with white chocolate to create a colour, or alternatively it can be painted or sprayed on all types of chocolate.

Edible Food Colour Pens

Edible food colour pens can be used to draw designs or embellishments on cakes or sugar work. They can also be used for practical applications, such as marking dowels or tracing templates.

tips for colouring

With all colours, make sure you add them slowly and gradually. You can always add more but you can't take it away. Use the tip of a cocktail stick to add tiny amounts of paste food colour at a time. Add liquid colour one drop at a time.

Don't use dust directly from the pot. Instead, use a small palette knife to put a little bit on a paint palette or a piece of kitchen paper. This allows you to better control how much is on your brush and is also ideal for mixing dusts.

If making a deep coloured flower paste or sugarpaste from white, consider, if possible, using both a paste colour and a dust colour of the same shade. The dryness of the dust will offset the wetness of the paste and vice versa, helping to maintain the flower paste or sugarpaste's consistency.

RECIPES

When it comes to baking, times are a guide only as all ovens vary. Check your cake 10 minutes before the baking time is up. Be guided by its colour, the spring back on the top of the cake when it's touched, whether it is coming away from the side of your tin, and by how clean the skewer is once you've inserted it in the centre to check.

All the oven temperatures provided in this book are based on conventional ovens.

For fan-assisted ovens, reduce the temperature by around 20°C.

CLASSIC VANILLA SPONGE CAKE

This classic sponge cake recipe can serve as the base for many flavours.
The vanilla can be swapped with, for example, lemon zest or coffee.

Ingredients

Unsalted butter: 225g (8oz)

Caster sugar: 225g (8oz)

Eggs: 4 medium

Vanilla extract: 1¹/₂tsp

Self-raising flour: 225g (8oz)

Equipment

Round cake tin: 20.5cm (8")

Stand mixer

Saucepan

This amount makes one 20.5cm (8")
cake, which can be split into two layers.

1 Preheat the oven to 160°C/325°F/ Gas Mark 3.

2 Line the bottom and side of a 20.5cm (8") round cake tin with baking paper.

3 Cream the butter and sugar together in a mixer until pale and fluffy.

4 Add the eggs one at a time and beat in well until they are fully combined. If the mixture curdles you can add a spoonful of flour.

5 Add the vanilla extract and mix until combined.

6 Sift in the flour and slowly mix until fully incorporated and there are no lumps or pockets of flour remaining.

7 Spoon the batter into the prepared tin. Place in the centre of the oven and bake for 55 minutes or until a skewer inserted in the middle comes out clean.

8 Leave the cake to cool in the tin for 10 minutes before removing and allowing it to cool completely on a wire cooling rack.

These are the amounts for two cakes, meaning the batter should be split between two tins. Each cake should provide two layers.

ROUND	10cm (4")	12.5cm (5")	15cm (6")	18cm (7")	20.5cm (8")	23cm (9")	25.5cm (10")	28cm (11")	30.5cm (12")
SQUARE		10cm (4")	12.5cm (5")	15cm (6")	18cm (7")	20.5cm (8")	23cm (9")	25.5cm (10")	28cm (11")
Number of tins	2	2	2	2	2	2	2	2	2
Unsalted butter	115g (4oz)	150g (5¹/₄oz)	225g (8oz)	340g (12oz)	450g (1lb)	565g (1lb 4oz)	675g (1lb 7³/₄oz)	900g (2lb)	1.125kg (2lb 7⁵/₈oz)
Caster sugar	115g (4oz)	150g (5¹/₄oz)	225g (8oz)	340g (12oz)	450g (1lb)	565g (1lb 4oz)	675g (1lb 7³/₄oz)	900g (2lb)	1.125kg (2lb 7⁵/₈oz)
Medium eggs	2	2²/₃	4	6	8	10	12	16	20
Vanilla extract	³/₄tsp	1tsp	1¹/₂tsp	2¹/₄tsp	3tsp	3³/₄tsp	4¹/₂tsp	6tsp	7¹/₂tsp
Self-raising flour	115g (4oz)	150g (5¹/₄oz)	225g (8oz)	340g (12oz)	450g (1lb)	565g (1lb 4oz)	675g (1lb 7³/₄oz)	900g (2lb)	1.125kg (2lb 7⁵/₈oz)
Baking time	35 mins	40 mins	45 mins	50 mins	55 mins	1 hr	1 hr 5 mins	1 hr 10 mins	1 hr 15 mins

DARK CHOCOLATE CAKE

This is an easy to make but delicious chocolate cake. The use of coffee in this recipe is optional, but if included, it will create a richer, more indulgent taste. It won't make your sponge taste like coffee, rather it will bring out the flavours of the chocolate.

Ingredients

Dark chocolate: 100g (3^1/$_2$oz)

Unsalted butter: 125g (4^3/$_8$oz)

Self-raising flour: 185g (6^1/$_2$oz)

Cocoa powder: 30g (1oz)

Golden caster sugar: 165g (5^7/$_8$oz)

Eggs: 2 large

Milk: 190ml (6^3/$_4$fl oz)

Vanilla extract: 1tsp

Salt: a pinch

Coffee: 1tsp (optional)

Equipment

Round cake tin: 20.5cm (8")

Saucepan

Mixing bowl

This amount makes one 20.5cm (8") cake, which can be split into two layers.

top tip

You can easily make a cake release mixture to use on the sides of your tins instead of baking paper.

Simply mix together 1tbsp vegetable oil, 1tbsp white vegetable fat and 1tbsp of flour, and then brush it over the sides of the tins. This amount will cover several tins.

If you are making a chocolate cake that will be served uncovered and untrimmed, either use cocoa instead of flour or sprinkle the sides of the tins with a little cocoa powder after the mixture has been applied.

1   Preheat the oven to 180°C/350°F/ Gas Mark 4.

2   Line the bottom and side of a 20.5cm (8") round cake tin with baking paper.

3   Put the butter and chocolate in a saucepan and melt over a low heat. Alternatively, melt in a heatproof bowl over a pan of simmering water (the bain-marie method).

4   Sift the flour and cocoa into a large mixing bowl. Add the sugar, eggs, milk and vanilla to the bowl, as well as the melted butter and chocolate. Whisk until smooth.

top tip

Wrapping a baking collar around your cake tins can help keep the cakes flat and reduce how well-done they are at the sides.

5   Pour the batter into the prepared cake tin. Place the cake in the centre of the oven and bake for 45 minutes or until a skewer inserted in the middle comes out clean.

6   Leave the cake to cool in the tin for 10 minutes before removing and allowing to cool completely on a wire cooling rack.

DARK CHOCOLATE CAKE AMOUNTS

These are the amounts for two cakes, meaning the batter should be split between two tins. Each cake should provide two layers.

ROUND	10cm (4")	12.5cm (5")	15cm (6")	18cm (7")	20.5cm (8")	23cm (9")	25.5cm (10")	28cm (11")	30.5cm (12")
SQUARE		10cm (4")	12.5cm (5")	15cm (6")	18cm (7")	20.5cm (8")	23cm (9")	25.5cm (10")	28cm (11")
Number of tins	2	2	2	2	2	2	2	2	2
Dark chocolate	50g (1^3/$_4$oz)	65g (2^1/$_4$oz)	100g (3^1/$_2$oz)	150g (5^1/$_4$oz)	200g (7oz)	250g (8^3/$_4$oz)	300g (10^1/$_2$oz)	400g (14oz)	500g (1lb 1^3/$_4$oz)
Unsalted butter	65g (2^1/$_4$oz)	85g (3oz)	125g (4^3/$_8$oz)	190g (6^3/$_4$oz)	250g (8^3/$_4$oz)	315g (11oz)	375g (13^1/$_4$oz)	500g (1lb 1^3/$_4$oz)	625g (1lb 6oz)
Self-raising flour	95g (3^3/$_8$oz)	125g (4^3/$_8$oz)	185g (6^1/$_2$oz)	280g (10oz)	370g (13oz)	465g (1lb^1/$_2$oz)	555g (1lb 3^1/$_2$oz)	740g (1lb 10oz)	925g (2lb ^{5}/$_8$oz)
Cocoa powder	15g (^{1}/$_2$oz)	20g (^{3}/$_4$oz)	30g (1oz)	45g (1^5/$_8$oz)	60g (2^1/$_8$oz)	75g (2^5/$_8$oz)	90g (3^1/$_8$oz)	120g (4^1/$_4$oz)	150g (5^1/$_4$oz)
Golden caster sugar	85g (3oz)	110g (3^7/$_8$oz)	165g (5^7/$_8$oz)	250g (8^3/$_4$oz)	330g (11^5/$_8$oz)	415g (14^5/$_8$oz)	495g (1lb 1^1/$_2$oz)	660g (1lb 7^1/$_4$oz)	825g (1lb 13oz)
Large eggs	1	1^1/$_3$	2	3	4	5	6	8	10
Milk	95ml (3^1/$_4$fl oz)	125ml (4^1/$_2$fl oz)	190ml (6^3/$_4$fl oz)	285ml (10fl oz)	380ml (13^1/$_4$fl oz)	475ml (16^3/$_4$fl oz)	570ml (1pt)	760ml (1pt 6^3/$_4$fl oz)	950ml (1pt 13^1/$_2$fl oz)
Vanilla extract	^{1}/$_2$tsp	^{2}/$_3$tsp	1tsp	1^1/$_2$tsp	2tsp	2^1/$_2$tsp	3tsp	4tsp	5tsp
Salt	Pinch	Pinch	Pinch	^{1}/$_4$tsp	^{1}/$_4$tsp	^{1}/$_4$tsp	^{1}/$_4$tsp	^{1}/$_2$tsp	^{1}/$_2$tsp
Coffee (optional)	^{1}/$_2$tsp	^{2}/$_3$tsp	1tsp	1^1/$_2$tsp	2tsp	2^1/$_2$tsp	3tsp	4tsp	5tsp
Baking time	25 mins	30 mins	35 mins	40 mins	45 mins	50 mins	55 mins	1 hr	1 hr 5 mins

PORTION GUIDE

The following is a guide to roughly how many portions you should get from a single tier of cake. **Wedding or finger portions are 2.5cm x 2.5cm (1" x 1"). Dessert or party portions are 2.5cm x 5cm (1" x 2").** The exact amount may well vary depending on how accurately the cake is cut.

	10cm (4")	12.5cm (5")	15cm (6")	18cm (7")	20.5cm (8")	23cm (9")	25.5cm (10")	28cm (11")	30.5cm (12")
Round 1x1 Finger portion	8	14	22	30	40	52	62	80	97
Round 1x2 Dessert portion	5	8	12	16	22	26	34	40	48
Square 1x1 Finger portion	16	25	36	49	64	81	100	121	144
Square 1x2 Dessert portion	8	12	18	24	32	40	50	60	72

This is an example of how a 12.5cm (5") round cake can be cut into finger or dessert portions:

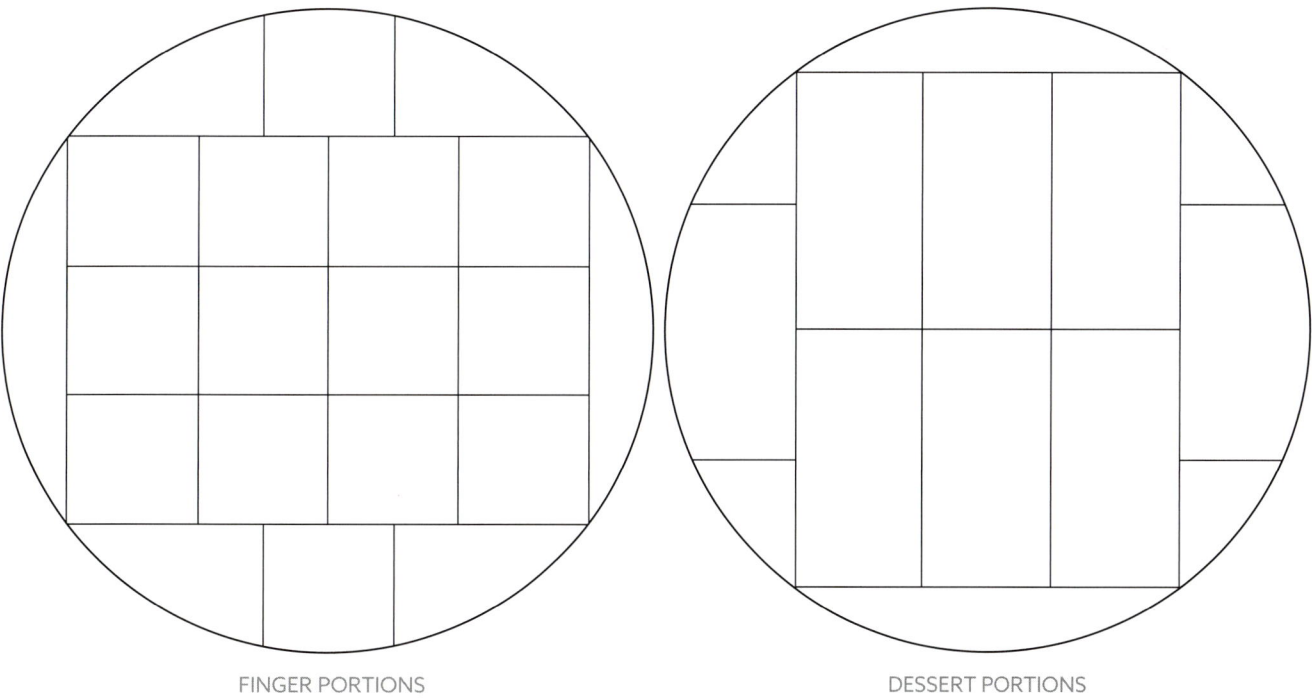

FINGER PORTIONS   DESSERT PORTIONS

FILLINGS AND COVERINGS

There are so many options to choose from when it comes to cake fillings and coverings. These recipes are what I typically use when making my cakes, so you can use them as a guide for you own. That being said, if you have a specific recipe you swear by or that is tailored to an allergy or intolerance then feel free to use that. Or get creative and experiment with different flavours and colours!

TRADITIONAL BUTTERCREAM

Traditional buttercream is a simple but tasty filling and covering for cakes, generally consisting of one part butter to two parts sugar plus flavouring. It is important to mix thoroughly until the sugar has dissolved so that the buttercream is not grainy.

Ingredients

Unsalted Butter: 260g (9^1/$_4$oz), at room temperature

Icing sugar: 520g (1lb 2^3/$_8$oz), sifted

Milk: a few drops (optional)

Equipment

Hand or stand mixer

Mixing bowl

Sieve

This can be used to fill two split, stacked 20.5cm (8") round cakes, equating to three layers of filling.

1 Cream the butter using a hand or stand mixer until it becomes light and has a fluffy consistency. This usually takes a few minutes.

2 Gradually add the sifted icing sugar to the butter and slowly beat them together until combined. Once combined, beat faster until the sugar has completely dissolved.

3 Add any flavourings to the mixture, such as vanilla, and continue to beat until the buttercream is fluffy and smooth.

4 This will keep for two weeks in an airtight container in the fridge.

top tips

If your buttercream is too stiff, add a drop of milk and beat until it softens. If it is too soft, add a tablespoon of sifted icing sugar and mix until combined.

Where possible, use cane icing sugar (ideally cornflour free) rather than beet icing sugar. It incorporates better, reducing the chance of grainy buttercream. If your buttercream is grainy, leave it for a few hours to allow the sugar granules to soften and then whisk again.

CHOCOLATE CONDENSED MILK BUTTERCREAM

This is a Russian buttercream with the addition of chocolate. Russian buttercream is a delicious, silky filling or covering made from butter and condensed milk. Incorporating chocolate lets you not only add flavour, but it also allows you to control the density. It has the advantage of there being no chance of graininess because the sugar component is already dissolved.

Ingredients

Unsalted butter: 380g (13^1/$_2$oz), at room temperature

Condensed milk: 305g (10^3/$_4$oz)

Chocolate (white, milk or dark): 155g (5^1/$_2$oz)

Equipment

Hand or stand mixer

Mixing bowl

Heatproof bowl

This can be used to fill two split, stacked 20.5cm (8") round cakes, equating to three layers of filling.

1 Cream the butter using a hand or stand mixer until it becomes light and has a fluffy consistency. This usually takes a few minutes.

2 Gradually add the condensed milk, beating slowly in the bowl. Increase the speed and beat until the butter and condensed milk are fully combined.

3 Melt the chocolate in a heatproof bowl over a pan of simmering water (the bain-marie method). Leave to cool.

4 Add the cooled, melted chocolate to the bowl and mix until combined.

5 This will keep for one week in an airtight container in the fridge.

top tips

If the buttercream splits after adding the condensed milk, the butter is probably too warm. Put the buttercream in the fridge for about 10 minutes and then beat again.

You can add more or less chocolate to get a firmer or looser buttercream.

GANACHE

Ganache is a delicious option for covering or filling a cake. As a covering, it can set hard enough to give a firm base for sugarpaste or it can be soft enough for a smooth layer of filling. For a filling ganache, reduce the amount of chocolate used to cream by one part – 1:1 for dark chocolate for example. A general rule of thumb is that ganache needs the consistency of peanut butter for coating a cake that's ready for covering and the consistency of Nutella for filling.

Ratios of chocolate to cream for a firm covering ganache are: **Dark** Chocolate 2:1, **Milk** Chocolate 2.5:1, **White** Chocolate 3:1

To cover a 20.5cm (8") diameter, 12.5cm (5") tall cake.

Ingredients

	Dark	Milk	White
Chocolate	520g (1lb 2^3/$_8$oz)	560g (1lb 3^3/$_4$oz)	585g (1lb 4^5/$_8$oz)
Whipping cream	260ml (9^1/$_4$fl oz)	220ml (7^3/$_4$fl oz)	195ml (6^3/$_4$fl oz)

Equipment

Milk pan/saucepan

Heatproof mixing bowl

Spatula

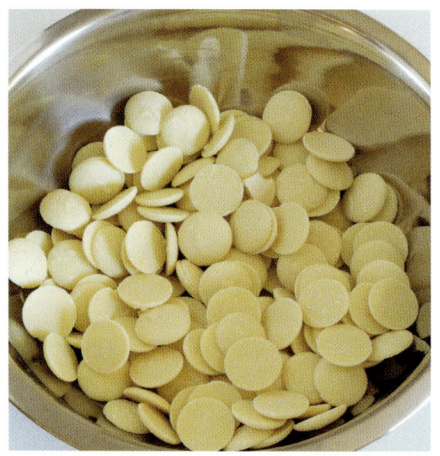  

1   If your chocolate is a bar, chop it into small pieces. This helps it melt more quickly. Place into your mixing bowl.

2   Heat the cream in the pan until it simmers. Do not let it boil!

3   Pour the hot cream over the chocolate and let it sit for a few minutes to soften the chocolate.

4   Gently stir with a spatula from the centre outwards until the chocolate has melted, leaving a silky smooth and glossy ganache.

5   Leave the ganache to cool at room temperature. Ganache usually keeps for two weeks in an airtight container in the fridge.

top tip

Split ganache can be brought back by vigorously whisking, either by hand or with a hand blender. If this does not work at first, rest the bowl over a pan of simmering water and whisk again. Another option is to add 1tbsp of milk and, again, whisk vigorously.

SUGAR SYRUP

Sugar syrup (also known as simple syrup) is used to keep cakes moist when they are assembled and can also be used to add or enhance flavour. It is easy to make and only has two ingredients: sugar and water, and always in a 1:1 ratio.

Ingredients

Caster sugar: 90g (3oz)

Water: 90ml (3¹/₄fl oz)

Flavourings (optional)

Equipment

Saucepan

Spoon

Pastry brush or squeeze bottle

To moisten a 20.5cm (8") diameter, 12.5cm (5") tall cake.

The syrup can be flavoured with extracts, such as vanilla or lemon or even with alcohol. Alternatively, the water can be substituted in part or in whole with liquids like coffee or fruit juices.

1   Put equal amounts of caster sugar and water (or substitute) into a saucepan.

2   Start stirring and bring the mixture to the boil. Keep stirring until all the sugar has dissolved.

3   Turn off and remove from the heat. Allow the mixture to cool down. At this point, add any extract flavourings such as vanilla or lemon.

4   Once cool, either apply the sugar syrup to the cake with a pastry brush or put it in a squeeze bottle and use that.

How much sugar syrup you apply to a cake depends on how moist the original cake is. Be careful not to use too much as this can make the cake too wet and too sweet. Spare sugar syrup can be stored in the fridge for several weeks.

The following is a rough guide to how much sugar syrup and buttercream/ganache covering and filling to make.

	10cm (4")	12.5cm (5")	15cm (6")	18cm (7")	20.5cm (8")	23cm (9")	25.5cm (10")	28cm (11")	30.5cm (12")
Sugar syrup	40ml (1$\frac{1}{2}$fl oz)	70ml (2$\frac{1}{2}$fl oz)	100ml (3$\frac{1}{2}$fl oz)	140ml (5fl oz)	180ml (6$\frac{1}{4}$fl oz)	220ml (7$\frac{3}{4}$fl oz)	280ml (9$\frac{3}{4}$fl oz)	340ml (12fl oz)	400ml (14fl oz)
Covering only	340g (12oz)	440g (15$\frac{1}{2}$oz)	550g (1lb 3$\frac{1}{2}$oz)	660g (1lb 7$\frac{1}{4}$oz)	780g (1lb 11$\frac{1}{2}$oz)	900g (2lb)	1.03kg (2lb 4$\frac{3}{8}$oz)	1.17kg (2lb 9$\frac{1}{4}$oz)	1.32kg (2lb 14$\frac{1}{2}$oz)
Three layers of filling only	210g (7$\frac{1}{2}$oz)	330g (11$\frac{5}{8}$oz)	470g (1lb $\frac{1}{2}$oz)	640g (1lb 6$\frac{1}{2}$oz)	840g (1lb 13$\frac{5}{8}$oz)	1.06kg (2lb 5$\frac{3}{8}$oz)	1.31kg (2lb 14$\frac{1}{4}$oz)	1.59kg (3lb 8oz)	1.89kg (4lb 2$\frac{5}{8}$oz)
Covering + three layers of filling	550g (1lb 3$\frac{1}{2}$oz)	770g (1lb 11$\frac{1}{8}$oz)	1.02kg (2lb 4oz)	1.3kg (2lb 13$\frac{7}{8}$oz)	1.62kg (3lb 9$\frac{1}{8}$oz)	1.97kg (4lb 5$\frac{1}{2}$oz)	2.35kg (5lb 9oz)	2.76kg (6lb 1$\frac{1}{8}$oz)	3.21kg (7lb 1$\frac{1}{4}$oz)

CAKE ASSEMBLY

It is important to split and assemble your cake with care; a well-covered cake depends on a well-prepared cake. Any unevenness or roughness at this stage will be reflected in the finished cake.

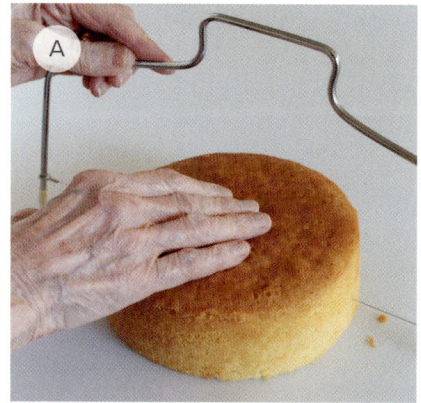

LAYERING A CAKE

1   Your cake layers need to be equal in height. The easiest way to do this is with a cake leveller – a height of about 2.5cm (1") is ideal. Set the height and cut through the cake. The bottom part will be your first layer, remove it and set it aside (A).

2   Cut a second layer from the remaining part of the cake and set it aside with the first layer. Repeat the process to cut your second cake.

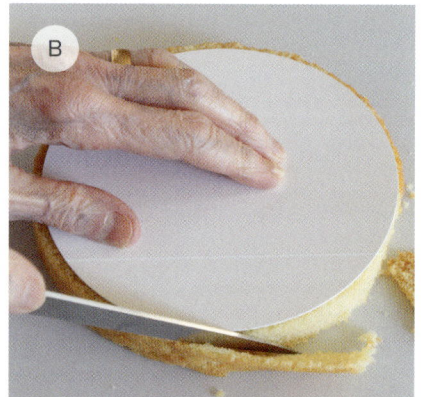

3   Use the first layers cut from each cake (those that include the base of the original cake) for the first and last layers of your cake: base down for the first layer and base up for the last layer.

4   The cake should be assembled on a cake board of the same size. However, the cake layers first need to be trimmed so that they are slightly smaller than the board itself. This leaves a space between the board and the cake that will be filled by buttercream or ganache. Make a trimming guide by cutting a circle of card 1cm (3/8") smaller than the board on which the cake will go.

5   Place the card guide centrally on top of one of the layers of cake. Using a sharp knife, cut around the guide to trim the layer to size. Be careful to keep the cuts vertical. Repeat this for each layer (B).

6   Place your first layer of cake centrally on the cake board. The natural stickiness of the cake means it should secure itself to the board. If it does not, spread a little buttercream or ganache in the middle of the board.

7   Brush all over the top of the cake layer with sugar syrup to help keep it moist (C). Spread your filling evenly on top of the cake (D). Alternatively, if you like, you can pipe a dam of buttercream or ganache around the perimeter of the cake and then spread or pipe the rest of the filling in the middle of it. Aim for a thickness of between 5mm (1/4") and 1cm (3/8").

8   Place the next layer of cake centrally on top of the filled layer and press down to secure (E). Rest a spare cake board on top of the cake and use a spirit level to make sure the cake is level. If it's not, press the raised side down and check again.

9   Repeat steps 7–8 for the remaining layers, except the last. With the last layer, brush the cut side with sugar syrup and then turn it over and place it on the cake with the original cake's base facing upwards.

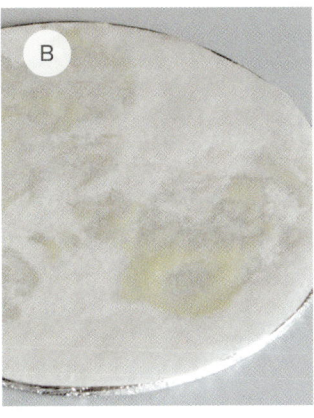

COATING A ROUND CAKE

1. Chill the cake in the fridge or freezer for at least 30 minutes to firm up.

2. First, the cake needs to be crumb-coated. This, as the term suggests, secures any crumbs on the trimmed sides and prepares the cake for its final coat. Use a palette knife to lightly coat the top and sides of your cake with your chosen covering – ganache or buttercream – and scrape around the cake with a cake scraper to remove any excess covering (A).

3. Return the cake to the fridge for another 30 minutes to allow the crumb coating to firm up.

4. Place a cake board (the same size as the one your cake is secured to) on a piece of baking paper and trace around it. Cut out the circle and stick it to the silver side of the board with a little of your covering (B). Put it in the fridge for the covering to firm up.

5. Remove the cake from the fridge. Use a little melted chocolate or your covering to temporarily fix the cake to the centre of an acrylic board or cake board of ideally at least 15cm (6") larger than your cake. To assist you when covering, place the cake and large board onto a turntable.

6. Generously coat the top of your cake with your covering. Use a long palette knife to smooth and level the top (C).

7. Remove the cake board with the baking paper from the fridge and place it paper side down centrally on top of your cake (D). Press the board down firmly and use a spirit level to make sure that it's level (E).

8. Hold a cake scraper vertically to line up the top and bottom boards all the way around the cake (F). Also make sure that no covering extends beyond them. Check that the board is still level.

9. Place the cake in the fridge to firm up for 10 minutes.

10. Remove the cake from the fridge and generously coat the side with your covering, ideally until it has fully filled the gap between the boards and the cake (G).

11. Hold a scraper vertically butted up against the two cake boards and sitting flush on the larger board. Draw

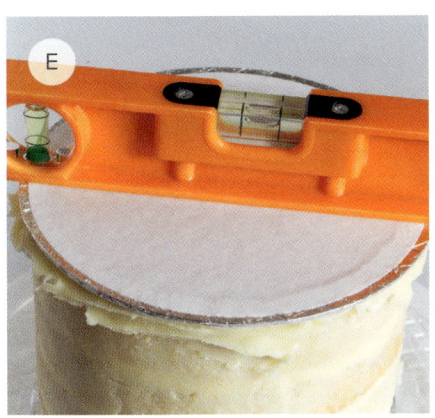

the scraper around the cake to remove the excess covering. Remove the scraped off covering from the scraper after each pass (H).

12 Use a spatula to fill in any gaps and use the scraper again to scrape around the cake once more.

13 Repeat step 12 until the cake is fully covered with no gaps (I).

14 Return the cake to the fridge for a final 30 minutes or until firm.

15 Remove the cake from the fridge. Slide a small spatula between the top cake board and the baking paper circle and lift the board off (J). Carefully peel off the baking paper (K).

16 If there are any gaps on the top or around the edge of the cake, fill them with covering and scrape them level (L).

COATING OTHER CAKE SHAPES

The method for coating other shaped cakes, such as a square or hexagon, is much the same as for a round cake, except care needs to be taken to make the corners neat. To do this, scrape along one side, clean the scraper, and then scrape along the next side of the cake. Continue this process for each side until you have a finish you are happy with.

COVERING CAKES

Before rolling out your sugarpaste always knead it well so that it is pliable, and then form it into roughly the shape you are going to roll out. Also lightly dust your work surface with cornflour – do not use too much as it will be absorbed into the paste and may dry it out.

I use spacers when rolling out my sugarpaste to achieve a consistent thickness. Spacers are either rings that fit around the ends of a rolling pin, or lengths of plastic that you lay either side of the sugarpaste and roll the rolling pin on them. I use spacers that are approximately 3mm (1/8") thick, as I find this leaves the paste robust enough to work with but thin enough not to overwhelm the flavours of the cake.

When rolling out the paste, lift it every three or four rolls to make sure that it's not sticking. If it feels like it is beginning to stick, you can dust over a little more cornflour at this point.

My preferred method of covering cakes is the panelling technique. It is relatively straightforward and is a fool-proof way of getting sharp edges.

There is also the over-the-top method, which is where you drape the paste centrally over the cake and smooth down.

It's up to you how you choose to cover your cake, so do what works easiest for you!

COVERING A DRUM

1   Roll out your sugarpaste (see the panelling table on page 38 for the amount to use) to a 3mm (¹/₈") thickness using spacers and a non-stick rolling pin.

2   Use a pastry brush to lightly dampen the top of the cake drum with a little cooled, boiled water. Alternatively, lightly smear the drum with some white vegetable fat.

3   Lay the sugarpaste over the drum, then smooth and press it down with a smoother. Use a sharp knife to neatly trim the excess paste away from around the edges. Set the drum aside to firm overnight.

4   Once the paste is firm, fix some 1.5cm (¹/₂") width ribbon around the edge of the drum using a non-toxic glue stick, being careful not to come into contact with the sugarpaste. Set the covered drum aside for later.

top tip

When working with sugarpaste, you always need more for working than that which actually ends up on the cake, so always re-knead and wrap up any clean excess sugarpaste for later use.

PANELLING TECHNIQUE

Covering A Round Cake

1   To cover the top of the cake, roll out your sugarpaste (see the table on page 38 for the amount) to a 3mm (¹/₈") thickness using a non-stick rolling pin and spacers.

2   Use a sharp knife to cut out a disc that is 2.5cm (1") larger than the diameter of your cake.

3   Using a pastry brush, lightly brush the top of the cake with a little cooled, boiled water or lightly smear with some white vegetable fat. Place the disc centrally on top of the cake and carefully trim away the excess from around the edge with a sharp knife (A).

4   To cover the side, roll out your sugarpaste (see the table on page 38 for the amount) to a thickness of 3mm (¹/₈"). Cut out a panel that is 1.5cm (¹/₂") taller than your cake and 2.5cm (1") longer than the circumference of your cake.

5   Lightly dampen around the side of the cake with cooled, boiled water or lightly smear with white vegetable fat. Gently roll up the panel of sugarpaste around a rolling pin and then wrap it around the side of the cake, making sure it sits flush with the base (B). Use a smoother to ensure that the paste is firmly attached.

6   Use a sharp knife to trim the overlapping ends so that they join neatly (C, D). Carefully trim away the excess paste from around the top of the cake (E). Use a smoother to ensure the edges are flush with the top of the cake.

7   Leave the covered cake to dry overnight. Allowing it to firm up a bit reduces the risk of accidental finger marks etc. when decorating and handling the cake.

top tip

You can flip your cake upside down before covering the sides if you wish so that you are trimming the bottom edge. To do this, tape a piece of wax paper around a cake board larger than your cake – make sure it has no wrinkles! Place the board paper side down on the top of your cake and then flip the cake and board over. Cover the side and trim the base (currently at the top). Turn the cake back over, remove the board and use smoothers to close any gaps between the side and the top, if necessary.

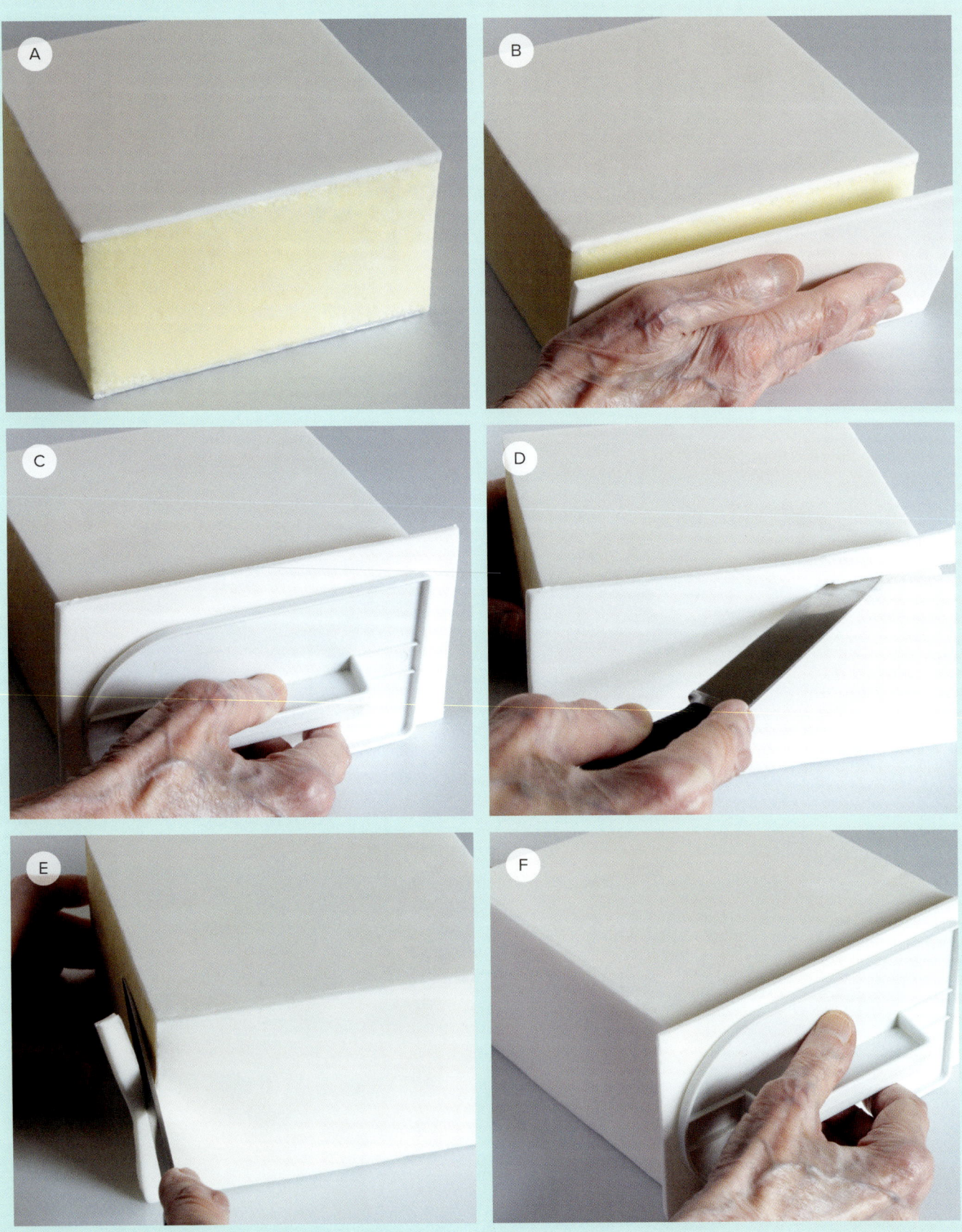

Covering A Square Cake

1 To cover the top of the cake, roll out your sugarpaste (see the table on page 38 for the amount) to a 3mm (1/8") thickness using a non-stick rolling pin and spacers.

2 Use a sharp knife to cut out a square that is 2.5cm (1") larger than the width of your cake.

3 Using a pastry brush, lightly brush the top of the cake with a little cooled, boiled water or lightly smear with some white vegetable fat. Place the square of sugarpaste on top of the cake centrally. Carefully trim away the excess from around the edges using a sharp knife (A).

4 Next, roll out the panels for the sides of the cake (see the table on page 38 for the amount for all four sides). Roll the sugarpaste to a 3mm (1/8") thickness. Cut out four panels that are 1.5cm (1/2") taller than your cake and 2.5cm (1") wider than the width of your cake. Make sure the edges that will be at the bottom are nice and straight.

5 Leave all four panels to firm up for an hour. This will make them easier to handle when applying to the cake.

6 The back of the cake is always covered first. Lightly dampen the back with a little cooled, boiled water or lightly smear with white vegetable fat. Take one of the panels and position its bottom edge centrally and flush with the base of the cake (B). Press the panel into place using a cake smoother (C).

7 Use a knife to trim the top edge of the panel level with the top of the cake. Next, trim the side edges flush with the sides of the cake (D, E).

8 Repeat steps 6–7 to attach the left and right side panels to the cake, and then finish by attaching the front panel to the cake in the same way (F). Attaching the panels in this order means that there are no seams on the front of the cake.

9 Use a smoother to ensure that each panel is positioned flush at the edges.

10 Leave the covered cake to dry overnight. Allowing the paste to firm up a bit reduces the risk of accidental finger marks etc. when decorating and handling the cake.

Covering Other Cake Shapes

Covering other cake shapes like hexagons or octagons can be approached in a few ways.

Firstly, the same way as a square cake. Start with the panel at the back; then work forwards, switching between the left and right sides of the cake; and finishing with the front panel.

An alternative panelling method is to cut the panels a few millimetres wider than the sides with a slight inward angle so that they slot together once applied to the cake. You can then refine the join with smoothers.

You can also wrap the cake as with a round cake and use smoothers to work the corners towards a point.

OVER-THE-TOP TECHNIQUE

Covering A Round Cake

1 Before you start, measure the diameter and the height of your cake. Add together the diameter and twice the height to get the minimum diameter sugarpaste circle you will need to roll out to cover the whole cake.

2 Roll out the sugarpaste (see the table on page 39 for the amount) to a 3mm ($^1/_8$") thickness using spacers and a non-stick rolling pin.

3 Using a pastry brush, lightly dampen the entire cake with a little cooled, boiled water or lightly smear with white vegetable fat.

4 Lightly dust the rolled paste with some cornflour. Now either fold the paste around a rolling pin or slip your hands (palms up) and forearms under the paste to lift it. Now drape the rolled paste over the cake, making sure that it completely covers the cake.

5 Smooth the paste down on the top of the cake with a smoother (A) and quickly use the edge of your hands to ensure the top 2.5cm (1") down the side is secured to the cake. This will stop the weight of the sugarpaste pulling and tearing around the edge.

6 Pull the 'skirt' out from around the side and work around the cake with your hands, pressing and smoothing the paste to the cake as you go (B).

7 Once the paste has been attached to the side, use a sharp knife to trim the excess paste away from the base (C).

8 Go around the covered cake with a smoother to finish the side and tidy up the trimmed base.

9 To sharpen the edge, use a pair of cake smoothers (either solid or flexible) to gently push the paste together where it meets at the edge of the top and the top of the side (D). The edge is not achieved in one go, so work around the cake several times until you get the crisp edge you are looking for (E).

Covering A Square Cake

1 Repeat steps 1–5 from Over-The-Top Technique: Covering A Round Cake, except instead of measuring the diameter you will need to measure the diagonal width of the cake (F, G).

2 Once the top edge has been secured, work on the corners next. Lift the paste out on adjacent sides so it spreads across the corner and press it into place, making sure that it's secured about 2.5cm (1") in on either side of the corner right down to the base (H, I). Repeat for each corner.

3 Flap out the 'skirt' on each side and work down from the top, smoothing it against the cake between the secured corners.

4 Repeat steps 7–9 from Over-The-Top Technique: Covering A Round Cake to finish the cake. Use the same technique on the corners as on the top to achieve the sharp edges (J).

> 66 All skills take practice and your first attempt is not likely to be your best. Sometimes there is more than one way of doing things. 99

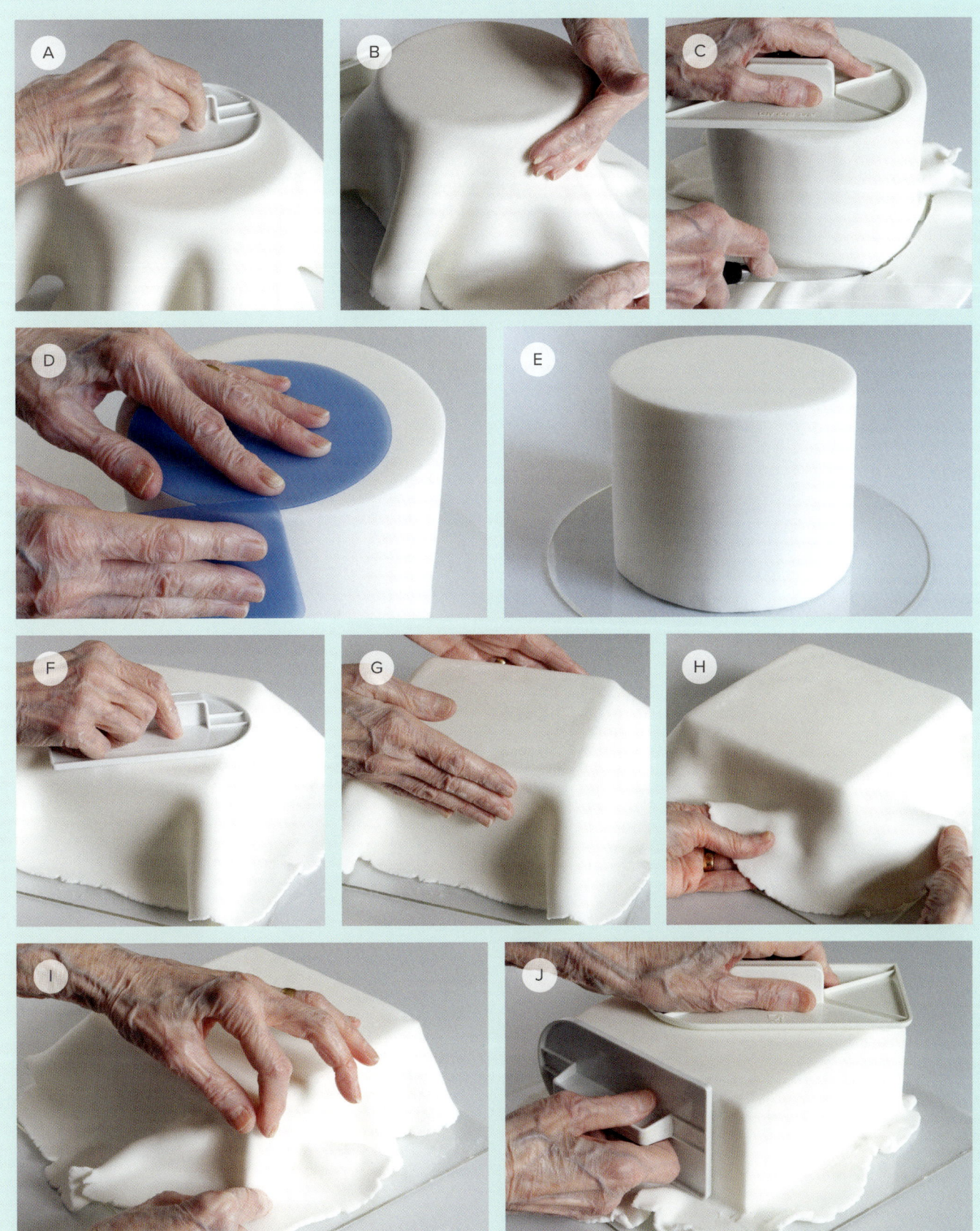

SUGARPASTE QUANTITIES

The following tables list the approximate amount of sugarpaste required to cover round and square cakes with both the panelling method and the over-the-top method. The panelling method will also be used to cover your round and square drums.

These figures expect a roll out thickness of 3mm ($1/8$"). If you roll out the paste thicker, the amount required will increase. For example, rolling out to a thickness of 6mm ($1/4$") would double the amount of sugarpaste required.

In each instance there will be sugarpaste left over, as a certain amount of working paste is required.

PANELLING

Use these quantities of sugarpaste for covering a round cake with the panelling technique, as well as for covering a round drum. For a square cake, add 25% to the weight for the same size round cake.

		10cm (4")	12.5cm (5")	15cm (6")	18cm (7")	20.5cm (8")	23cm (9")	25.5cm (10")	28cm (11")	30.5cm (12")
TOP PANEL OR DRUM ▶		75g (2⅝oz)	105g (3¾oz)	135g (4¾oz)	175g (6⅛oz)	215g (7½oz)	260g (9¼oz)	310g (11oz)	360g (12¾oz)	420g (14⅞oz)
SIDE PANEL	5cm (2")	225g (8oz)	265g (9⅜oz)	310g (11oz)	350g (12⅜oz)	395g (14oz)	435g (15⅜oz)	480g (1lb 1oz)	520g (1lb 2⅜oz)	565g (1lb 4oz)
	7.5cm (3")	265g (9⅜oz)	320g (11¼oz)	370g (13oz)	420g (14⅞oz)	470g (1lb ½oz)	525g (1lb 2½oz)	575g (1lb 4¼oz)	625g (1lb 6oz)	675g (1lb 7¾oz)
	10cm (4")	310g (11oz)	370g (13oz)	430g (15⅛oz)	490g (1lb 1¼oz)	550g (1lb 3½oz)	610g (1lb 5½oz)	670g (1lb 7⅝oz)	730g (1lb 9¾oz)	790g (1lb 11⅞oz)
	12.5cm (5")	355g (12½oz)	425g (15oz)	495g (1lb 1½oz)	560g (1lb 3¾oz)	630g (1lb 6¼oz)	700g (1lb 8¾oz)	765g (1lb 11oz)	835g (1lb 13½oz)	905g (2lb)
	15cm (6")	400g (14oz)	480g (1lb 1oz)	555g (1lb 3½oz)	630g (1lb 6¼oz)	710g (1lb 9oz)	785g (1lb 11¾oz)	860g (1lb 14⅜oz)	940g (2lb 1⅛oz)	1.02kg (2lb 4oz)
	18cm (7")	445g (15¾oz)	530g (1lb ¾oz)	615g (1lb 5¾oz)	700g (1lb 8¾oz)	785g (1lb 11¾oz)	875g (1lb 14⅞oz)	960g (2lb 1⅞oz)	1.04kg (2lb 4⅝oz)	1.13kg (2lb 7⅞oz)
	20.5cm (8")	490g (1lb 1¼oz)	585g (1lb 4⅝oz)	680g (1lb 8oz)	770g (1lb 11⅛oz)	865g (1lb 14½oz)	960g (2lb 1⅞oz)	1.05kg (2lb 5oz)	1.15kg (2lb 8½oz)	1.24kg (2lb 11¾oz)

OVER-THE-TOP

Use these quantities of sugarpaste for covering a round cake with the over-the-top technique. For covering a drum, use the table on page 38.

For a square cake, add 50% to the weight for the same size round cake.

HEIGHT ▼ / WIDTH ▶	10cm (4")	12.5cm (5")	15cm (6")	18cm (7")	20.5cm (8")	23cm (9")	25.5cm (10")	28cm (11")	30.5cm (12")
5cm (2")	215g (7$\frac{1}{2}$oz)	260g (9$\frac{1}{4}$oz)	310g (11oz)	360g (12$\frac{3}{4}$oz)	420g (14$\frac{7}{8}$oz)	480g (1lb 1oz)	545g (1lb 3$\frac{1}{4}$oz)	615g (1lb 5$\frac{3}{4}$oz)	690g (1lb 8$\frac{3}{8}$oz)
7.5cm (3")	310g (11oz)	360g (12$\frac{3}{4}$oz)	420g (14$\frac{7}{8}$oz)	480g (1lb 1oz)	545g (1lb 3$\frac{1}{4}$oz)	615g (1lb 5$\frac{3}{4}$oz)	690g (1lb 8$\frac{3}{8}$oz)	770g (1lb 11$\frac{1}{8}$oz)	855g (1lb 14$\frac{1}{8}$oz)
10cm (4")	420g (14$\frac{7}{8}$oz)	480g (1lb 1oz)	545g (1lb 3$\frac{1}{4}$oz)	615g (1lb 5$\frac{3}{4}$oz)	690g (1lb 8$\frac{3}{8}$oz)	770g (1lb 11$\frac{1}{8}$oz)	855g (1lb 14$\frac{1}{8}$oz)	940g (2lb 1$\frac{1}{8}$oz)	1.03kg (2lb 4$\frac{3}{8}$oz)
12.5cm (5")	545g (1lb 3$\frac{1}{4}$oz)	615g (1lb 5$\frac{3}{4}$oz)	690g (1lb 8$\frac{3}{8}$oz)	770g (1lb 11$\frac{1}{8}$oz)	855g (1lb 14$\frac{1}{8}$oz)	940g (2lb 1$\frac{1}{8}$oz)	1.03kg (2lb 4$\frac{3}{8}$oz)	1.13kg (2lb 7$\frac{7}{8}$oz)	1.23kg (2lb 11$\frac{3}{8}$oz)
15cm (6")	690g (1lb 8$\frac{3}{8}$oz)	770g (1lb 11$\frac{1}{8}$oz)	855g (1lb 14$\frac{1}{8}$oz)	940g (2lb 1$\frac{1}{8}$oz)	1.03kg (2lb 4$\frac{3}{8}$oz)	1.13kg (2lb 7$\frac{7}{8}$oz)	1.23kg (2lb 11$\frac{3}{8}$oz)	1.34kg (2lb 15$\frac{1}{4}$oz)	1.44kg (3lb 2$\frac{3}{4}$oz)
18cm (7")	855g (1lb 14$\frac{1}{8}$oz)	940g (2lb 1$\frac{1}{8}$oz)	1.03kg (2lb 4$\frac{3}{8}$oz)	1.13kg (2lb 7$\frac{7}{8}$oz)	1.23kg (2lb 11$\frac{3}{8}$oz)	1.34kg (2lb 15$\frac{1}{4}$oz)	1.44kg (3lb 2$\frac{3}{4}$oz)	1.56kg (3lb 7oz)	1.67kg (3lb 11oz)
20.5cm (8")	1.03kg (2lb 4$\frac{3}{8}$oz)	1.13kg (2lb 7$\frac{7}{8}$oz)	1.23kg (2lb 11$\frac{3}{8}$oz)	1.34kg (2lb 15$\frac{1}{4}$oz)	1.44kg (3lb 2$\frac{3}{4}$oz)	1.56kg (3lb 7oz)	1.67kg (3lb 11oz)	1.8kg (3lb 15$\frac{1}{2}$oz)	1.92kg (4lb 3$\frac{3}{4}$oz)

DOWELLING AND STACKING CAKES

It is vital when stacking cakes on top of each other that the supporting cakes are dowelled. Dowels support the weight of the tiers being stacked; cake alone would not be strong enough, especially when multiple tiers are added.

Dowels are available in plastic or wood and come in varying thicknesses. Plastic tube dowels can be cut using good kitchen scissors, while solid plastic or wooden dowels require garden secateurs – these must be kept for the exclusive use of dowel cutting!

1   First, attach the bottom cake tier to the cake drum, if one is being used. To do this, spread a little royal icing in the middle of the drum and place the cake centrally on top, making sure the back of the cake (if it has one) is in line with the ribbon join on the drum. Use a spirit level to check the cake is level.

2   Next, the area within which the dowels are to be placed needs to be marked. Centrally position a cake board the same size as the next upper tier (unless an offset tier is required) on top of the cake. Gently press the board down or lightly scribe around it with a scriber tool to leave a circle guide. Remove the board from the cake when finished.

3   Use the table below to determine how many dowels are needed for the circle size that has been marked. If you wish, you can add a further central dowel for extra stability.

4   Use a cocktail stick to mark the points within the circle – make the marks about 1.25cm ($^1/_2$") inside the perimeter of the circle.

5   Insert a cake dowel into the cake at one of the points until it stops at the board. Mark the height of the cake on the dowel with an edible ink pen (A).

6   Remove the dowel and cut it to length. Use this dowel as a guide to mark and cut the rest of your dowels to the exact same length.

7   Insert each cut dowel into the cake at the marked points (B). Place a spare cake board over the dowelled cake and use a spirit level to check that it is level. If it's not, trim or re-cut the dowels to the appropriate height.

8   Spread some royal icing over the centre of the dowelled area (C). Carefully place the upper tier in position, making sure that its back (if it has one) is at the back.

top tip

If you cannot hold a cake by its sides due to decoration, simply lift the cake with a wide spatula or a cake lifter and gently place your other hand on top for stability.

The following table specifies how many dowels are required under a tier. Arrange the dowels in a circle and equally spaced apart.

10cm (4")	12.5cm (5")	15cm (6")	18cm (7")	20.5cm (8")	23cm (9")	25.5cm (10")	28cm (11")	30.5cm (12")
3	4	4	5	5	6	6	7	7

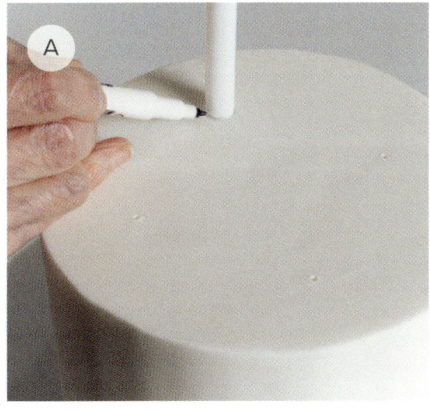
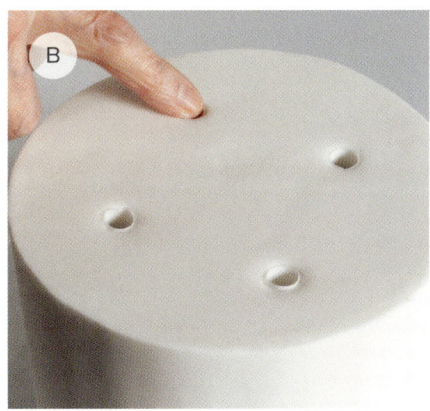
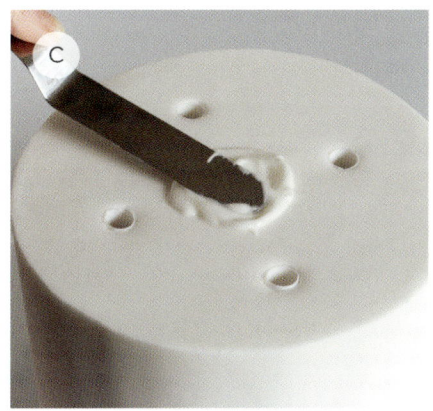

LET LOVE
grow

Combining two symbols of true love – hearts and red roses
– this clean and contemporary cake design is the perfect
way to show your loved ones you care.

YOU WILL NEED

Edibles

Round, filled sponge cake covered with ganache/buttercream with a sharp edge finish, secured on a cake board of the same size (see page 29), 10cm (4") deep: 15cm (6") wide

SK Professional Paste Food Colours: Leaf Green and Rose

SK Fairtrade Sugarpaste: 660g (1lb 7^1/$_4$oz) Bridal White

SK Sugar Florist Paste (SFP): 140g (5oz) White

SK HD Sugar Modelling Paste: 90g (3^1/$_8$oz) Red

SK Essentials Edible Glue

SK Professional Instant Mix Royal Icing: 50g (1^3/$_4$oz) White

SK Designer Paste Food Colour: Olive

Equipment

Round cake board: 15cm (6")

Round cake drums: 2 x 20.5cm (8")

1.5cm (^{1}/$_2$") width satin ribbon: 69cm (27") Bridal White

Templates: page 226

Round polystyrene separator, 2.5cm (1") deep: 7.5cm (3")

Cocktail sticks: 2

FMM Multi Ribbon Cutter

Heart cutters: 1.2cm (^{1}/$_2$") and 3.2cm (1^1/$_4$")

Floral wires: 24-gauge Nile green and 18-gauge white

FMM Rose Leaf Cutter: 3.1cm (1^1/$_4$")

Modelling tool: medium ball

SK-GI Silicone Veiner Rose - Tea: Large Leaf

Full-width floral tape: Nile green

Drinking straws: 3mm (^{1}/$_8$")

Fluted cookie cutter: 5.8cm (2^1/$_4$")

SEE PAGES 11–15 FOR ESSENTIAL EDIBLES AND EQUIPMENT

Covering The Cake Drum

1   Knead a small amount of Rose paste food colour into 660g (1lb 7$^1/_4$oz) of Bridal White sugarpaste to create a pale pink shade.

2   Roll out 250g (8$^3/_4$oz) of the pale pink sugarpaste and cover the 20.5cm (8") cake drum (see technique on page 32). Set the drum aside to firm overnight.

3   Fix the Bridal White ribbon around the edge of the drum (see technique on page 32).

Covering The Cake

1   Using the panelling method, roll out 135g (4$^3/_4$oz) of the pale pink sugarpaste and cut out a 17.5cm (6$^7/_8$") disc. Attach the disc to the top of the cake and trim away the excess (see technique on page 32).

2   To cover the side of the cake, roll out 430g (15$^1/_4$oz) of the pale pink sugarpaste and cut out an 11.5cm x 50cm (4$^1/_2$" x 19$^3/_4$") panel. Roll up the panel of sugarpaste and wrap it around the cake (see technique on page 32). Set the cake aside to harden overnight.

Adding The Stripes

1   Transfer the stripe template to a piece of food-safe card and cut it out. Carefully fold it at the base of the triangular end and trim the long section to the height of the cake.

2   Trace and cut out the round spacing template and place it on a spare cake drum that is at least 20.5cm (8") wide. Place the cake on the template, making sure that it is positioned centrally. As you add stripes, rotate the drum rather than the cake so the template doesn't shift.

3   Place a 2.5cm (1") deep x 7.5cm (3") diameter round separator in the centre of the cake and temporarily fix it in place using two sterilised pins or cocktail sticks.

top tip

If you do not have a separator, a straight cookie cutter or ring of stiff card can be used instead.

4   Roll out 20g ($^3/_4$oz) of White SFP to a thickness of approximately 2mm ($^1/_{16}$"). Use a ribbon cutter (or a ruler and cutting wheel) to cut out a 1.2cm ($^1/_2$") wide x 17.5cm (6$^7/_8$") long strip (A). Use a sharp knife or razor blade to make one end of the strip pointed by cutting away both sides at a 45° angle (B).

5   Place the card template on the cake so that its right edge is level with one of the divisions on the spacing template (C). Lightly brush some cooled, boiled water over the side and top of the cake where the strip will go (D). Attach a strip to the cake, using the guide to keep it straight. Fold the strip over the top of the cake, keeping it against the guide, and press it into place so that the pointed end is upright against the separator, forming one slat of the picket fence (E).

6   Repeat step 4 to prepare a second strip. Move the card template so that its right edge is in line with the next division on the spacing template and attach the second strip in the same way as step 5.

7   Repeat step 6 to make and attach the remaining strips to the cake.

8   Once all the vertical strips have been attached, cut out a 5mm ($^1/_4$") wide x 26cm (10$^1/_4$") long strip of White SFP. Lightly brush a little cooled, boiled water on the fence posts, just below the angled tops. Wrap the strip around the fence posts, gently pressing it onto each post to secure. Trim the ends to fit.

9   Leave the strips to firm overnight before very carefully removing the polystyrene separator.

Attaching The Small Hearts

1   Roll out 20g ($^3/_4$oz) of Red modelling paste to a 2mm ($^1/_{16}$") thickness. Use a 1.2cm ($^1/_2$") heart cutter to cut out 21 hearts (F).

2   Use a small paintbrush to dab a little edible glue over the back of one heart and attach it to the cake, centring it horizontally and vertically in the gap between two strips.

3   Skip the next gap between strips and attach a second heart centred in the gap after that. Repeat and carry on attaching single hearts in every other gap.

4   Add two hearts in each empty gap between strips, placing them so that they are approximately 1.5cm ($^1/_2$") down from the top of the cake and 1.5cm ($^1/_2$") up from the base.

Making The Leaves

1   Colour 10g ($^1/_4$oz) of White SFP a fresh green colour using a mixture of Leaf Green and Olive paste food colours. Cut a piece of 24-gauge Nile green floral wire into quarters.

2   Very thinly roll out a small piece of the fresh green-coloured SFP and cut out two leaves using a 3.1cm (1$^1/_4$") Rose Leaf cutter.

3   Lightly brush one side of the first leaf with a little edible glue. Lay a wire along the length of the glued leaf, starting at the top and extending past

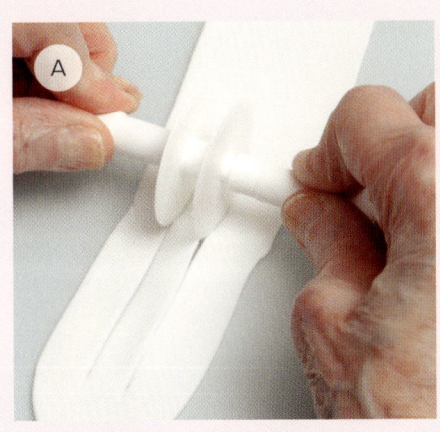

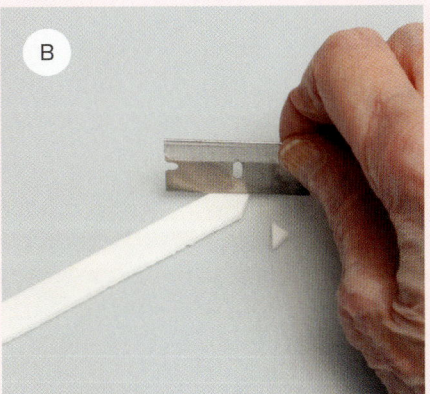

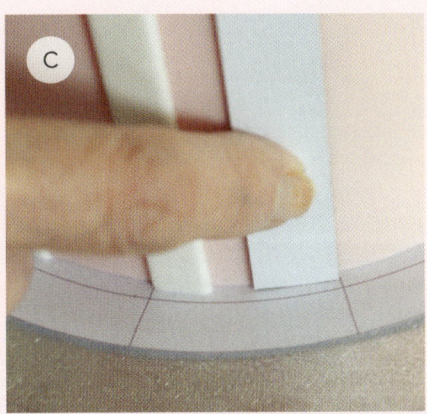

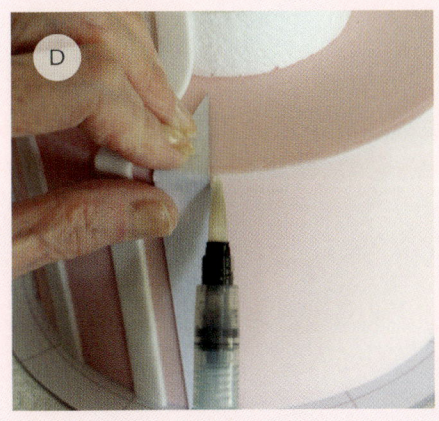

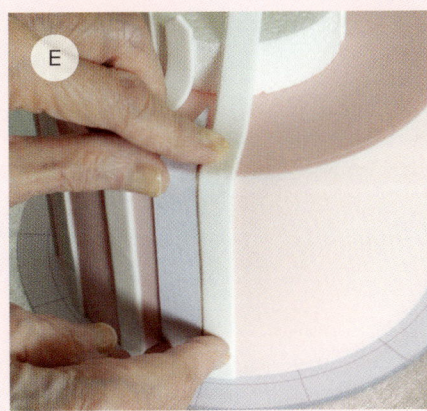

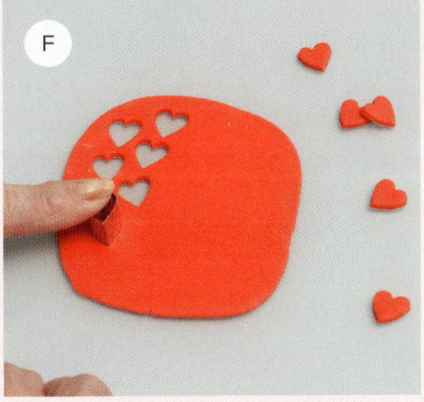

the base. Place the second leaf on top of the first, sandwiching the wire between them, and press the two together (G).

4   Place the leaf on a foam pad and thin the edges with a medium ball tool (H). Press the leaf firmly between the two halves of a Tea Rose Leaf veiner to texture (I). Remove and shape the leaf with your fingers to create a natural sense of movement (J).

5   Repeat steps 2–4 to make a total of four wired leaves. Allow all the leaves to firm overnight.

Making The Stems

1   Bend the end of an 18-gauge white floral wire around a 1.25cm ($^1/_2$") thick rolling pin or pen to make a loop (K, L).

2   Bind the wire with Nile green floral tape, starting just below the loop and continuing 7.5cm (3") down the wire. Repeat the binding several times until the stem reaches a thickness of approximately 4mm ($^3/_{16}$") (M).

3   Bind 1.2cm ($^1/_2$") below the section already covered to a roughly 3mm ($^1/_8$") thickness that will fit snugly in a drinking straw.

4   Repeat steps 1–3 to make a second stem, this time only wrapping the tape 6cm ($2^3/_8$") down the wire.

5   Trim the wires so there is 7.5cm (3") of wire remaining below the bound section on each stem.

Making The Heart 'Roses'

1   Roll out 40g ($1^1/_2$oz) of Red modelling paste to a 5mm ($^1/_4$") thickness. Lay a piece of cling film over the paste and cut out a heart through it using a 3.2cm ($1^1/_4$") heart cutter (N). Repeat to cut out a second heart.

2   Hold the looped end of a stem against the flat side of one of the hearts so the top of the taped section sits at the base of the heart (O).

3   Place the flat side of the second heart on top of the first heart, sandwiching the wire loop between the two (P). Gently press the hearts together and use your finger to smooth the join. Use a little edible glue to adhere them together, if needed.

4   Repeat steps 1–3 to add a heart to the second wire stem.

top tip

Cutting out a heart through cling film gives the shape a rounded edge.

Adding The Leaves

1   Hold one of the stems so the heart is face on and use some Nile green tape to fix one leaf on each side, positioning them so the point that the wire exits the leaf sits approximately 1.5cm ($^1/_2$") below the base of the heart. Fold the leaves out at right angles as if they were arms.

2   Repeat step 1 to add a pair of leaves to the second stem.

Assembling The Cake

1   Spread a little royal icing in the middle of the covered drum and secure the cake centrally on top. Make sure that the join in the strip around the fences and the ends of the ribbon are aligned.

2   Colour 80g ($2^3/_4$oz) of White SFP a similar green shade to the leaves using a combination of Leaf Green and Olive paste food colours. Roll the green paste out to a 2mm ($^1/_{16}$") thickness and cut out a fluted disc using a 5.8cm ($2^1/_4$") cookie cutter.

3   Brush a little cooled, boiled water over the central 5cm (2") on the top of the cake and carefully place the disc in the centre of the fence circle.

4   Cut two 3mm ($^1/_8$") straws to the height of the cake. With the front of the cake facing you, insert the straws down through the green section: place the first 1.25cm ($^1/_2$") to the left of the centre of the cake and place the second 2.5cm (1") to the right of the first.

5   With the front of the cake still facing you, insert the shorter heart stem in the straw to the left of the centre until the thicker part of the bound stem reaches the cake. Insert the longer heart stem likewise in the other straw. Adjust the stems so that the hearts are leaning against each other.

IMPORTANT NOTE: Ensure that the recipient of the cake is aware that it contains inedible elements and that the heart flower decorations must be removed before the cake is served.

LOST IN THE
lavender fields

This pretty, single tier cake would look lovely on your table for a summer party or wedding. To really set the scene, you could adorn the table with some fresh lavender to add instant style and enhance the cake.

YOU WILL NEED

Edibles

Round, filled sponge cake covered with ganache/buttercream with a sharp edge finish, secured on a cake board of the same size (see page 29), 18cm (7") deep: 15cm (6") wide

SK Professional Paste Food Colours: Fern, Holly/Ivy (Dark Green) and Mint (Xmas Green)

SK Sugar Florist Paste (SFP): 165g (5⁷/₈oz) White

SK Fairtrade Sugarpaste: 50g (1³/₄oz) Bridal White, 110g (3⁷/₈oz) Palm Green and 855g (1lb 14¹/₄oz) Sweet Lavender

White vegetable fat

SK Paste Food Colours: Brown and Purple

SK Essentials Edible Glue

SK Professional Instant Mix Royal Icing: 100g (3¹/₂oz) White

SK Professional Dust Food Colour: Lilac (optional)

Equipment

Template: page 227

Food-grade card

Pizza wheel cutter

Round cake drum: 23cm (9")

SK High-Quality Paintbrush: no. 4

Razor blade

1.5cm (¹/₂") width satin ribbon: 1m (1yd 3³/₈") Emerald Green

Round cake board: 15cm (6")

A4 paper: 2 sheets

Modelling tool: scribing needle

Orchard Products Calyx Cutter: 1.9cm (³/₄")

Cardboard tube

Floral wires: 26-gauge Nile green

Orchard Products Six-Petal Cutter: 1.9cm (³/₄")

Half-width floral tape: Nile green

SEE PAGES 11–15 FOR ESSENTIAL EDIBLES AND EQUIPMENT

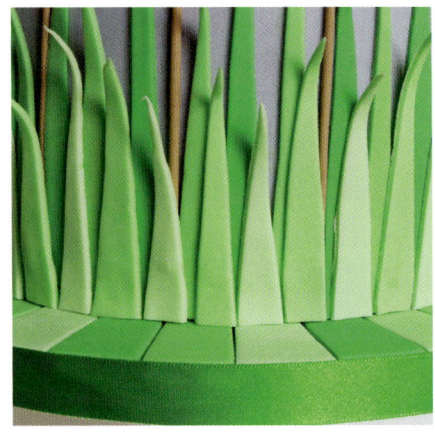

Mixing The Greens

1   Use a little Mint (Xmas Green) and Fern paste food colours to colour 55g (2oz) of White SFP as near to the green shade of the Palm Green sugarpaste as you can. You want to add the same amount of each paste food colour. Start with a small amount of the colours and keep adding more to the SFP until you get close enough to the Palm Green shade.

2   Knead the green SFP mixture together with 110g (3⁷/₈oz) of Palm Green sugarpaste. You want to have a 1:2 ratio. Adding SFP to sugarpaste makes it slightly firmer when working with it.

3   Divide the green SFP-sugarpaste mixture into four pieces of the following weights: 60g (2¹/₈oz), 60g (2¹/₈oz), 30g (1oz) and 15g (¹/₂oz). Wrap up and set one of the 60g (2¹/₈oz) pieces aside – this will be used as is.

4   Knead together 25g (>³/₄oz) of White SFP and 50g (1³/₄oz) of Bridal White sugarpaste. This will be used to lighten two of the remaining three pieces of the green SFP-sugarpaste mixture while retaining their ratio of SFP to sugarpaste.

5   Knead the 30g (1oz) piece of green SFP-sugarpaste together with 30g (1oz) of the white SFP-sugarpaste mix to make a lighter green.

6   Knead the 15g (¹/₂oz) piece of green SFP-sugapaste together with 45g (1⁵/₈oz) of the white SFP-sugapaste (a 1:3 ratio) to make the lightest green shade.

7   Slightly darken the other 60g (2¹/₈oz) piece of the green SFP-sugapaste using a small amount of Mint (Xmas Green) paste food colour and a tiny bit of Holly/Ivy (Dark Green) paste food colour.

8   Wrap up each colour with some cling film until it's needed. You will end up with a 60g (2¹/₈oz) piece of dark green paste, a 60g (2¹/₈oz) piece of light green paste, a 60g (2¹/₈oz) piece of very pale green paste and a 60g (2¹/₈oz) piece of the original green SFP-sugarpaste mixture that you set aside earlier.

Covering The Cake Drum

1   Trace the segment template onto a piece of food-grade card and cut it out with scissors.

2   On a non-stick board, roll out the dark green paste to a 3mm (¹/₈") thickness. Place the template on top of the paste and use a pizza wheel cutter to cut out eight segments in total (A). Gather and knead your dark green offcuts into a ball and wrap up to use later for the grass.

3   Repeat step 2 to cut out eight segments of each of the three remaining shades of green: the light green, the very pale green and the original green SFP-sugarpaste mixture. You want to end up with 32 pieces in total. Leave all the cut segments to firm up for half an hour.

4   Arrange the pieces around the outer edge of the cake drum, but do not secure them in place yet. Try to get a balanced distribution of shades and make sure you don't have two pieces of the same colour next to each other (B).

5   Once you are happy with the arrangement, make sure all the pieces are lined up neatly with each other and the edge of the drum. If necessary to make things fit, trim one of the pieces or cut a new piece to fill a gap. If this is needed, treat this area as the back of the drum.

6   Remove one segment and use a no. 4 paintbrush to lightly paint the area on the drum with a little white vegetable fat. Attach the segment back in its place and gently press down to secure it to the drum. Repeat to attach all the remaining pieces to the drum, one at a time.

7   Once finished, check that no pieces overlap the edge of the drum. If they do, carefully trim them with a razor

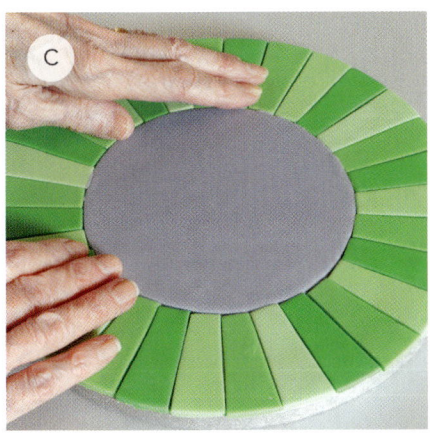

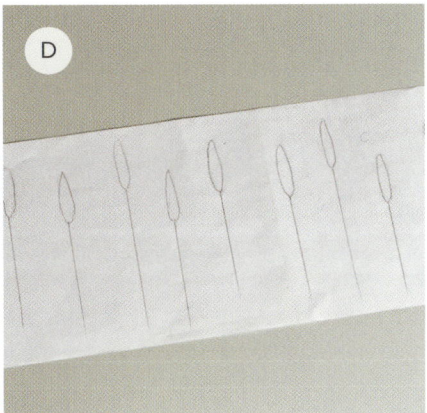

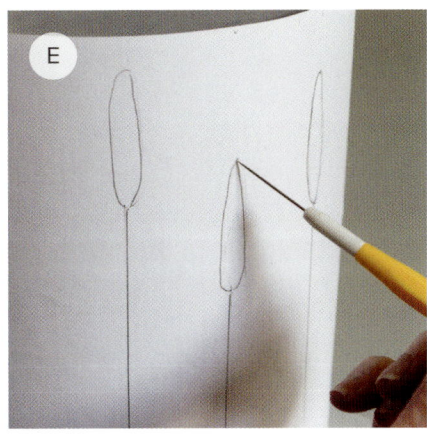

top tip

Using a little white vegetable fat instead of cooled, boiled water to attach sugarpaste to a drum allows the paste to be repositioned if necessary.

blade. Keep and wrap up all your leftover individual green-coloured pastes to use later for the grass.

8   Measure the circle left by the segments in the centre of the drum – it should be about 12.5cm (5") in diameter.

9   Roll out 105g (3³/₄oz) of Sweet Lavender sugarpaste to a 3mm (¹/₈") thickness. Cut out a disc from the paste to a slightly smaller size than what you measured in the centre of the drum. Keep the offcuts.

10   Lightly brush the gap left in the centre of the drum with some white vegetable fat. Position the disc of Sweet Lavender paste in the centre of the drum – it does not matter if there's a little gap around it as this will be covered by the cake and won't be seen. Use your hands and a smoother to press the paste down firmly to adhere it to the drum (C).

11   Fix some Emerald Green ribbon around the edge of the drum (see technique on page 32).

Covering The Cake

1   For the top of the cake, roll out 135g (4³/₄oz) of Sweet Lavender sugarpaste and cut out a 18cm (7") disc. Attach the disc to the top of the cake and trim away the excess (see technique on page 32).

2   To cover the side of the cake, roll out the remaining 615g (1lb 5³/₄oz) of Sweet Lavender sugarpaste and cut out a 50cm x 19cm (19³/₄" x 7¹/₂") panel. Roll up the panel of sugarpaste and wrap it around the cake (see technique on page 32). Set the cake aside to harden overnight.

top tip

If you are decorating all the way around a cake, it's often useful to plan it first on paper to be sure that the spacing works.

Planning The Lavender Positions

1   Tape the short ends of two pieces of A4 paper together. Cut a rectangle from the paper so it measures the height of the cake by the circumference of the cake, approximately 18cm x 50cm (7" x 19³/₄").

2   Use a pencil to lightly sketch out positions for the lavender along the length of the paper – the lavender heads should be roughly 1.25cm x 5cm (¹/₂" x 2"). Treat the centre of the paper as the front of the cake. Draw them around 3cm – 5cm (1¹/₈" – 2") apart and at varying heights, but keep them in the top half of the cake. It should take 12 to go all the way round the cake.

3   Once you are happy with the positions, draw them in more firmly. You can also add the stalks if you like (D).

4   Wrap the paper around the cake with the sketched lavender positions at the top, and tape the two ends together at the back of the cake in line with the seam.

5   Use a scribing tool to mark the top of each head of lavender onto the sugarpaste covering the cake (E). If you like, you can also mark partway down the stems for a guide when attaching them.

top tip

Give the scribing tool a little wiggle to ensure the marks can be seen clearly when the paper is removed. Don't worry about the marks showing as the lavender will cover them once it's been added.

Making The Lavender On The Side

1   Colour 75g (2⁵/₈oz) of White SFP a lavender shade using a little Purple paste food colour.

2   Roll out a small piece of the purple SFP to a thickness of about 1mm (<1/₁₆") and use a 1.9cm (³/₄") calyx cutter to cut out a lavender flower.

3   Carefully fold two adjacent petals upwards using your fingers (F). Set the flower aside to dry.

4   Repeat steps 2–3 to make 60 lavender flowers in total.

Making The Lavender Stems

1   Mix a little Brown paste food colour with 6.5g (¹/₄oz) of White SFP to achieve a pale brown shade.

2   Take a 1cm (³/₈") ball of the pale brown SFP and use your hands to roll the paste into a rope, about 2mm (¹/₁₆") thick (G, H). Set the rope aside to dry, making sure that it is left straight. Repeat to make 11 more lavender stems.

top tip

To save time you can use wholewheat spaghetti for the stems, just remember to remove it before the cake is served!

Attaching The Lavender

1   Dip the no. 4 paintbrush into some edible glue and wipe off the excess on a piece of kitchen paper. Brush a little glue on the back of one of the folded lavender flowers (I).

2   Use one of the scribed guide marks to position the flower in place on the side of the cake. Make sure the folded petals are at the bottom of the flower facing downwards and that the top petal covers the guide mark.

3   Following the same technique as in step 2, glue a second flower directly below the first so the tip of the second flower's top petal just touches the bottom of the flower above.

4   Repeat step 3 to attach three more petals below the first two.

5   Repeat steps 1–4 to attach all the lavender flowers to the cake on the remaining 11 guide marks (J).

Attaching The Stems

1   Take a stem and trim it so that it is about 2.5cm (1") shorter than the gap between a lavender head and the base of the cake. The stem does not need to reach down to the base of the cake because that area will be covered by the grass.

2   Brush a little edible glue along the length of one side of the stem. Attach it to the cake directly underneath the chosen lavender head, making sure that the stem is vertical (K).

3   Repeat steps 1–2 to attach the remaining lavender stems to the cake.

Making The Grass

1   Take the remaining dark green paste you set aside earlier and roll it into a strip, approximately 10cm (4") deep and 2mm (¹/₁₆") thick.

2   Use a pizza wheel to cut back and forth over the paste at angles, cutting blades of grass about 1.5cm (¹/₂") wide at their widest point (L). Cut about 20–25 blades in total. Keep and wrap up your offcuts.

3   Separate the grass blades and trim them to be between 7cm – 10cm (2³/₄" – 4") long.

4   Lay the individual blades down with their tips resting against a cardboard tube, or equivalent, to give them a slight curve (M). Leave them to dry for an hour.

5   Repeat steps 1–4 to make some more blades of grass that are the same size, this time using the remaining original green SFP-sugarpaste mixture (the second darkest shade).

6   Repeat steps 1–4 again using the remaining light green and very pale green pastes, but this time trim them to be between 5cm – 7cm (2" – 2³/₄") long.

top tips

You can attach the grass to the cake before or after it's attached to the drum, but you may find it easier to move the cake before the grass is attached.

You can use both sides of the tube to shape and dry the blades of grass. If the tube will not stay still, press small wedges of paste either side of it to keep it in place.

Attaching The Grass

1   The two darkest shades of green form the inner layer of grass. When attaching the grass, start next to the join at the back of the cake. Brush a little edible glue on the flat back part of one of the darker pieces of grass and attach it to the cake (N), ensuring it sits flush with the bottom. Make sure to avoid going over any of the stems.

2   Continue gluing on the darker two shades of grass until you have gone all the way round (O). You can alternate the shades or add them randomly, but if you do, don't have too many of the same colour next to each other. If required, trim any blades shorter.

3   Attach the two lighter and shorter shades of grass as an outer layer. Position the second layer of grass so that their points sit in the gaps between the inner layer's blades. As with the inner layer, you can alternate the shades or do them randomly.

Making The Lavender Posy

1   Cut eight pieces of 26-gauge Nile green floral wire into 15cm (6") lengths and bend a small closed hook in one end of each (P).

2   Take a small piece of the purple SFP you made earlier, about the size of two round headed pins, and shape the SFP into an oval so it looks like a plump grain of rice.

top tip

To add a bit of variety to the lavender, colour the SFP for the lavender tips with a little bit of Lilac dust food colour.

3   Dip the hooked end of a cut wire into edible glue and wipe off the excess. Push the hook into one tapered end of the oval piece of purple SFP and pinch the paste closed around it (Q).

4   Roll out a piece of the purple SFP to a thickness of about 1mm ($<1/16$") and cut out a blossom using a 1.9cm ($3/4$") Six-Petal cutter (R).

5   Lightly brush the centre of the blossom with a little edible glue and then push the wired centre down through the middle of the blossom. Slide the blossom up the wire until it reaches the SFP tip at the top (S). Gently pinch the petals up around the paste (T).

6   Repeat step 4 to cut out one or two more blossoms. Lightly brush the centre of the loose blossom(s) with edible glue. Slide a blossom up the same wire until it nestles against the first blossom. Gently pinch the petals up around the paste. Repeat to attach a second flower if cut (U).

7   Repeat step 4 to cut out another three or four blossoms. Glue and slide one of the flowers up the wire until it is about 8mm ($5/16$") below the previous group of blossoms (V). Slide the remaining blossoms up the wire until they nestle against the first set;

again, lightly brushing the centre of the loose blossoms with a little edible glue.

8   Repeat step 7 three more times to give you five groups of blossoms on the wire (W). Set the lavender aside to dry.

9   Once dry, cover the exposed wire below the flowers with half-width Nile green floral tape.

10   With the remaining cut wires, repeat steps 2–9 to give you eight lavender stems in total.

11   Once the stems have dried, bind them all together in a bunch with half-width Nile green tape (X).

12   To finish, tie a bow around the stem just below the lavender with the remaining Emerald satin ribbon (Y).

Assembling The Cake

1   Spread a little royal icing in the middle of the covered drum. Secure the cake centrally on the drum, making sure the join at the back of the cake is in line with the ribbon join on the drum.

2   Lay the lavender posy on top of the cake, positioning it so that it's pointing to the front right.

top tip

Not attaching a flower arrangement to the top of the cake means that it can be saved as a keepsake.

RAINBOW
spheres

This playful cake surrounded by spheres would brighten any occasion, from birthday celebrations to wedding receptions.

Edibles

Round, filled sponge cake covered with ganache/buttercream with a sharp edge finish, secured on a cake board of the same size (see page 29), 7.5cm (3") deep: 10cm (4") wide

Round, filled sponge cake covered with ganache/buttercream with a sharp edge finish, secured on a cake board of the same size (see page 29), 15cm (6") deep: 12.5cm (5") wide

SK Fairtrade Sugarpaste: 85g (3oz) Bridal Rose, 1.27kg (2lb 12$^3/_4$oz) Bridal White, 85g (3oz) Glamour Red, 45g (1$^5/_8$oz) Spa Blue, 170g (6oz) Sunshine Yellow and 85g (3oz) Zesty Orange

SK Professional Paste Food Colour: Vine

White vegetable fat

SK Essentials Edible Glue

SK Professional Instant Mix Royal Icing: 100g (3$^1/_2$oz) White

Equipment

Polystyrene balls: 6 x 1.8cm ($^3/_4$") and 6 x 2.5cm (1")

Cocktail sticks: 13

Non-toxic glue stick

Polystyrene block

Round cake drum: 23cm (9")

Round cake boards: 10cm (4") and 12.5cm (5")

Modelling tool: scribing needle

Sterilised pins: 2

Coloured pencils: blue, green, orange, pink, red and yellow

Round cutters: 6mm ($^1/_4$"), 1cm ($^3/_8$"), 1.25cm ($^1/_2$"), 1.6cm ($^5/_8$"), 2.2cm ($^7/_8$") and 2.8cm (1$^1/_8$")

1.5cm ($^1/_2$") width satin ribbon: 76cm (30") Bridal White

SEE PAGES 11–15 FOR ESSENTIAL EDIBLES AND EQUIPMENT

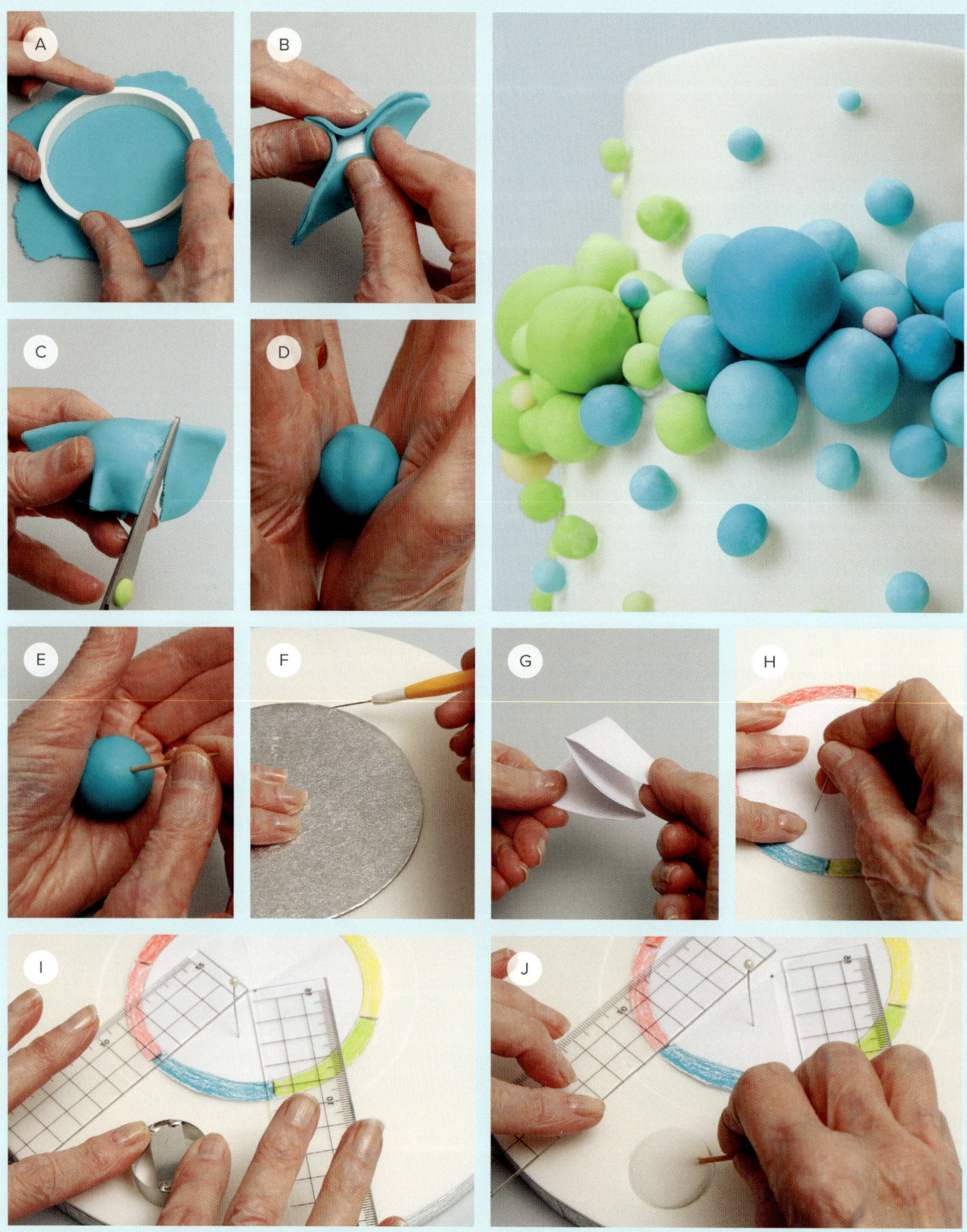

Mixing The Sugarpaste Colours

1   You will be using six base colours for this project: yellow, orange, red, pink, blue and green. The Sunshine Yellow, Zesty Orange, Glamour Red and Bridal Rose sugarpaste colours will be used straight from the packet as they are.

2   To make the blue base colour, mix 45g (1⁵/₈oz) of Spa Blue sugarpaste with 45g (1⁵/₈oz) of Bridal White sugarpaste. Wrap up and set aside until needed.

3   To make the green, knead a little Vine paste food colour into 85g (3oz) of Sunshine Yellow sugarpaste to achieve a light green shade. Wrap up and set aside.

4   This design also requires two paler shades of each base colour of sugarpaste. To make them, mix 35g (1¹/₄oz) of each of the six base colours with an equal amount of Bridal White sugarpaste to make six medium tones.

5   Mix one third of each of the six medium tones with an equal amount of Bridal White sugarpaste to make six pale tones. Individually wrap up all the colours until needed to prevent them from drying out.

Making The Spheres

1   Roll out 30g (1oz) of the darkest tone of blue sugarpaste to a 2mm (¹/₁₆") thickness and cut out an 8cm (3¹/₈") disc (A). Place a 2.5cm (1") polystyrene ball in the centre of the disc and gather the sugarpaste around it (B). Use sharp scissors to cut off the excess sugarpaste (C). Gently roll the ball between your palms until the gathered paste has melded together and there are no visible seams (D).

2   Cut one third off a cocktail stick. Brush 1cm (³/₈") at the cut end

with non-toxic glue and push it into the base of the sphere (E). Insert the other end of the cocktail stick into a block of polystyrene to dry.

3   Repeat steps 1–2 using a 1.8cm (³/₄") polystyrene ball and a 6cm (2³/₈") disc of the darkest blue sugarpaste.

4   Roll two 1.25cm (¹/₂") diameter balls of dark blue sugarpaste and two 1.25cm (¹/₂") diameter balls of medium blue sugarpaste. Roll the balls between your palms until they are smooth with no seams. Allow them to firm on a piece of food-grade foam.

5   Roll at least five 1cm (³/₈") diameter balls and at least five 7mm (¹/₄") diameter balls of both medium and light blue sugarpaste. Allow the balls to firm.

6   Repeat steps 1–5 using the Bridal Rose, Glamour Red, Zesty Orange, Sunshine Yellow and green sugarpaste colours. Allow the spheres to firm for at least 24 hours.

Covering The Cake Drum

1   Lightly cover the 23cm (9") cake drum with white vegetable fat. Roll out 300g (10¹/₂oz) of Bridal White sugarpaste and cover the drum (see technique on page 32). Set the drum

aside to firm overnight. Don't attach the ribbon at this stage.

2   Place a 12.5cm (5") cake board in the centre of the covered drum and draw around it with a scribing tool. This will create a guide as to where the cake will sit and therefore how much of the drum needs to be decorated (F).

3   Cut out a 10cm (4") disc of paper. Fold the paper in half and then into thirds to make a six-sectioned guide (G). Use coloured pencils to colour in the rim of each of the six sections, starting with blue and then continuing clockwise with pink, red, orange, yellow and green.

4   Place the paper in the centre of the drum as a guide to the segment colours and secure it with two sterilised pins (H).

5   Use a 2.8cm (1¹/₈") round cutter to cut out a disc of sugarpaste from the centre of the blue segment (I). Use a cocktail stick to lift the cut circle off the drum (J).

top tip

While you work with each section, it may help to lay some rulers or strips of paper on the drum in line with the guidelines to show you how wide the segment is at the edge of the board.

6 Roll out a small piece of the darkest blue sugarpaste to a 3mm ($^1/_8$") thickness. Cut out a 2.8cm (1$^1/_8$") disc and turn it over; the underside of the cut discs makes for a cleaner fit in the holes. Carefully insert the blue disc into the hole (K). Gently use your fingers to press it into place.

7 Repeat steps 5–6 to cut out a 2.2cm ($^7/_8$") or 1.6cm ($^5/_8$") circle on one side of the blue circle and replace with a disc of dark or medium blue sugarpaste.

8 Continue filling the blue segment with a selection of 2.2cm – 6mm ($^7/_8$ – $^1/_4$") discs and the three tones of blue sugarpaste (L). Try to create smaller circles in lighter tones of blue as you work out towards the edge of the segment and don't make the edges of the section too neat – let some circles overlap into the pink and green segments and leave room for some of those circles to overlap into the blue segment. Add some blue circles running over the edge of the drum (M), trimming the inserted disc to size.

9 Repeat steps 5–8 to complete the remaining segments using the respective colours of sugarpaste. Vary how far each colour's main circle sits between the edge of the drum and the 12.5cm (5") circle. Remove the paper guide once finished (N).

Covering The Cakes

1 You will be using the panelling method to cover the cakes. For the top tier, roll out 75g (2$^5/_8$oz) of Bridal White sugarpaste and cut out a 12.5cm (5") disc. Place the disc on top of the 10cm (4") wide cake and trim away the excess (see technique on page 32). For the bottom tier, repeat to cover the top of the 12.5cm (5") wide cake with a 15cm (6") disc using 105g (3$^3/_4$oz) of the Bridal White sugarpaste.

2 To cover the sides, start with the 10cm (4") cake. Roll out 265g (9$^1/_4$oz) of Bridal White sugarpaste and cut out a 34cm x 9cm (13$^3/_8$" x 3$^1/_2$") panel. Gently roll up the panel and wrap it around the cake (see technique on page 32).

3 Repeat step 2 to cover the side of the 12.5cm (5") cake. This time, roll out 480g (1lb 1oz) of Bridal White sugarpaste and cut a 42cm x 16.5cm (16$^1/_2$" x 6$^1/_2$") rectangle. Once both cakes are covered, leave them to dry overnight.

Decorating The Top

1 Cut out two irregularly placed 1.2cm ($^1/_2$") circles from the sugarpaste covering the top of the 10cm (4") cake, taking care not to cut down into the buttercream or ganache. Use a cocktail stick to remove the circles from the cake.

2 Roll out a small piece of the remaining darkest green sugarpaste to a 3mm ($^1/_8$") thickness. Cut out two 1.2cm ($^1/_2$") discs and turn them over.

Carefully insert the green discs into the holes on top of the cake, using your fingers to gently press them into place.

3 Repeat steps 1–2 to add more green circles to the top of the cake, working outwards and adding a selection of 1cm ($^3/_8$") medium and light green circles, followed by a selection of 6mm ($^1/_4$") medium and light green circles (O).

Assembling The Cake

1 Attach the 12.5cm (5") cake centrally on top of the covered drum. Dowel the cake, spacing them evenly within a central 10cm (4") circle. Attach the 10cm (4") cake centrally on top (see technique on page 41).

Attaching The Spheres

1 Measure the circumference of the bottom cake tier and divide the result by six.

2 Roll out a small piece of each darkest shade of sugarpaste into thin sheets and cut out strips that are 1.25cm ($^1/_2$") wide and slightly longer than the length calculated in step 1. Make 30° cuts at the ends of each strip, angling them inwards (P). This will help the strips fit the curve of the cake.

3 Lightly brush the exposed top edge of the bottom tier with edible glue. Attach the cut strips to the cake, arranging the colours in the opposite direction to the covered drum (Q). Finish with the red and orange strips at the back of the cake.

4 Insert the cocktail stick of the large red sphere into the red section on the cake (R). Add the second largest red sphere to the red section in the same way, positioning it at a different height to the larger sphere and not immediately adjacent to it (S).

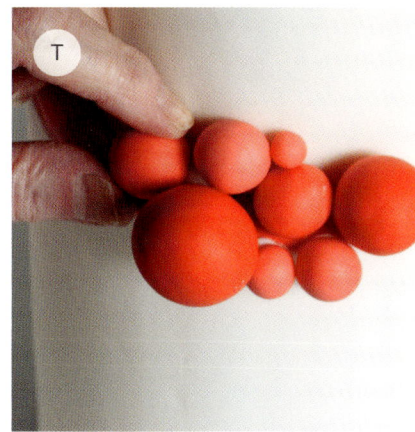

5   Use some royal icing to attach the remaining spheres to the red section, above and below the first two (T). Start with the largest spheres and work down to the smallest.

6   Repeat steps 4–5 to attach the other coloured spheres you made earlier around the cake. When securing the large spheres for each colour, place them at varying heights and in varying positions within their sections.

7   Fill any gaps in the sections with remaining spheres, rolling new ones from the leftover sugarpaste if required. Also add some small spheres to the sides of the cakes with royal icing, overlapping neighbouring colour sections slightly in some places.

8   To finish, fix the Bridal White ribbon around the edge of the drum (see technique on page 32). Position the ends of the ribbon at the point where the red and orange segments meet.

top tip

A nice touch would be to make accompanying cake pops in the same selection of colours. Just make sure to keep them separate from the polystyrene spheres!

TURQUOISE
treasure

Clean lines, bold colours and gold accents make this cake a star showstopper. Depending on the season, the fantasy flower arrangement could be easily adapted by using pastel shades or warmer tones.

YOU WILL NEED

Edibles

Square, filled sponge cakes covered with ganache/buttercream with a sharp edge finish, secured on cake boards of the same size (see page 30), 12.5cm (5") deep: 12.5cm (5") and 15cm (6") wide

SK Fairtrade Sugarpaste: 100g (3^1/$_2$oz) Bridal White and 1.8kg (3lb 15^1/$_2$oz) Frosted Leaf

SK Designer Metallic Lustre Dust Food Colour: Classic Gold

Clear alcohol, e.g. vodka or gin

SK Sugar Florist Paste (SFP): 50g (1^3/$_4$oz) White

SK Paste Food Colour: Black

SK Essentials Edible Glue

PME Piping Gel

Sugar pearls: 2mm (^{1}/$_{16}$") black

SK Professional Paste Food Colour: Poinsettia (Xmas Red)

SK Essentials Confectioners' Glaze

PME Edible Glaze Spray

SK Professional Instant Mix Royal Icing: 100g (3^1/$_2$oz) White

Equipment

Square cake drum: 20.5cm (8")

1.5cm (^{1}/$_2$") width satin ribbon: 87cm (34^1/$_4$") Honey Gold

Square cake boards: 12.5cm (5") and 15cm (6")

Square polystyrene separator, 2.5cm (1") deep: 10cm (4")

White card: 10cm (4") square

Non-toxic glue stick

CelStick: 6mm (^{1}/$_4$")

Templates: page 227

Floral wires: 26-gauge Nile green, and 22-, 24- and 26-gauge white

Modelling tools: dresden and medium ball

Cupped formers

Food-grade foam drying mat

SK High-Quality Paintbrush: no. 4

Round cutter: 1.5cm (^{1}/$_2$")

Half-width floral tape: Nile green and white

Oak leaf cutter (or similar): 6.5cm (2^1/$_2$")

SK-GI Silicone Veiner Rose - Tea: Very Large Leaf

SEE PAGES 11–15 FOR ESSENTIAL EDIBLES AND EQUIPMENT

Covering The Cake Drum

1 Roll out 315g (11oz) of Frosted Leaf sugarpaste and cover the 20.5cm (8") cake drum (see technique on page 32). Set the drum aside to firm overnight.

2 Fix the Honey Gold ribbon around the edge of the drum (see technique on page 32).

Covering The Cakes

1 You will be using the panelling method to cover the cakes. For the top tier, roll out 175g (6¹/₈oz) of Frosted Leaf sugarpaste and cut out a square for the top of the cake. Also cut out four panels for the sides of the cake using 530g (1lb 2³/₄oz) of Frosted Leaf sugarpaste (see technique on page 35).

2 Attach the square to the top of the 12.5cm (5") wide cake and then, one at a time, attach the panels to the sides (see technique on page 35).

3 Repeat steps 1–2 to cover the top and sides of the 15cm (6") cake, this time using 220g (7³/₄oz) of Frosted Leaf sugarpaste for the top and 620g (1lb 5³/₄oz) for the sides. Once both cakes are covered, leave them to dry overnight.

top tip

You can leave the sugarpaste panels to firm for a while, even overnight, to make them easier to handle and trim.

Covering The Separator

1 Stick the square of white card to the bottom of the polystyrene separator using non-toxic glue. Use a small CelStick to pierce a hole in one narrow side of the separator, 5cm (2") deep and 1.5cm (¹/₂") in from the edge.

2 As you did with the cakes, use the panelling method and 100g (3¹/₂oz) of Bridal White sugarpaste to cover the sides of the separator with rectangles (see technique on page 35).

3 Use the CelStick to poke through the paste and expose the hole. Leave the separator to firm overnight.

4 Once the sugarpaste is firm, mix some Classic Gold lustre dust with a little clear alcohol and paint each side gold. Apply three or four layers of paint, allowing it to dry fully between coats.

top tip

Only mix up enough gold paint as you need at the time. The alcohol content means it can dry out quite quickly and become too thick to paint smoothly.

Making The Petals

1 Roll out a small piece of White SFP to a 1.5mm (¹/₁₆") thickness over a groove on a non-stick board. Use the small petal template and a cutting wheel or knife to cut out the petal, ensuring that the thicker ridge of paste runs through the centre.

2 Cut a 24-gauge white floral wire into thirds. Hold the petal along the ridge, dip one end of a piece of wire in edible glue, wipe off the excess and then carefully insert the wire through the ridge.

3 Transfer the wired petal to the non-stick board. Drag the broad end of a dresden tool from near the base of the wired petal towards the top, continuing to drag it over the edge of the petal (A). Press firmly but not hard enough to go through the paste. Continue adding lines on either side of the centre, fanning them out but concentrating them at the top of the petal. Leave the petal to firm in a cupped former overnight.

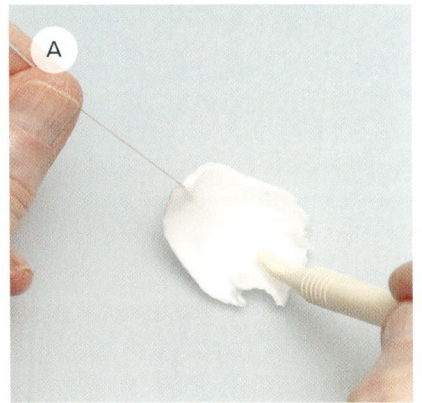

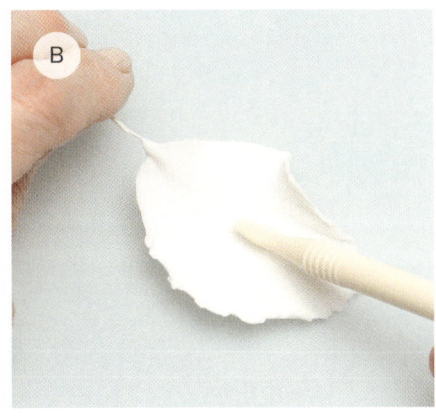

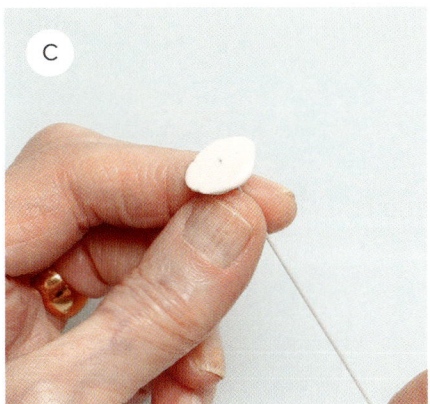

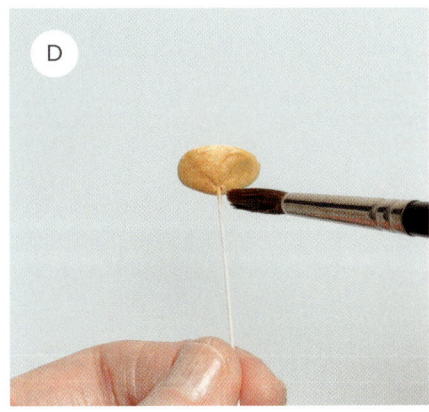

4   Repeat steps 1–3 to make three more small petals and five large petals (B). Leave the large petals to firm on a foam drying mat so they have a less cupped shape than the smaller petals.

Making The Centre

1   Roll a piece of White SFP into a flattened cone shape, 1.5cm (1/2") wide at the base and 8mm (5/16") tall from base to tip.

2   Cut a 24-gauge white floral wire into thirds. Bend a small hook in one end of a cut piece of wire and insert the hook into the point of the cone so it is embedded in the paste (C). Leave the wired cone to firm overnight.

3   Once the cone is firm, mix some Classic Gold lustre dust and clear alcohol together to form a paint. Using the no. 4 paintbrush, proceed to paint the underside of the cone gold (D).

4   Knead a little Black paste food colour into a small amount of White SFP to make a dark grey shade. Roll the grey SFP out into a thin sheet, cut out a disc using a 1.5cm (1/2") round cutter and glue it to the flat side of the cone (E).

5   Brush the grey disc with some piping gel, leave it to get tacky, then dip it into a pot of black sugar pearls (F). Carefully set aside.

top tip

If you don't have black sugar pearls, colour some White SFP black and roll little balls from it. Leave them to dry and then glaze them.

Assembling The Flower

1   Hold a petal between your forefinger and thumb at the point where the wire enters the paste. Gently bend the wire down until it's at a 90° angle to the petal. Repeat this for the remaining eight wired petals.

2   One at a time, use some half-width white floral tape to bind the four smaller petals around the flower centre. Make sure they are evenly distributed, taping directly underneath the petals where the wire enters.

3   Tape the five larger petals around the smaller ones following the same technique as in step 2. Arrange them evenly and tape all the way down the main wire (G). Set aside until assembly.

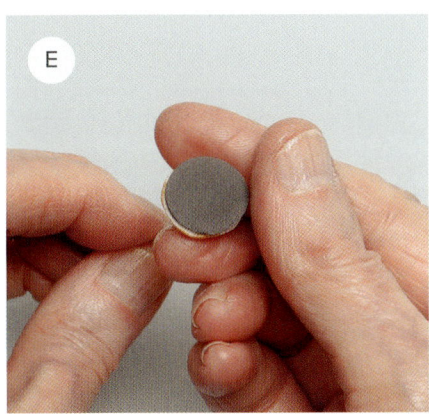

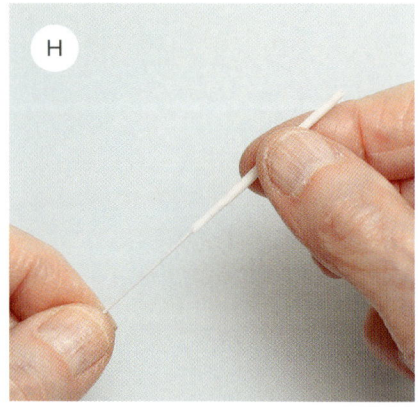

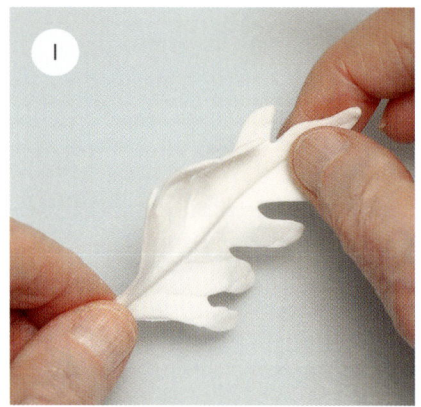

Making The Large Leaves

1   Cut a 24-gauge white floral wire into thirds. Knead a small piece of White SFP well to soften it, before sliding it onto the end of a cut wire. Work the paste down the wire, rolling it between your fingers until it is about 4cm (1½") long (H). Pull away any excess SFP.

2   Roll out a piece of White SFP to a 2mm (¹⁄₁₆") thickness and use an oak leaf cutter (or similar) to cut out a leaf. Keep and wrap up your offcuts.

3   Place the leaf on a foam pad and run a medium ball tool around the edges to thin and broaden the shape.

4   Lightly moisten one side of the wired paste with cooled, boiled water and press it onto the centre of the leaf with the uncovered wire at the base.

5   With the wired side facing down press the leaf firmly in between the two halves of the Tea Rose Leaf veiner to texture. Take care not to pull it by the wire when removing it from the veiner.

6   Use your fingers to shape the leaf and give it some movement (I). Set aside on a foam drying mat to firm.

7   Using one of the remaining cut wires, repeat steps 1–6 to make a second leaf.

8   Once the leaves are firm, mix some Classic Gold lustre dust and clear alcohol to make a paint. Paint both sides of each leaf gold and continuing 5cm (2") down the wires (J). Set the leaves aside to dry thoroughly before applying a second coat of gold paint.

Making The Small Leaves

1   Roll out a piece of White SFP to a 1.5mm (¹⁄₁₆") thickness over a groove on the non-stick board. Cut out a leaf using the small leaf template, ensuring the thicker ridge of paste runs through the centre. Place the leaf on the foam pad and thin the edges with the medium ball tool.

2   Cut three 26-gauge white floral wires into fifths to give you 15 pieces. Hold the leaf along the ridge, dip the end of a cut wire in edible glue, wipe off the excess and then carefully insert it through the ridge.

3   Press the wired leaf between the two halves of the Tea Rose Leaf veiner to texture. Remove and use your fingers to slightly twist the end of the leaf to create a little movement.

4   Using the remaining cut wires, repeat steps 1–3 to make 12 small leaves in total. Set them aside to firm overnight.

5   Once firm, use the Classic Gold lustre dust and clear alcohol solution to paint two coats of gold paint to both sides of each leaf and continuing along the top of the wire. Set aside to dry.

6   Use half-width white floral tape to bind the small leaves into two stems of six, spacing and staggering them evenly as you work (K). To finish, take the gold paint and cover the length of the stems gold.

Making The Berries

1   Cut four lengths of 24-gauge Nile green floral wire into thirds to give you 12 pieces. Bend a small closed hook in one end of 11 cut wires. You won't need the leftover wire piece.

2   Colour a small amount of White SFP a bright red shade using some Poinsettia (Xmas Red) paste. Divide the red SFP into 11 balls that are 1cm (³⁄₈") in diameter.

3　Take a cut wire and pierce the straight end through the centre of a ball, sliding it down until only the tip of the hook is visible at the top of the berry.

4　Repeat step 3 to wire all the berries using the remaining wires. Allow all the berries to firm overnight.

5　Once firm, dip the 11 berries in Confectioners' Glaze and allow them to dry.

6　When the glaze has dried, use half-width Nile green floral tape to bind the berries together in two bunches. You don't want to start taping directly under the berries; by leaving about 1cm ($^3/_8$") of wire beneath the berries untaped, you will be able to reposition them at different angles after taping (L).

Making The Wire Embellishment

1　Cover the entire length of a 22-gauge white floral wire with half-width white floral tape. Next, use a Classic Gold lustre dust and clear alcohol solution to paint the wire gold.

2　Once the paint has dried, lightly spray the covered wire with edible glaze. When dry, cut the wire in half and bend each piece into a curve.

Assembling The Arrangement

1　On the main flower stem, fix the two bundles of berries on opposite sides of the flower using half-width white tape. Tape a large leaf and a spray of small leaves on either side of each bunch of berries. Tape a curved wire behind each berry and leaf arrangement, with the lower one curving round to the left and the upper one curving round to the right.

2　To finish, use wire cutters to trim the taped stem to a 5cm (2") length.

Assembling The Cake

1　Attach the 15cm (6") cake centrally on top of the covered drum. Dowel the cake, spacing them evenly within a central 10cm (4") square, and attach the 10cm (4") separator on top (see technique on page 41). Make sure the prepared hole is at the front.

2　It is easier to attach the flower before attaching the top tier. To do this, pipe a little royal icing into the hole in the separator and insert the stem. If necessary, use pliers to push it further into the separator and ensure it is securely fixed in place. Arrange the leaves and berries so they are well spaced.

3　Spread a small amount of royal icing over the top of the separator and place the 12.5cm (5") cake on top, making sure it's centred.

top tip

It is a good idea to leave the separator to set for a while after attaching it to the cake so that it does not move around while you are attaching the flower spray.

SHADES
of grey

This subtle grey cake with soft pink and green hues from the delicate roses and eucalyptus branches gives off a very nonchalant, chic vibe that would be suitable for any time of year.

YOU WILL NEED

Edibles

Round, filled sponge cake covered with ganache/buttercream with a sharp edge finish, secured on a cake board of the same size (see page 29), 15cm (6") deep: 12.5cm (5") wide

Round, filled sponge cake covered with ganache/buttercream with a sharp edge finish, secured on a cake board of the same size (see page 29), 7.5cm (3") deep: 15cm (6") wide

SK Fairtrade Sugarpaste: 1.34kg (2lb 15^1/$_4$oz) Dove Grey

SK Sugar Florist Paste (SFP): 180g (6^1/$_4$oz) White

SK Professional Paste Food Colours: Holly/Ivy (Dark Green), Olive and Rose

SK Professional Dust Food Colours: Holly/Ivy (Dark Green), Sunflower and Vine

SK Paste Food Colour: Brown

Rainbow Dust ProGel Professional Food Colour: Grey

SK Essentials Edible Glue

PME Edible Glaze Spray

SK Professional Instant Mix Royal Icing: 100g (3^1/$_2$oz) White

Equipment

Round cake boards: 12.5cm (5") and 15cm (6")

Round cake drum: 20.5cm (8")

1.5cm (^{1}/$_2$") width satin ribbon: 69cm (27") Dove Grey

Polystyrene balls: 6 x 3cm (1^1/$_8$"), 8 x 3.5cm (1^3/$_8$") and 5 x 4cm (1^1/$_2$")

Floral wires: 24- and 30-gauge Nile green, and 18-gauge white

Tweezers

Cream matt pointed head stamens: 32 small

Floral tape: half-width and quarter-width Nile green, and full-width white

Carnation cutter: 4cm (1^3/$_4$")

SK High-Quality Paintbrush: no. 4

Safety razor blade

SK Multi Flower Cutter Set 1A, Round Petal/Leaf: nos. 2–4

Modelling tools: dresden, medium ball, small ball and veining

Deep soft sponge scourer

FMM Rose Calyx Cutter, Set of 3: 4cm (1^3/$_4$")

FMM Rose Leaf Cutters, Set of 3: 2.6cm (1"), 3.4cm (1^3/$_8$") and 4.3cm (1^3/$_4$")

SK-GI Silicone Veiner Rose - Tea: Large Leaf

Katy Sue Flower Pro Wedding Foliage Mould: Seeded Eucalyptus Leaves

Posy picks: various sizes

SEE PAGES 11–15 FOR ESSENTIAL EDIBLES AND EQUIPMENT

Covering The Cake Drum

1 Roll out 250g (8³/₄oz) of Dove Grey sugarpaste and cover the 20.5cm (8") cake drum (see technique on page 32). Set the drum aside to firm overnight.

2 Secure the Dove Grey ribbon around the edge of the drum (see technique on page 32). Set the covered drum aside for later.

Covering The Cakes

1 You will be using the panelling method to cover the cakes. For the top tier, roll out 105g (3³/₄oz) of Dove Grey sugarpaste and cut out a 15cm (6") disc. Place the disc on top of the 12.5cm (5") wide cake and trim away the excess (see technique on page 32). For the bottom tier, repeat to cover the top of the 15cm (6") wide cake with an 18cm (7") disc using 135g (4³/₄oz) of Dove Grey sugarpaste.

2 To cover the sides, start with the 12.5cm (5") wide cake. Roll out 480g (1lb 1oz) of Dove Grey sugarpaste and cut a 42cm x 16.5cm (16¹/₂" x 6¹/₂") panel. Roll up the panel and wrap it around the cake (see technique on page 32).

3 Repeat step 2 to cover the side of the 15cm (6") wide cake. This time, roll out 370g (13oz) of Dove Grey sugarpaste and cut out a 50cm x 9cm (19³/₄" x 3¹/₂") panel. Set both cakes aside to dry overnight.

top tip

If you don't have a carnation cutter for the ruffled centre pieces, you could use a small fluted pastry or cookie cutter as an alternative.

Making The Rose Centres

1 Colour 125g (4³/₄oz) of White SFP a very light fresh pink shade using some Rose paste food colour. You will be using this throughout the project, so make sure you keep your offcuts and wrap up the paste when you aren't working to prevent it from drying out.

top tip

When mixing pale colours for a flower, always make them lighter than you think you need. As the petals layer up and as shadows get introduced, the colour will intensify.

2 Use a sharp knife to cut a 3.5cm (1³/₈") polystyrene ball in half (A).

3 Roll out a 2cm (³/₄") ball of the pink SFP to a 1mm (<¹/₁₆") thickness.

4 Brush the surface of one half of the cut polystyrene ball (excluding the cut side) with a little edible glue. Lay the SFP on the ball and smooth it around the shape. Pull off the excess that goes onto the cut side.

5 Roll out a 1.5cm (¹/₂") ball of the pink SFP to a 1mm (<¹/₁₆") thickness.

6 Brush the cut face of the ball with edible glue. Stick the paste to the face and remove the excess that goes over onto the sides. Knead together the offcuts with the remaining pink SFP and wrap up.

7 Cut a 7.5cm (3") length of 18-gauge white floral wire and make an open hook in one end.

8 Take around eight pointed head cream stamens and fold them in half to give you 16 heads. Bind the

bottom 1cm (³/₈") of the stamens with half-width Nile green floral tape (B).

9 Use the no. 4 paintbrush to dust the heads with some Sunflower dust food colour. Optionally, lightly brush the tips of the stamen heads with a little Brown paste food colour.

10 Hook the wire between the stamens, pull it against the taped section and squeeze it closed with pliers (C). Bind the wire to the stamens using half-width Nile green tape.

11 Push the end of the wire down centrally through the face of the halved pink ball and pull it through until the tops of the stamens sit about 1cm (³/₈") above the paste (D).

12 Roll out a small piece of the pink SFP to a 1mm (<¹/₁₆") thickness. Cut out a flower shape using a 4cm (1¹/₂") carnation cutter (E).

13 Drag a dresden tool outwards over the fluted sections to stretch and thin them (F). There is no need to worry about keeping them neat.

14 Use a safety razor blade to cut the shape into four equal pieces (G). Scrunch up each piece with your fingers, keeping the thinned areas at the top (H).

15 Brush a little edible glue on the face of the pink rose base surrounding the stamens. Secure the scrunched pieces all around the stamens so they are positioned just a little higher than them (I).

16 Repeat steps 12–15 to attach more petals to the centre. Do this until the whole face of the rose base has been filled (J).

17 Repeat steps 3–16 to make a second rose centre with the other half of the cut polystyrene ball.

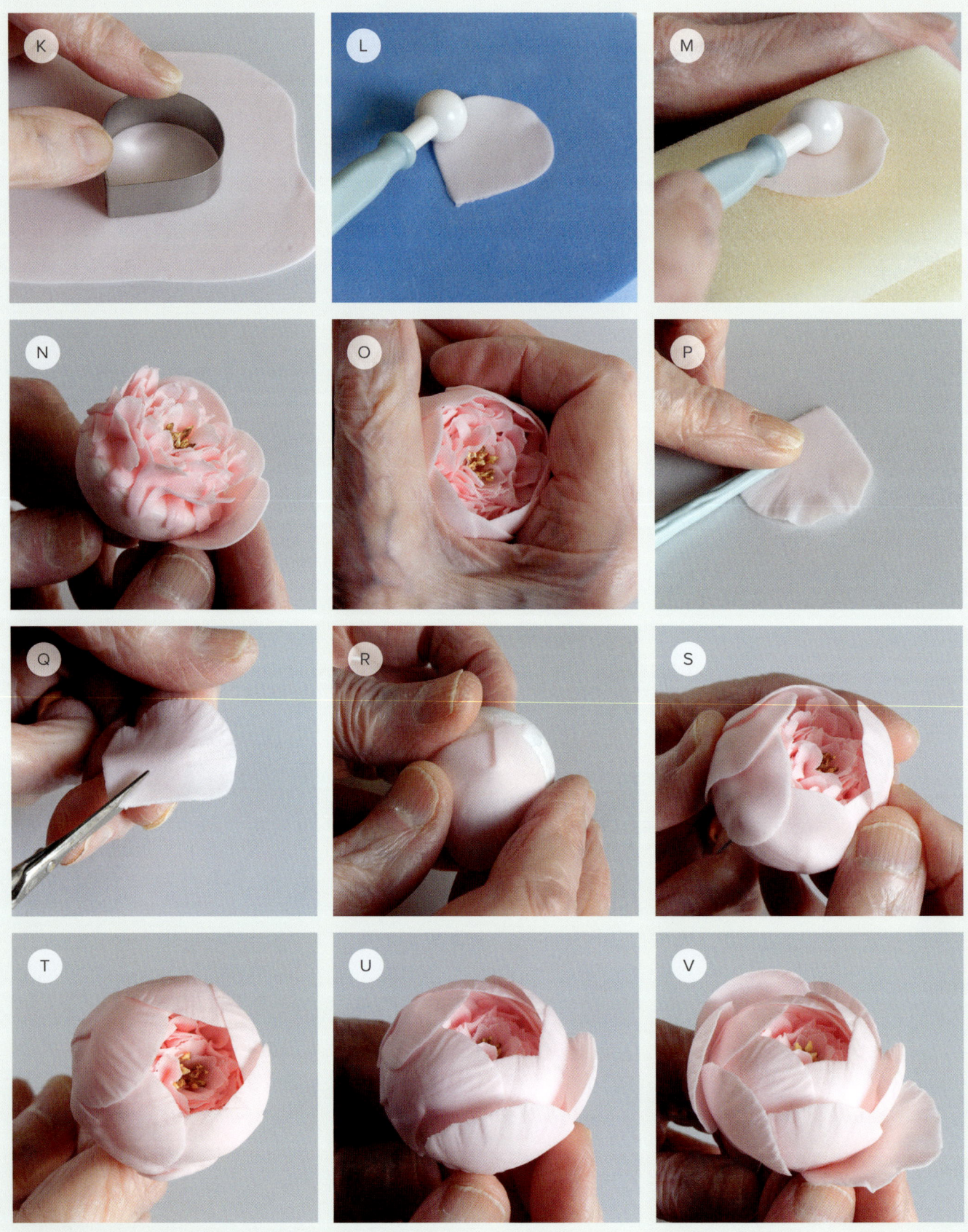

Making The Rose Petals

Layer One

1   Roll out a small piece of the pink SFP from earlier to a 1mm (< $^1/_{16}$") thickness and cut out a rose petal using a 3cm (1$^1/_8$") round petal cutter (K).

2   Place the petal on a foam pad and thin the edges with a medium ball tool (L).

3   Move the petal to the sponge side of a scourer and cup it using the medium ball tool again (M).

4   Repeat steps 1–3 to make eight rose petals in total.

5   Brush the lower half of one petal with some edible glue. Attach it to the first rose centre so it is positioned about 3mm ($^1/_8$") above the ruffled top.

6   Repeat step 5 to attach the remaining petals to the centre, making sure they are spaced evenly and that the final petal tucks under the first so they all overlap each other (N). Finish by curling your fingers and thumb around the petals to curve them inwards over the ruffled centre (O).

7   Repeat steps 1–6 to attach the first layer of petals to the second rose centre.

Layer Two

1   Repeat steps 1–2 from Rose Petals: Layer One to make another petal of the same size.

2   Lightly texture the petal using a veining tool. Keep the tool pointing towards the base of the petal as you roll it back and forth (P).

3   Make a 1cm ($^3/_8$") cut upwards from the pointed base of the petal with a pair of scissors (Q).

4   Cross the cut ends over each other and place the petal on a 3cm (1$^1/_8$") polystyrene ball (R). Press the ball and petal into your cupped hand to shape and curve the petal. Leave the petal to dry until slightly firm.

5   Repeat steps 1–4 to make six petals in total.

6   Brush the lower half of a petal with some edible glue. Attach the petal to the flower, positioning its base about halfway up the first layer of petals.

7   Repeat step 6 to attach the remaining petals, making sure that each one overlaps the next (S). The attached petals should curve over the centre to leave an opening of about 1.5cm – 2cm ($^1/_2$" – $^3/_4$") in size (T).

8   Repeat steps 1–7 to attach the second layer of petals to the second rose centre.

Layer Three

1   Repeat steps 1–4 from Rose Petals: Layer Two to make six petals using a 3.3cm (1$^1/_4$") round petal cutter. Allow them to dry on 3.5cm (1$^3/_8$") polystyrene balls.

2   Brush the lower third of a petal with edible glue and attach it to

the flower. Ensure its top is roughly level with the previous layer but that it stands about 1cm ($^3/_8$") away.

3   Repeat step 2 to attach the remaining five petals around the flower, making sure they are evenly spaced and that each petal overlaps the next one (U).

4   Repeat steps 1–3 to attach the third layer of petals to the second rose centre.

Layer Four

1   Repeat steps 1–4 from Rose Petals: Layer Two to make five petals using a 4.2cm (1$^5/_8$") round petal cutter. Allow them dry on 4cm (1$^1/_2$") polystyrene balls. This time, give the outer edge of each petal a bit of undulation when left to dry.

2   Brush the lower quarter of a petal with edible glue and attach it to the underside of the flower, flaring out about 1.5cm ($^1/_2$") away from the previous petals.

3   Repeat step 2 to attach the remaining four petals, spacing them evenly and with each overlapping the next (V).

4   Repeat steps 1–3 to attach the final layer of petals to the second rose centre.

the excess. Holding the leaf between your fingers, gently insert the glued wire 1cm (³/₈") into the ridge at the base of the leaf.

5   Place the leaf on the foam pad and thin the edges with the medium ball tool.

6   Place the leaf between the two halves of a Tea Rose Leaf veiner and press down firmly to texture. Remove from the veiner and use your fingers to shape the leaf to give it some movement. Set aside to dry.

7   Repeat steps 2–6 to make one 2.6cm (1") leaf and three 3.4cm (1³/₈") leaves using the respective Rose Leaf cutters.

8   Once the leaves are dry, brush them with some Holly/Ivy (Dark Green) dust. Steam the leaves to set the colour and, once dry, spray them with edible glaze.

Making The Rose Calyxes

1   Colour a 2cm (³/₄") ball of White SFP with a combination of Olive and Holly/Ivy (Dark Green) paste food colours to achieve a green shade.

2   Roll out half of the green SFP to a 1mm (<¹/₁₆") thickness and cut out a calyx with a 4cm (1¹/₂") Rose Calyx cutter.

3   Thin the calyx edges with the medium ball tool on the foam pad.

4   Take one rose and brush a little edible glue on the area around the wire on the underside of the flower. Slide the calyx centrally up the wire and press it into place.

5   Finally, bind down the length of the main stem with half-width Nile green floral tape.

6   Using the remaining green SFP, repeat steps 2–5 to attach a calyx to the second rose.

Making The Rose Leaves

1   Colour a 2cm (³/₄") ball of White SFP with a little Olive paste food colour to achieve a green shade.

2   Roll a small piece of the green SFP to a 1mm (<¹/₁₆") thickness over a groove on the non-stick board.

3   Remove the paste from the board and cut out a leaf using a 4.3cm (1³/₄") Rose Leaf cutter, taking care to place the cutter centrally over the ridge. Keep your offcuts.

4   Cut a 7.5cm (3") length of 30-gauge Nile green floral wire. Dip the end of the wire in edible glue and wipe off

Assembling The Rose Leaves

1   Bind the large leaf to one of the rose flowers just below the calyx with some quarter-width Nile green tape.

2   The remaining four leaves will make two branches. Cut two 18cm (7") lengths of 24-gauge Nile green wire.

3   Take one of the cut wires and bind down the length, about the first 5cm (2"), with quarter-width Nile green tape.

4   Attach the smallest leaf, making sure it sits flush against the main wire, before taping on a medium leaf approximately 2.5cm – 5cm (1" – 2") below. Continue taping down the wire until you reach the end.

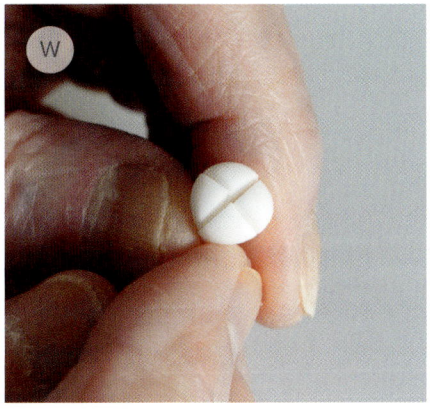

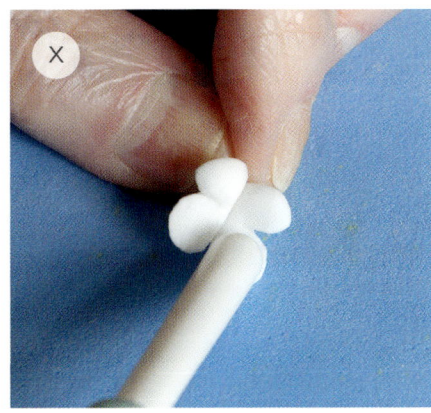

5 Take the second cut wire and repeat steps 3–4 to make a second branch using the remaining two medium leaves. Make some gentle curves in the branches to give them life.

6 If you want, you can add a few little twigs to the branches. To do this, fold a 5cm (2") piece of quarter-width Nile green tape over the branch and twist the two ends together to form a twig.

Making The Filler Flowers

1 Roll a 1cm ($^3/_8$") ball of White SFP into a teardrop shape. Use a safety razor blade to carefully divide the wide section of the teardrop into quarters (W). Fold out each quarter and pinch them flat.

2 Lay the flower down on its side on the foam pad and use a small ball

tool to thin and shape each individual petal (X).

3 Cut a 7.5cm (3") length of 30-gauge Nile green floral wire and bend a small hook in one end.

4 Slide the wire down through the middle of the flower (Y) until the hook nestles in the centre. Taper the paste around the wire under the flower.

5 Using the no. 4 paintbrush, dust the bottom of the flower with a little Vine dust to blend it into the wire, fading out the colour as you work up (Z).

6 Repeat steps 1–5 to make about 18 flowers in total. Vary the size of the ball you start with; you want to finish with a selection of flower sizes.

7 To make an opening bud, shape an 8mm ($^5/_{16}$") ball of White SFP into

a teardrop. Use a safety razor blade to divide the paste into quarters, but this time only ease the quarters apart a little and gently pinch the tops to taper them.

8 Cut a 7.5cm (3") length of 30-gauge Nile green floral wire and bend a small closed hook in one end. Dip the hook in edible glue and wipe off the excess. Insert the hooked end into the bottom of the bud and taper the paste around it.

9 Repeat steps 7–8 to make two or three more opening buds. You can vary the size of the starting ball, and for some, just mark a cross in the top rather than cutting it.

10 Repeat step 5 to dust the base of the opening buds.

11 To make a closed bud, shape a roughly 5mm ($^1/_4$") ball of White

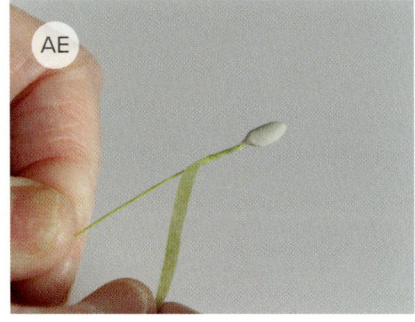

SFP into an oval. Repeat to make four or five closed buds of varying sizes.

12 Repeat step 8 to wire each of the closed buds.

13 To finish, repeat step 5 to dust the closed buds.

Assembling The Filler Flowers

1 Gather together five or six flowers of varying sizes, as well as two or three opening or closed buds.

2 When assembling, start with a closed bud. Bind another bud or two (closed or opening) to it with quarter-width Nile green tape, spaced about 1cm (³/₈") apart (AA).

3 Start binding on some of the open flowers, going from smallest to largest. As with the buds, space them about 1cm (³/₈") apart and vary the side of the wire that you put them on (AB).

4 Continue binding down to the end of the wires until completely covered with tape.

5 Repeat steps 1–4 to make two more sprays of filler flowers.

Making The Eucalyptus Leaves

1 Colour 35g (1¹/₄oz) of White SFP with a combination of Holly/Ivy (Dark Green) and Grey paste food colours to achieve a pale green shade.

2 Shape a 1cm (³/₈") ball of the pale green SFP into a long flat oval. Press into a Seeded Eucalyptus Leaves mould, use your fingers to push it up to all the edges and then smooth it down (AC).

3 Cut a 7.5cm (3") length of 30-gauge Nile green wire. Dip one end in edible glue and wipe off the excess. Slide the glued wire along the channel in the mould and up 1cm (³/₈") into the leaf (AD).

4 Carefully remove the leaf from the mould and pinch the base closed around the wire. Slightly curve the leaf with your fingers, with the veined side on the outside, to add a little movement. Set aside to dry.

5 Repeat steps 2–4 to make about 18 leaves in a mixture of the two sizes: 4cm (1¹/₂") and 5cm (2"). Set aside until assembly.

6 Cut a 7.5cm (3") length of 30-gauge Nile green wire and make a tiny closed hook in one end.

7 Shape a roughly 4mm (³/₁₆") ball of the pale green SFP into an oval. Insert the hooked wire into one end of the oval and pinch it closed.

8 Bind down the wire from directly underneath the bud with quarter-width Nile green tape (AE).

9 Repeat steps 6–8 to make 10 buds in total and set aside.

Assembling The Eucalyptus

1 Cut two 15cm (6") lengths of 24-gauge Nile green floral wire.

2 Bind five eucalyptus buds to the end of a piece of cut wire using quarter-width Nile green tape. Position the leaves on the main stem so they are at varying heights but not equally spaced.

3 Tape a pair of eucalyptus leaves on opposite sides of the wire, about 1.5cm (¹/₂") down from the top of the

stem, making sure to have the veined side facing up.

4 Repeat step 3 to add three or four pairs of leaves, each spaced about 2cm (^{3}/$_4$") apart from the previous pair (AF). Tape down to the end of the wire.

5 Repeat steps 2–4 to make a second eucalyptus branch using three or four pairs of the remaining leaves.

6 If you have any leaves left over, bind these into a small spray with quarter-width Nile green tape.

Assembling The Cake

1 Attach the 15cm (6") cake centrally on top of the covered drum. Dowel the cake, spacing them evenly within a 12.5cm (5") circle that is positioned towards the back of the cake. Attach the 12.5cm (5") cake on top (see technique on page 41).

Attaching The Arrangement

1 Make several hooped pins by covering 6cm (2^3/$_8$") lengths of 18-gauge white floral wire with some full-width white tape and bending them into a U-shape.

2 Hold the roses against the cake in roughly the positions you want them. Gently mark the points at which the stems will be inserted.

3 Insert the two eucalyptus branches into posy picks, fixing them in place with a little leftover sugarpaste or royal icing inside the picks. Attach the picks to the top of the bottom tier: one pointing left and the other pointing right. Leave about a 7.5cm (3") gap between the base leaves for the roses. Insert the small eucalyptus spray into a posy pick and attach upright in front of where the rose on the right will go. Trim the length if required.

4 Insert the two rose leaf branches into posy picks and attach to the cake. Have the one with the small leaf going upwards almost to the top of the top tier, and have the other curving downwards over the bottom tier.

5 Attach the filler flowers to the cake using posy picks. Place one to the left of the gap for the roses, and secure two in front of the small eucalyptus spray.

6 Using posy picks, insert the two roses where you marked earlier. Position the one with the large leaf attached standing and pointing upwards and slightly forward. Position the second rose pointing slightly left and upwards.

top tip

Fix flowers to cakes by inserting them into posy picks, or into trimmed drinking straws sealed at the base with hardened melted chocolate or royal icing. Make sure the straws are always longer than the wires. Alternatively, if you have some Safety Seal, you can use that instead.

SWEET
as can be

This sweet sugar spray of tulips, primrose and forsythia flowers adorned on a classic white cake is suitable for all kinds of celebrations.

Edibles

Round, filled sponge cake covered with ganache/buttercream with a sharp edge finish, secured on a cake board of the same size (see page 29), 18cm (7") deep: 12.5cm (5") wide

Round, filled sponge cake covered with ganache/buttercream with a sharp edge finish, secured on a cake board of the same size (see page 29), 10cm (4") deep: 10cm (4") wide

SK Fairtrade Sugarpaste: 1.2kg (2lb 10^1/$_4$oz) Bridal White

SK Sugar Florist Paste (SFP): 155g (5^1/$_2$oz) White

SK Professional Dust Food Colours: Daffodil (Yellow), Edelweiss (White), Leaf Green, Rose and Sunflower

SK Professional Paste Food Colour: Leaf Green

SK Designer Paste Food Colour: Olive

SK Neonz Paste Food Colours: Pink and Purple

SK Essentials Edible Glue

SK Professional Instant Mix Royal Icing: 100g (3^1/$_4$oz) White

Equipment

Templates: page 227

Round cake boards: 10cm (4") and 12.5cm (5")

Round cake drum: 18cm (7")

1.5cm (^{1}/$_2$") width satin ribbon: 61cm (24") Bridal White

Floral wires: 24- and 26-gauge Nile green, and 18-, 26- and 33-gauge white

SK High-Quality Paintbrush: no. 4

Floral tape: full-width brown, and full-width, half-width and quarter-width Nile green

Modelling tools: dresden, large ball, medium ball and small ball

SK Multi Flower Cutter Set 1B, Round Petal/Leaf: no. 5

Aluminium foil

Safety razor blade

Food-grade card

PME Modelling Tools: Cutting Wheel and Taper Cones 5/6 Star

Deep soft sponge scourer

CelStick: 6mm (^{1}/$_4$")

FMM Primrose Cutters: 2.1cm (^{7}/$_8$") and 2.8cm (1^1/$_8$")

Posy picks: various sizes

SEE PAGES 11–15 FOR ESSENTIAL EDIBLES AND EQUIPMENT

Covering The Cake Drum

1   Roll out 200g (7oz) of Bridal White sugarpaste and cover the 18cm (7") cake drum (see technique on page 32). Set the drum aside to firm overnight.

2   Fix the Bridal White ribbon around the edge of the drum (see technique on page 32).

Covering The Cakes

1   You will be using the panelling method to cover the cakes. For the top tier, roll out 75g (2⅝oz) of Bridal White sugarpaste and cut out a 12.5cm (5") disc. Place the disc on top of the 10cm (4") cake and trim away the excess (see technique on page 32). For the bottom tier, repeat to cover the top of the 12.5cm (5") cake with a 15cm (6") disc using 105g (3¾oz) of the Bridal White sugarpaste.

2   To cover the sides, start with the 10cm (4") cake. Roll out 310g (10¾oz) of Bridal White sugarpaste and cut out a 34cm x 11.5cm (13⅜" x 4½") panel. Roll up the panel and wrap it around the cake (see technique on page 32).

3   Repeat step 2 to cover the side of the 12.5cm (5") cake. This time, roll out 530g (1lb 2¾oz) of Bridal White sugarpaste and cut out a 42cm x 19cm (16½" x 7½") rectangle. Once both cakes are covered, leave them to dry overnight.

top tip

This centrepiece would also work well being made with square cake tiers instead of round ones!

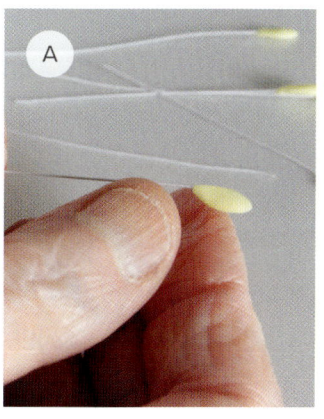
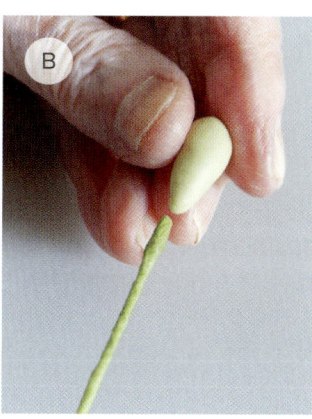
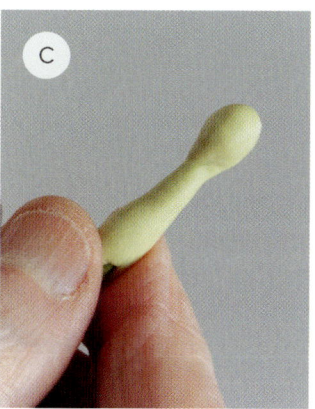
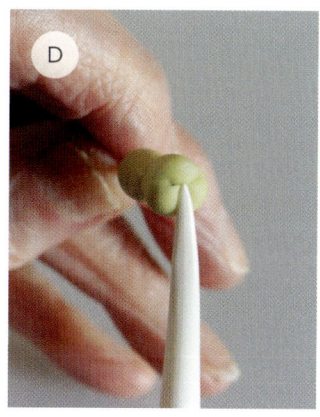

Making The Parrot Tulip Centre

1   Cut six 5cm (2") lengths of 33-gauge white floral wire. Colour a 1cm ($\frac{1}{8}$") ball of White SFP a yellow shade using a little Daffodil (Yellow) dust. Divide the ball into six equal pieces.

2   Roll one of the six pieces of yellow SFP into a ball and attach it to one end of a cut wire. Roll the ball and wire between your fingers into a rice grain shape and then pinch to flatten (A). Repeat for the five remaining pieces and wire. Leave the stamens to dry.

3   Use a no. 4 paintbrush to dust the top of each stamen with a little Sunflower dust colour and set aside.

4   Cut a 7.5cm (3") length of 18-gauge white floral wire. Cover the entire wire with half-width Nile green tape, wrapping it round the first 1cm ($\frac{3}{8}$") of the wire an extra time to make it a bit thicker.

5   Colour a 1.5cm ($\frac{1}{2}$") ball of White SFP a pale green shade using some Olive paste food colour. Roll the ball into a teardrop shape.

6   Insert the thick end of the taped wire up into the thin end of the teardrop (B). Work the paste between your fingers until it resembles a bowling pin – a narrow centre and with the lower portion being slightly longer (C).

7   Use a dresden tool to mark three indents from the centre outwards on the top of the paste (D). Gently pinch the three sections to flatten them slightly (E).

8   Bind the six stamens evenly around the centre with quarter-width Nile green tape. Position them so they are sitting about 1cm ($\frac{3}{8}$") above the top of the centre (F).

Making The Parrot Tulip Petals

1   Mix 30g (1oz) of White SFP with a combination of Pink and Purple neon paste food colours to achieve a deep pinky-purple shade.

2   Roll out a 2cm ($\frac{3}{4}$") ball of the pinky-purple SFP to a thickness of about 1mm ($<\frac{1}{16}$") over a groove on a non-stick board (G).

3   Remove the paste from the board and lay it ridged side up. Cut out a petal using a 5.5cm ($2\frac{1}{4}$") round petal cutter, making sure the length of the cutter is centred over the ridge (H).

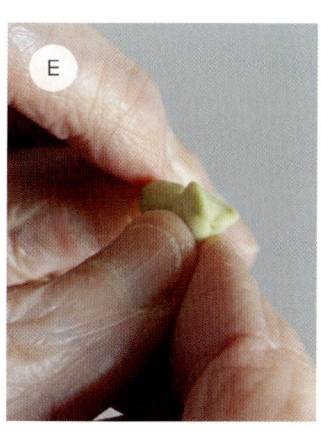

Knead the offcuts back with the remaining paste and wrap up for later.

4   Use the very tip of a petal cutter to cut away tiny pieces from around the edge of the petal (I).

5   Lay the petal ridged side up on a foam pad. Drag a medium ball tool firmly across the cut edges to thin and frill them (J). Use the dresden tool to drag marks from the ridge to the edge of the petal (K).

6   Cut a 7.5cm (3") length of 26-gauge white floral wire. Dip one end in edible glue and wipe off the excess. Holding the bottom of the petal between your finger and thumb, insert the glued end of the wire about 1cm ($^3/_8$") into the ridged part of the petal (L).

7   Place the petal ridged side down in a food-grade cupped former to dry (M). I used a 6cm ($2^3/_8$") long egg mould to dry my flowers, but for convenience, you could shape some aluminium foil around a large egg to make your own formers.

8   Repeat steps 2–7 to make five more parrot tulip petals. Leave all the petals to dry overnight.

top tip

To make long pieces of half or quarter-width floral tape without a tape cutter, cut a length of full-width tape, fold it over on itself lengthwise a few of times (being careful to keep an end free), then cut the folded piece into halves or quarters with scissors and unfold it.

Assembling The Parrot Tulip

1   Take a petal and bend the wire down by 45°. Bind the petal to the flower centre using full-width Nile green tape, with the bottom of the petal flush against the base of the centre. Bind approximately 2.5cm (1") down the stem (N). Repeat with two more parrot tulip petals, making sure they are evenly spaced around the centre.

2   Take one of the remaining petals and bend the wire down by 90°. Position the petal so it's flush against the previous petal row and sits in line with the gap between two of them. Bind it to the main stem with full-width Nile green tape.

3   Repeat step 2 for the remaining two petals. When attaching the final petal, bind right down to the bottom of the stem.

Making The Closed Tulips

1   Colour 55g (2oz) of White SFP a light pink shade using a little Pink neon paste colour.

2   Roll 10g ($^1/_4$oz) of the light pink SFP into a teardrop shape. Use a safety razor blade to make three evenly spaced 1cm ($^3/_8$") cuts on the narrow tip of the teardrop (O).

3   Gently pinch each cut section to define and separate them, before pinching them the opposite way to flatten into petal tips (P). Smooth the petal tips upwards so they line up neatly but are still separate (Q).

4   Cut a 12.5cm (5") length of 18-gauge white floral wire and bend a hook in one end. Dip the hooked end in edible glue and wipe off the

excess. Insert the wire into the wide base of the tulip cone and pinch the paste closed around the wire.

5   Repeat steps 2–4 to make two more tulip cones.

6   Trace the tulip petal template onto a piece of food-grade card and cut it out.

7   Roll out a 1.5cm ($^1/_2$") ball of the pale pink SFP to a thickness of about 1mm ($<^1/_{16}$"). Cut out a tulip petal shape using the template and a small cutting wheel. Knead the offcuts back with the remaining pink SFP and wrap up.

top tip

When using a cutting wheel to cut out petals or leaves, turn your board 180° after cutting the first half so you aren't cutting across yourself for the second half.

8   Use the medium ball tool to thin the edges of the petal on a foam pad. Firmly mark a line from the tip of the petal down to the base with the dresden tool (R).

9   Transfer the petal to the sponge side of a scourer and use a large ball tool to cup the petal, concentrating on the lower half (S).

10   Repeat steps 7–9 to make two more petals.

11   Dip the clean no. 4 paintbrush into edible glue and wipe off the excess. Lightly brush the lower two thirds of a petal with glue and attach the petal to a tulip cone, positioning it flush against the wire underneath. Attach the remaining two petals around the bud in the same way, making sure they are evenly spaced (T).

12 Repeat steps 7–11 to make two more closed tulips with the other cones. Leave all three closed tulips to dry.

13 Mix a little Edelweiss (White) and Rose dusts together on a paper towel. Use the clean no. 4 paintbrush to dust the lower half of each tulip, fading the dust out as it moves up the petals. Finally, dust the underside of each tulip with a little Leaf Green dust.

14 Knead a mixture of Leaf Green and Olive paste food colours into 40g (1¹/₂oz) of White SFP to make a light fresh green shade. This light green SFP will be used throughout the rest of the project.

15 To make a thick stem, take a 1.2cm (¹/₂") ball of the light green SFP and slide it up the main wire of one of the tulips until it is directly below the flower. Twiddle the paste between your finger and thumb to work it about 7.5cm (3") down the wire. Pinch off any excess and wrap it up with the remaining paste. Repeat for the two other tulips and leave the stems to dry.

Making The Tulip Leaves And Stems

1 Trace the tulip leaf template onto a piece of food-grade card and cut it out.

2 Roll out 10g (¹/₄oz) of the light green SFP you made earlier to a thickness of about 1mm (<¹/₁₆"). Roll it into a strip that is both long and wide enough for the leaf template.

3 Use the leaf template and a cutting wheel to cut out a leaf shape. Knead the offcuts back with the remaining paste and wrap up. Use the medium ball tool to thin the edges of the leaf.

4 Cut an 18cm (7") length of 24-gauge Nile green wire. Take a pea-sized ball of the light green SFP and knead until it is very soft. Once pliable, push the paste onto one end of the wire. Roll the paste between your finger and thumb to work it down the wire until it covers about 7.5cm (3") of it. Pinch off any excess and knead it back with the remaining paste.

5 Lightly brush one side of the wired paste with edible glue. Firmly press the paste section of the wire centrally to the back of the leaf, making sure the lowest part of the paste is in line with the base of the leaf (U). Pinch the paste to the wire at the base.

6 Use your fingers to gently bend the leaf and wire a little to give it some shape. Remember, the wire needs to be on the underside (V).

7 Repeat steps 2–6 to make two more tulip leaves. Set the leaves aside to dry overnight.

8 To make the stems, roll the remaining light green SFP into a 5mm (¹/₄") wide rope. Cut a 10cm (4") and a 15cm (6") piece from the rope and leave both to dry.

top tip

If you want to vein the tulip leaves you can use a dried corn husk to texture.

Making The Primroses

1 Colour 15g (¹/₂oz) of White SFP a light yellow shade using a little Daffodil (Yellow) dust food colour.

2 Roll a 1.5cm (¹/₂") ball of the light yellow SFP into a teardrop shape. Pinch out the bottom section of the teardrop to leave a mound in the paste, shaped like a witch's hat (W).

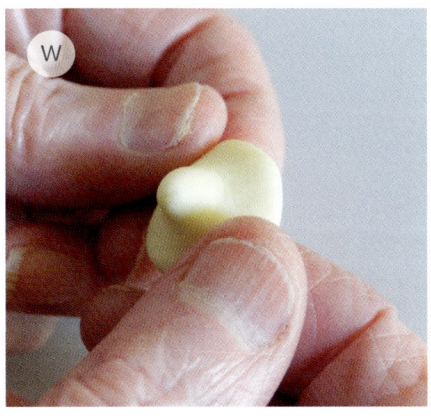

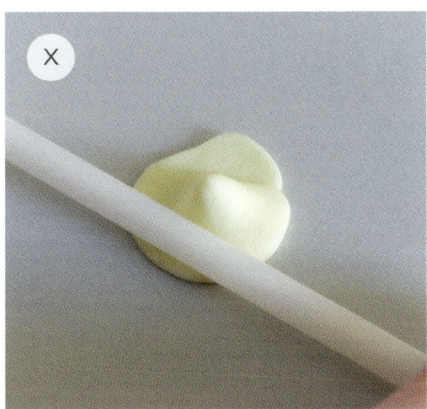

3   Place the paste flat side down on the non-stick board and use a small CelStick to thin out the pinched section until it is about 4cm (1½") in diameter (X). You should end up with a disc with a raised mound in the centre.

4   Place the 2.8cm (1⅛") Primrose cutter centrally over the raised section of the paste and press down firmly to cut it out (Y). Remove the flower from the cutter. Knead the offcuts back with the remaining paste and wrap up.

5   Lay the petal on the foam pad with the flat side facing towards you.

Holding the raised part at the back, use a medium ball tool to thin and slightly curl each individual petal. Next, press a Taper Cones 5/6 Star tool firmly in the centre of the flower to create divisions (Z).

6   Cut a 9cm (3½") length of 26-gauge Nile green floral wire and bend a small open hook in one end. Dip the hooked end of the wire in edible glue and wipe off the excess. Slide the wire down through the middle of the flower until the hook nestles in the centre but is still slightly visible (AA). To finish, use your fingers to taper the paste underneath the petals to the wire. Set aside to dry.

7   Repeat steps 2–6 to make nine more primroses. Make around half of them using the 2.8cm (1⅛") Primrose cutter and the other half using the 2.1cm (⅞") Primrose cutter. Leave all the flowers to dry overnight.

8   Using a no. 4 paintbrush, lightly dust the middle 1cm (⅜") of the flowers with some Sunflower dust. Finish by lightly dusting the very centre and the tapered bottom of the flowers with a little Leaf Green dust (AB).

9   Use some full-width Nile green floral tape to bind the primroses together in two bunches: one bunch of seven flowers and one bunch of three. Position them however you like, with them all level or at slightly different heights. Tape all the way down to the end of the wires to cover them.

Making The Forsythia Flowers

1   Colour 10g (¼oz) of White SFP a warm yellow shade using some Sunflower dust.

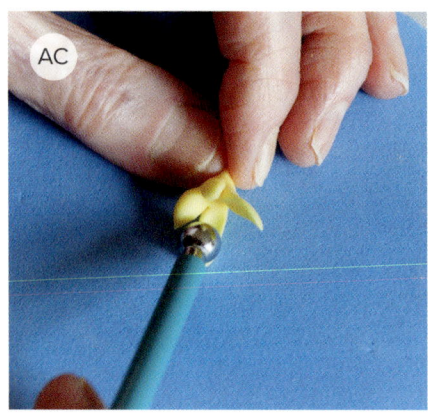

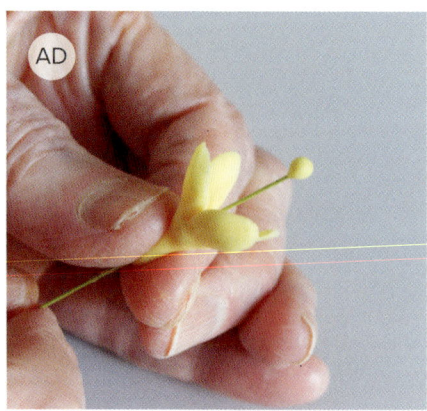

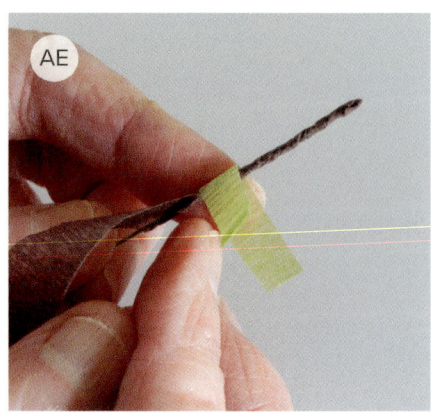

2   Take a 1cm (³/₈") ball of the warm yellow SFP and shape it into a teardrop. Holding the narrow end, use a small pair of sharp scissors to cut the rounded end in half to a depth of about 5mm (¹/₄"). Next, cut each of those halves in half to give you four petal sections.

3   Pinch each petal section flat and place the flower on the foam pad. Holding the narrow end, use a small ball tool to thin and elongate each petal section (AC). To finish, lightly pinch the tip of each individual petal to make a gentle point.

4   Cut a 5cm (2") length of 26-gauge Nile green floral wire and make a small closed hook in one end. Dip the hooked end of the wire into edible glue and wipe off the excess.

5   Roll a pin-sized piece of the yellow SFP into a tiny ball and push the

hooked end into the paste. Thread the wire down through the centre of the flower until the ball sits flush in the middle (AD). Use your fingers to taper the paste underneath the petals to the wire.

6   Repeat steps 2–5 to make 10 more forsythia flowers. Leave all the flowers to dry overnight.

7   Use the no. 4 paintbrush to dust the tapered base of each flower with Leaf Green dust. This will help blend it into wire.

Assembling The Forsythia Branches

1   Cut an 18cm (7") length of 24-gauge Nile green floral wire and cover roughly the first 3cm (1¹/₈") of wire with some full-width brown floral tape.

2   Cut a 2.5cm (1") length of full-width Nile green tape. Fold the tape over the wire at the lowest covered part and give it a couple of twists to make a small leaf extending away from the wire (AE, AF).

3   Take a forsythia flower and bind it to the branch up against the small leaf using some brown tape (AG).

4   Continue binding down the wire adding a small leaf and a flower roughly every 3cm (1¹/₈") until you have five flowers on the branch (AH). Also add little twigs every now and again by folding a small length of brown tape over the wire and twisting the ends together.

5   Repeat steps 1–4 to make two more branches, but this time attaching only three flowers to each.

top tip

Sometimes a bare branch with twigs is handy to balance an arrangement; it will add something but not too much.

Assembling The Cake

1 Attach the 12.5cm (5") cake centrally on top of the covered drum. Dowel the 12.5cm (5") cake, spacing them evenly within a central 10cm (4") circle. Attach the 10cm (4") cake centrally on top (see technique on page 41).

Attaching The Flowers, Leaves And Branches

1 Insert each wired element into posy picks, fixing them in place with a little leftover sugarpaste or royal icing inside the picks.

2 Mark a point just to the right of the front centre at the top of the 12.5cm (5") wide tier. This is where the parrot tulip will go.

3 Insert the long forsythia branch upright into the top of the 12.5cm (5") wide cake just to the left of the marked point.

4 Insert one of the pink tulips upright, about 2.5cm (1") to the right of the forsythia.

5 Insert one of the tulip leaves just behind the pink tulip and tilt it slightly to the right.

6 Insert a second tulip leaf into the top of the 12.5cm (5") wide cake, bending it to point out to the left and downwards slightly.

7 Insert the last tulip leaf into the top of the 12.5cm (5") wide cake, bending it so that it points down and is to the left of the forsythia.

8 Brush one side of the 15cm (6") tulip stem with edible glue and attach it to the front of the bottom tier. Make sure it is level with the top and roughly below the point marked for the parrot tulip. Attach the second stem the same way, roughly below the pink tulip.

9 Insert the parrot tulip at the point marked. Add the remaining pink tulips either side of the parrot tulip with one pointing right and one pointing down and left.

10 Add the remaining forsythia branches either side of the parrot tulip: one pointing up and right, and the other pointing down and left.

11 Finally, add the small primrose posy to the upper left of the parrot tulip and the large posy to the right and below the parrot tulip.

ORANGE
blossom beauty

The delicate sugar blossoms on this cake are a sweet serenade to its namesake tree, and the hanging modelled oranges are reminiscent of taking a stroll through a sun-drenched orange grove.

Edibles

Round, filled sponge cake covered with ganache/buttercream with a sharp edge finish, secured on a board of the same size (see page 29), 5cm (2") deep: 12.5cm (5") wide

Round, filled sponge cake covered with ganache/buttercream with a sharp edge finish, secured on a board of the same size (see page 29), 12.5cm (5") deep: 18cm (7") wide

SK Fairtrade Sugarpaste: 440g (15^1/$_2$oz) Bridal White and 1.1kg (2lb 6^7/$_8$oz) Lullaby Blue

SK Professional Instant Mix Royal Icing: 100g (3^1/$_2$oz) White

White vegetable fat

SK Essentials Edible Glue

SK Professional Dust Food Colours: Holly/Ivy (Dark Green), Sunflower and Vine

SK Sugar Florist Paste (SFP): 190g (6^3/$_4$oz) White

SK Professional Paste Food Colours: Holly/Ivy (Dark Green), Poppy, Sunflower and Vine

SK Dust Food Colour: Orange

PME Clear Edible Glaze Spray

Equipment

Round cake drum: 25.5cm (10")

1.5cm (^{1}/$_2$") width satin ribbon: 84cm (33") Bridal White

3mm (^{1}/$_8$") width satin ribbon: 1m (1yd 3^3/$_8$") Bridal White

Templates: page 227

Floral wires: 24- and 26-gauge dark green, and 18- and 26-gauge white

Cream matt pointed head stamens: 15 small

Floral tape: full-width Nile green, dark green and white, and quarter-width dark green

SK High-Quality Paintbrushes: nos. 4 and 10

Cream matt round head stamens: 40 small

Modelling tools: dresden, medium ball and small ball

CelStick: 6mm (^{1}/$_4$")

FMM Rose Calyx Cutter: 3cm (1^1/$_8$")

Tweezers

Cocktail sticks: 3

Polystyrene balls: 3 x 2.5cm (1")

Posy picks: various sizes

SEE PAGES 11–15 FOR ESSENTIAL EDIBLES AND EQUIPMENT

Covering The Cake Drum

1 Roll out 350g (12^1/$_4$oz) of Lullaby Blue sugarpaste and cover the 25.5cm (10") cake drum (see technique on page 32).

2 Fix the 1.5cm (^{1}/$_2$") width Bridal White ribbon around the edge of the drum and set aside for later (see technique on page 32).

Covering The Cakes

1 Use the panelling method to cover the cakes. For the top tier, roll out 105g (3^3/$_4$oz) of Bridal White sugarpaste and cut out a 15cm (6") disc. Secure the disc on top of the 12.5cm (5") wide cake and trim away the excess (see technique on page 32). Repeat to cover the top of the 18cm (7") cake, this time using 175g (6oz) of Lullaby Blue sugarpaste and cutting out a 20.5cm (8") disc.

2 For the side of the 12.5cm (5") wide cake, roll out 265g (9^3/$_8$oz) of Bridal White sugarpaste and cut out a 42cm x 6.5cm (16^1/$_2$" x 2^1/$_2$") panel. Roll up the panel and wrap it around the cake (see technique on page 32). Repeat to cover the side of the 18cm (7") cake, this time using 560g (1lb 3^3/$_4$oz) of Lullaby Blue sugarpaste and cutting out a 57cm x 14cm (22^1/$_2$" x 5^1/$_2$") rectangle. Set both cakes aside to dry overnight.

Adding The Orange Segment Design

1 Transfer the orange segment template onto a piece of food-grade card and cut it out.

2 Roll out 70g (2^1/$_2$oz) of Bridal White sugarpaste to a thickness of 2mm (^{1}/$_16$"). Leave the rolled out sugarpaste aside to firm up for an hour – this will make it easier for you to cut out the orange segments cleanly.

3 Take your firmed sugarpaste and use a sharp knife to cut around the template. Cut out 10 orange segments (A).

4 Arrange the segments around the circumference top of the 12.5cm (5") wide cake. This will act as a guide of how your orange design will look.

5 Once you're happy with the positioning, take one segment at a time and rub a little white vegetable fat over the middle on the back. Then return each segment to their position on top of the cake.

6 Refine the positions so that the segment pieces are about 5mm (^{1}/$_4$") in from the edge and so they are evenly spaced (B).

top tip

Attaching decorations to cakes using white vegetable fat allows you to adjust their positions easier than if you used edible glue or water.

Making The Main Flower Centre

1 Cut a 10cm (4") length of 18-gauge white floral wire and bend a 5mm (^{1}/$_4$") open hook in one end (C).

2 Gather the 15 cream pointed head stamens in a bunch and fold them in half. Hook the hooked end of the wire over the folded section of the stamen bunch and close the hook up (D).

3 Secure the stamen bunch and wire together with some full-width white floral tape, starting from about 1.25cm (^{1}/$_2$") below the top of the stamens (E).

4 Dip a no. 4 paintbrush into some edible glue and wipe off the excess. Brush the top of the stamens with a little

glue and dip them in some Sunflower dust food colour. Gently shake off the excess dust from the stamens, before leaving the flower centre to dry (F).

Making The Main Flower Petals

1 Transfer the small and large petal templates onto a piece of food-grade card and cut them out.

2 Roll out a small piece of White SFP, about 1mm (<^{1}/$_16$") thick, over one of the grooves on the non-stick board.

3 Use the small petal template and a sharp knife to cut out a petal, making sure it's centred over the groove and the narrow end of the template is at the edge of the board (G).

4 Cut a 10cm (4") length of 26-gauge white floral wire. Dip one end of the cut wire in some edible glue and wipe off the excess. Insert the wire about 2cm (^{3}/$_4$") into the raised groove at the base of the petal (H).

5 Transfer the petal to a foam pad and use a medium ball tool to thin the edges to give it some movement (I). Place the petal in a cupped former to dry – this will ensure the petal keeps its realistic shape. You can use a paint palette for this if you don't have a former!

6 Repeat steps 2–5 to make three more small petals. Repeat steps 2–5 again, this time using the larger template to make five large petals. Allow the petals to dry overnight.

Assembling The Main Flower

1 Hold the base of each petal between your finger and thumb and bend their wires down by roughly 90˚.

2   Bind the four small petals to the flower centre using full-width Nile green floral tape. Make sure they are evenly spaced around the centre and that the base of each petal is positioned about 1.25cm ($^1/_2$") below the top of the stamens (J).

3   Bind the five large petals to the flower centre using full-width Nile green tape. Make sure the large petals are evenly spaced around the centre and that they are sitting flush against and in between the first layer (K).

Making The Blossoms

1   For the blossom centres, colour a pea-sized piece of White SFP a pale green using a little Vine paste food colour.

2   Cut a 7.5cm (3") length of 26-gauge dark green floral wire and make a small closed hook in one end.

3   Take a small ball of the pale green SFP, about the size of a round headed pin, and insert the hooked end of the wire into it. Pinch the SFP underneath to adhere it to the wire (L).

4   To finish the centre, brush a little edible glue over the top of the SFP and dip in some Sunflower dust.

5   Repeat steps 2–4 to make seven more blossom centres.

6   To make a blossom, lightly press a 1.25cm ($^1/_2$") ball of White SFP into a 5mm ($^1/_4$") hole in the foam pad (M).

7   Use a small CelStick to roll out the protruding SFP to form a Mexican hat mound. Remove the SFP from the hole, turn it over and roll it even thinner, making sure you don't roll over the raised Mexican hat (N).

8   With the little Mexican hat mound facing upwards, use a 3cm ($1^1/_8$") Rose Calyx cutter to cut out a blossom from the SFP. Make sure the mound is in the centre of the cutter when you are cutting out the blossom (O).

9   On the flat part of the foam pad, gently thin the petals of the blossom using a small ball tool.

10   Slide a wired centre down through the face of the blossom until it nestles into the SFP. Pinch the SFP underneath so it adheres to the wire (P).

11   Use your fingers to slightly curl back the petals to give the blossom some shape.

12   Cut off the ends of five cream round head stamens, making them about 1.25cm ($^1/_2$") long.

13   Use tweezers to insert the five cut stamens into the SFP around the centre of the blossom, leaving them sticking up roughly 1cm ($^3/_8$") (Q).

14   Repeat steps 6–13 to make eight blossoms in total.

Making The Leaves

1   Transfer the leaf template onto a piece of food-grade card and cut it out.

2   Mix 60g (2oz) of White SFP with some Holly/Ivy (Dark Green) and Vine paste food colours to achieve a dark green. You'll be using this throughout the project so make sure you keep all your trimmings and wrap up the SFP to prevent it from drying out.

3   Cut some 26-gauge dark green floral wire into 20 pieces, each piece measuring a length of 8cm ($3^1/_8$").

4   Roll out a 1.5cm ($^1/_2$") ball of dark green SFP over a groove on the non-stick board. Cut out a leaf shape using the template, making sure the template is positioned centrally over the groove.

5   Transfer the leaf to the foam pad and, with the central ridge facing upwards, thin the edges with the medium ball tool (R).

6   Dip the end of a cut wire in edible glue and wipe off the excess. Carefully insert the wire about 2cm ($^3/_4$") into the raised groove of the leaf (S).

7   Press a dresden tool into the SFP to mark a line up and along the centre of the leaf. To finish, use your fingers to gently bend or twist the leaf a little – this will give it some character and movement. Set the leaf aside to dry.

8   Repeat steps 4–7 to make 20 leaves in total.

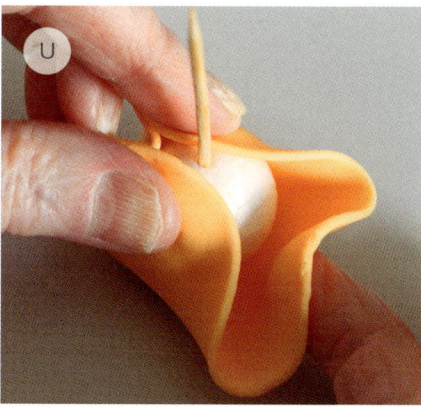

Making The Oranges

1   Colour 50g (1³/₄oz) of White SFP
an orange colour. Start off with a
little Sunflower paste food colour to
give the SFP a yellow base shade, before
adding some Poppy paste food colour
to gradually build up the colour to an
orange.

2   Roll out 12g (³/₈oz) of the orange
SFP mixture to a thickness of
2mm (¹/₁₆").

3   Push a cocktail stick up through
the centre of a 2.5cm (1")
polystyrene ball, making sure it doesn't
exit the other side. Then brush over the
ball with a little edible glue.

4   Place the polystyrene ball in the
middle of the rolled orange SFP,
with the cocktail stick pointing upwards
(T). Gather the orange SFP up around

the ball (U). Use a pair of scissors to trim
away the bulk of the excess SFP from the
side and base.

5   Remove the cocktail stick and
neaten up the SFP, making sure to
close any gaps (V). Roll the ball between
your palms to smooth out the SFP.

6   Reinsert the cocktail stick into the
ball and use the rounded end of a
paintbrush to stipple indents all over
the ball to make the orange's texture
(W). Finish by using the dresden tool to
mark some creases around the cocktail
stick (X).

top tip

This cake would also work well with
lemons or limes. Just use a slightly
smaller polystyrene ball and elongate
the ends of the covering sugarpaste.

7   Repeat steps 2–6 to make a second
orange.

8   Repeat steps 2–6 again to make a
third larger orange, but this time do
steps 2–5 twice to give it a second layer.
Leave all the oranges to dry overnight.

9   Use the no. 10 paintbrush to
dust the dried oranges liberally
with some Orange dust (Y). Steam the
oranges to set the dust colour and allow
them to dry. Once dry, spray the oranges
with some edible glaze spray and set
aside to dry once more.

10   Cut a 24-gauge dark green floral
wire in half. Cut one piece in half
again so you are left with one half length
and two quarter length pieces of wire.

11   Make a closed 5mm (¹/₄") hook on
one end of each piece of cut wire.
Bind the top 1cm (³/₈") of the hooked

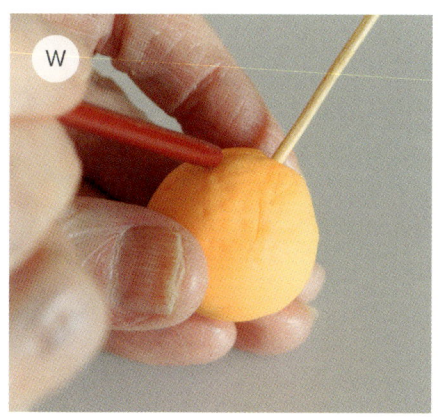

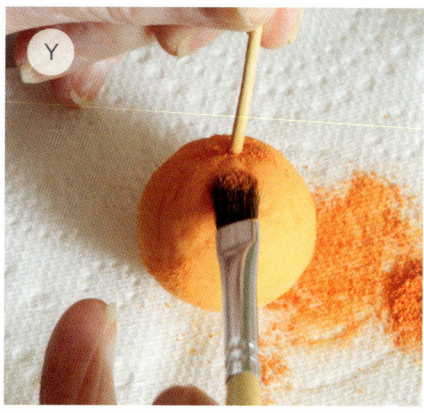

end of the wires with some full-width dark green floral tape until each piece is about the width of the cocktail sticks. Cover the remainder of each wire with a single layer of dark green tape.

11   Carefully remove the cocktail sticks from the oranges. Use the no. 4 paintbrush to apply a little glue to the thick end of each wire. Insert the long piece of wire into the hole of one of the smaller oranges, and insert the shorter wires into the remaining two oranges.

12   Use a little White SFP to lighten a small amount of the leftover green SFP mixture you used to make the leaves. Flatten three tiny balls of this lighter green SFP to make 5mm ($^1/_4$") discs. Use a cocktail stick to poke a hole in the centre of each disc.

13   Brush a tiny bit of glue on each orange around the base of the

wire. Slide the green discs down the wires and attach one to each orange, making sure they sit flush against the orange.

Making The Budding Oranges

1   Colour a 2cm ($^3/_4$") ball of White SFP green using some Holly/Ivy (Dark Green) and Vine paste food colours. You want to make it a bit lighter than the colour of the leaves. Also colour a 2cm ($^3/_4$") ball of White SFP orange using some Sunflower and Poppy paste food colours.

2   Roll out three or four balls of each colour, ranging from 6mm – 1.25cm ($^1/_4$" – $^1/_2$") in size.

3   Cut a 10cm (4") length of 26-gauge dark green floral wire for each ball. Make a small closed hook in one end of each wire.

4   Insert the hooked end of a wire into each ball and close the SFP up around the wire by pinching them together. Leave them all to dry.

5   Using the no. 10 paintbrush, dust part of the green balls with some Orange dust. Dust part of the orange balls with a mixture of Vine and Holly/Ivy (Dark Green) dust food colours. Steam each of the dusted balls to fix the colour in place. Once they are dry, spray them with some edible glaze and set aside.

Assembling The Blossoms, Leaves And Oranges

1   Make a spray using the two shorter stemmed oranges, five leaves, a budding orange and a blossom. Start by binding the two oranges together with some quarter-width dark green tape, making sure one is offset from the other. Next, add five leaves to the wire a little further down the stem, then attach a budding orange and a blossom beneath the leaves (Z).

2 Make a second spray using the longer stemmed orange. Bind three leaves, two blossoms and one budding orange to the orange stem using some quarter-width dark green tape. Start off by binding the leaves to the orange stem, gradually taping the two blossoms and one budding orange to the wire as you go down.

3 Bind the two sprays together using some quarter-width dark green tape, making sure the first spray is positioned below the second. Continue taping all the way down the wires, leaving you with a stem about 7.5cm – 10cm (3" – 4") long.

4 Make three small sprays from the remaining pieces, each spray consisting of one or two blossoms, three to five leaves, and one to three budding oranges. Following the technique in steps 1–2, bind the pieces together with some quarter-width dark green tape. Leave a stem of about 7.5cm – 10cm (3" – 4") long at the end.

Assembling The Cake

1 Attach the 18cm (7") cake centrally on top of the covered drum. Dowel

top tip

If you don't have quarter-width tape you can use a tape cutter to cut the tape into the appropriate width.

the cake, spacing them evenly within a central 12.5cm (5") circle and attach the 12.5cm (5") wide cake centrally on top (see technique on page 41).

2 Tie some 3mm (¹/₈") wide Bridal White ribbon around the base of the cake. Make a small bow and trim off the tails so they aren't visible from the front. Check that the ribbon is sitting flush with the drum.

Attaching The Sprays

1 Cut three 7.5cm (3") lengths of 18-gauge white floral wire. Cover the wires with full-width dark green tape.

2 Bend each of the wires in half to make three U-shaped pins, about 6mm (¹/₄") wide.

3 Lay the large spray on top of the bottom tier with its stem pointing

to the left and with the majority of the spray hanging down in front of the right half of the cake. Hook a wire pin around the stem and push it into a posy pick in the top the cake so that it is pinned to the top of the base tier.

4 Insert one of the small sprays vertically into a posy pick and attach to the top of the base tier. It should be positioned about halfway between the front and the left of the cake. It should also rise above the top of the top tier by about 7.5cm (3"). Trim the length if necessary.

5 Use some wire pins and posy picks to attach a spray to the top of the base tier so that it droops down just to the left of the large spray. You can bend the wire if necessary.

6 Pin the final spray into a posy pick in the top of the base tier, this time pointing towards the left and leaving enough space for the main flower to sit between it and the other sprays.

7 To finish, insert the main flower into a posy pick and attach it in the gap between the sprays, angling it very slightly to the left.

SPRING
wedding

Take inspiration from your own garden's fresh greenery and bright floral colours for an elegant spring wedding cake. With tasteful bouquets of poppies and daisies, this cake is jazzed up with a combination of circular and hexagonal tiers.

YOU WILL NEED

Edibles

Round, filled sponge cakes covered with ganache/buttercream with a sharp edge finish, secured on cake boards of the same size (see page 29), 12.5cm (5") deep: 10cm (4") and 15cm (6") wide

Round, filled sponge cake, 12.5cm (5") deep: 12.5cm (5") wide

SK Fairtrade Sugarpaste: 2.1kg (4lb 10oz) Bridal White

SK Professional Instant Mix Royal Icing: 100g (3^1/$_2$oz) White

SK Sugar Florist Paste (SFP): 160g (5^1/$_2$oz) White

SK Professional Paste Food Colours: Holly/Ivy (Dark Green), Leaf Green, Rose and Sunflower

SK Essentials Edible Glue

Equipment

Round cake drums: 20.5cm (8") and 23cm (9")

1.5cm (^{1}/$_2$") width satin ribbon: 1.45m (1yd 21") Bridal White

Round cake boards: 10cm (4") and 15cm (6")

Hexagonal cake boards: 2 x 12.5cm (5") point to point

Silikomart Rolling Pin: Lines

Floral wires: 24-gauge Nile green, and 18- and 28-gauge white

Tweezers

Circle cutter: 1.25cm (^{1}/$_2$")

SK Multi Flower Cutter Set 1A, Round Petal/Leaf: no. 1

Modelling tools: dresden, medium ball and veining

CelCakes CelFormers: small

Half-width floral tape: Nile green

Tapestry canvas or similar

PME Daisy Marguerite Plunger Cutter: 2.7cm (1^1/$_{16}$")

Dimple foam drying tray

Fine Cut Daisy Leaf Cutter: 3.2cm (1^1/$_4$")

SK-GI Silicone Veiner Rose - Tea: Medium Leaf

Cutting wheel

Posy picks: medium

2.5cm (1") width satin ribbon: 88cm (34^3/$_4$) yellow

SEE PAGES 11–15 FOR ESSENTIAL EDIBLES AND EQUIPMENT

Covering The Cake Drums

1   Roll out 250g (8³/₄oz) of Bridal White sugarpaste and cover the 20.5cm (8") drum. Next, cover the 23cm (9") drum using 300g (10¹/₂oz) of Bridal White sugarpaste (see technique on page 32). Set both drums aside to firm overnight.

2   Fix the Bridal White ribbon around the edge of each cake drum (see technique on page 32).

3   To stack the drums, spread a little royal icing in the centre of the 23cm (9") drum. Place the 20.5cm (8") drum centrally on top, lining up the ribbon joins at the back. Set aside for later.

Preparing The Hexagonal Cake

1   Place the 12.5cm (5") wide cake on a 12.5cm (5") hexagonal cake board (measured point to point). Put a second hexagonal cake board on top of the cake to use as a guide, making sure it's lined up with the first board.

2   Using the boards as a guide, trim the cake into a hexagon. Remove the top board and trim the cake slightly smaller than the base board to allow for a buttercream or ganache coating.

3   Coat the cake with ganache or buttercream, ensuring you create a sharp edge finish (see technique on page 30). Chill for at least 30 minutes before covering.

Covering The Round Cakes

1   You will be using the panelling method to cover the cakes. For the top tier, roll out 75g (2⁵/₈oz) of Bridal White sugarpaste and cut out a 12.5cm (5") disc. Place the disc on top of the 10cm (4") cake and trim away the excess

(see technique on page 32). For the bottom tier, repeat to cover the top of the 15cm (6") cake with an 18cm (7") disc using 135g (4³/₄oz) of Bridal White sugarpaste.

2 To cover the sides, start with the 10cm (4") cake. Roll out 355g (12¹/₂oz) of Bridal White sugarpaste and cut a 34cm x 14cm (13³/₈" x 5¹/₂") panel. Roll up the panel and wrap it around the cake (see technique on page 32).

3 Repeat step 2 to cover the side of the 15cm (6") cake. This time, roll out 495g (1lb 1¹/₂oz) of Bridal White sugarpaste and cut out a 50cm x 14cm (19³/₄" x 5¹/₂") rectangle. Once both cakes are covered, leave them to dry overnight.

Covering The Hexagonal Cake

1 Use the panelling method to cover the hexagonal cake. Roll out 105g (3³/₄oz) of Bridal White sugarpaste, cut out a 15cm (6") disc and secure on top of the cake (see technique on page 35).

2 For the sides, roll a 10cm x 15cm (4" x 6") rectangle of Bridal White sugarpaste to a 3mm (¹/₈") thickness. With the short end of the sugarpaste towards you, mark the paste using a ribbed rolling pin, pressing firmly and evenly.

3 Trim a horizontal line along the bottom of the ribbed texture. Measure the width of one side of the hexagonal cake, before cutting the sugarpaste to the nearest whole rib to the required width.

top tip

If necessary, gently and evenly stretch or squeeze the paste to widen or narrow it to the correct width.

4 Lightly brush one side of the cake with cooled, boiled water. Lift the ribbed panel and align its base centrally with the bottom of the cake. Gently secure to the cake, being careful not to flatten the ribbing. Trim the top of the paste level with the top of the cake.

5 Repeat steps 2–4 to attach five more side panels to the cake.

Making The Californian Poppy Centres

1 Cut eight pieces of 24-gauge Nile green wire to 25.5cm (10") lengths. These will be used for the flower centres.

2 Pinch one end of a cut wire with a pair of pliers and twist it round the tip of the pliers to make a small circle on the end of the wire like a lollipop (A).

3 Bend the circle down so it lays flat against the wire. Finally, bend the wire down 90° at the point it crosses the middle of the circle, so the circle is on the end of the wire like a plate spinning on a stick (B).

4 Colour 5g (<¹/₄oz) of White SFP a green shade using a little Holly/Ivy (Dark Green) and Leaf Green paste food colours. Secure a pea-sized ball of the green SFP to the circle end of the wire and flatten slightly.

5 Lightly pinch all over the flat centre with tweezers to texture it (C).

6 Mix 20g (³/₄oz) of White SFP with a little Sunflower paste food colour to make a yellow shade. You'll be using this yellow SFP throughout the project, so make sure you keep your offcuts and wrap up the paste as you work to prevent it from drying out.

7 Thinly roll a small piece of the yellow SFP and cut out a yellow disc

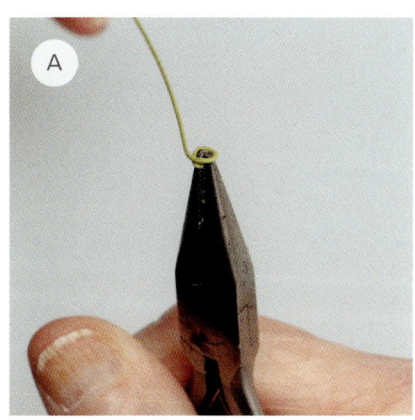

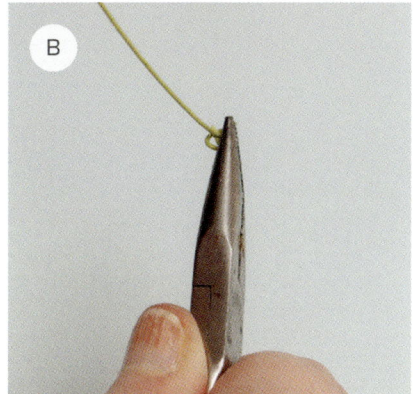

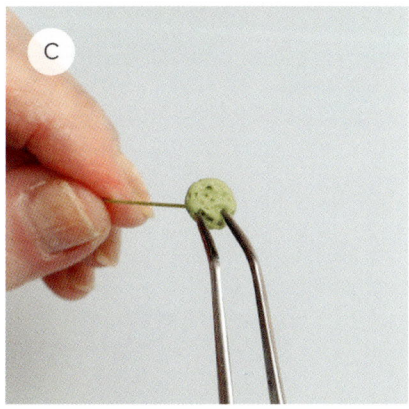

using a 1.25cm ($^{1}/_{2}$") circle cutter (D). Lightly brush a little edible glue on the underside of the textured centre. Slide the yellow disc up the wire and press it into place.

8 Snip round the exposed part of the yellow disc with scissors to give it some detail (E).

9 Repeat steps 2–8 to make a total of eight centres. Set aside to dry.

Making The Californian Poppy Petals

1 Roll a small piece of the yellow SFP you made earlier to a 2mm ($^{1}/_{16}$") thickness over one of the grooves on a non-stick board. Cut out a petal using a 2cm ($^{3}/_{4}$") round petal cutter, making sure the thicker ridge of paste runs through the centre (F).

2 Cut an 8cm ($3^{1}/_{8}$") length of 28-gauge white floral wire, dip the end in edible glue and wipe off the excess. Hold the ridge in the centre of the petal between your finger and thumb, and then insert the wire about 1cm ($^{3}/_{8}$") into it (G).

3 On the non-stick board, thin each side of the petal using a veining tool (H). Place the petal in a cupped former to dry.

4 Repeat steps 1–3 to make five more yellow petals. Next, use the same method to make six white, six pink and six orange petals. For the pink flowers, mix a little Rose paste into 10g ($^{1}/_{4}$oz) of White SFP. For the orange flowers, colour 10g ($^{1}/_{4}$oz) of White SFP with a mixture of Sunflower and Rose paste colours. Use 10g ($^{1}/_{4}$oz) of White SFP as is for the white flowers. Once you've wired all the petals, leave them to dry overnight.

Assembling The Californian Poppy

1 One at a time, hold each petal between your finger and thumb at the point the wire enters and bend the wires down 90˚.

2 Take one flower centre and bind three petals of the same colour to the wire stem using half-width Nile green floral tape. Make sure the petals are butted up against the base of the centre and evenly spaced. Continue taping down the entire length of the main wire until fully covered.

3 Repeat step 2 to attach the remaining petals to the other seven centres.

Making The Daisies

1 Repeat steps 1–4 from Making The Californian Poppy Centres to make the daisy centres. This time, cut 12 pieces of 24-gauge Nile green wire to 25.5cm (10") lengths and attach the yellow SFP from earlier to the circle end of the wires.

2 Take a daisy centre and press the flattened paste onto a piece of tapestry canvas or similar to texture it (I, J).

3 Roll out a little White SFP to a 2mm ($^{1}/_{16}$") thickness and cut out a flower using a 2.7cm ($1^{1}/_{16}$") Daisy Plunger cutter.

4 Use a razor blade to divide each of the individual petals into two (K). Place the daisy on a foam pad and use a dresden tool to separate and thin the individual petals (L).

5 Place the daisy in an irregular former or on a dimple foam drying tray to shape (M). Leave for an hour to firm.

6 Brush the underside of the centre with a little edible glue and thread the wire down through the middle of the daisy until it nestles in its centre.

7 Repeat steps 2–6 to make the remaining 11 daisies. Leave them to dry overnight.

Making The Leaves

1 Colour 70g ($2^{1}/_{2}$oz) of White SFP a green shade using some Holly/Ivy (Dark Green) and Leaf Green paste food colours.

2 Roll a small piece of the green SFP to a 1mm ($<^{1}/_{16}$") thickness over one of the grooves on the non-stick board. Cut out a leaf using a 3.2cm ($1^{1}/_{4}$") Daisy Leaf cutter, making sure the thick ridge of paste runs through the centre.

3 Cut a 25.5cm (10") length of 24-gauge Nile green wire, dip the end in edible glue and wipe off the excess. Hold the ridge in the centre of the leaf and insert the wire about 1cm ($^{3}/_{8}$") into it.

4 Place the leaf on the foam pad and thin the edges gently with a medium ball tool. Press the thinned leaf firmly between the two halves of a Tea Rose Leaf veiner to texture. Carefully remove the leaf and shape it with your fingers to give it some movement.

5 Repeat steps 2–4 to make nine leaves in total. Set the leaves aside to dry overnight.

Making The Grass

1 Take the leftover green SFP you made for the leaves and mix in a little White SFP to achieve a lighter green shade.

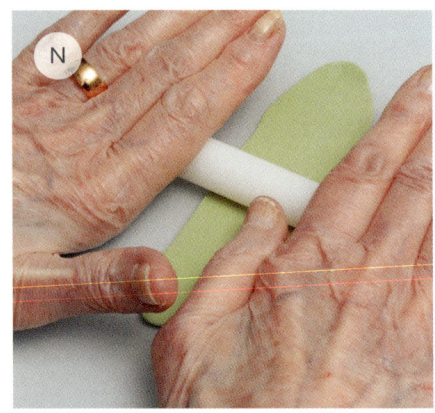

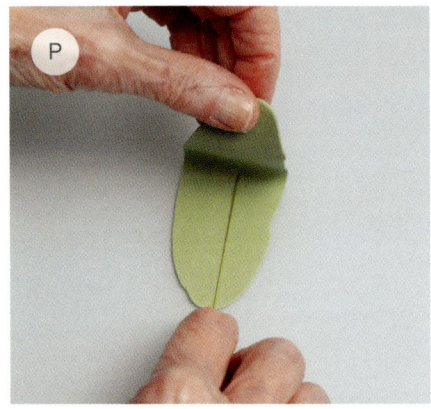

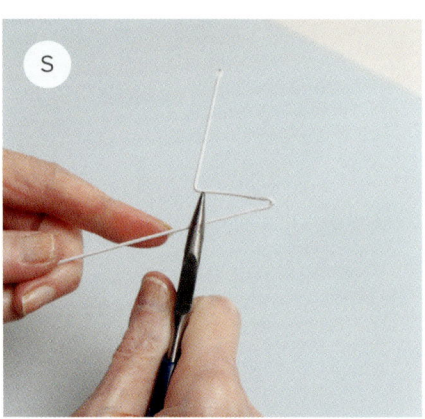

2 Take the light green SFP and thinly roll out a 20.5cm (8") long strip (N). Very lightly brush one half of the paste with edible glue.

3 Place a 25.5cm (10") long piece of 26-gauge Nile green wire along the glued half of the paste (O). Fold the opposite half of the paste over the wire so it is laying on top of it (P). Use a rolling pin to press the paste firmly together (Q).

4 Use a cutting wheel to cut a 6mm (¹⁄₄") wide blade of grass from the folded paste (R). Be careful to avoid cutting the wire.

5 Repeat steps 2–4 to make six blades of grass. Shape them with your fingers and then set aside to dry overnight.

Making The Wire Attachment

1 Take an uncut 18-gauge white floral wire and make a 90° bend 5cm (2") along its length.

2 Bend the wire 180° back on itself, 3cm (1¹⁄₈") along from the bend (S).

3 Next, bend the wire 90° at the point level with the 5cm (2") section (T). This will give you a long wire with a 3cm (1¹⁄₈") prong that is 5cm (2") from the top (U).

4 Make a second prong 2.5cm (1") below the first prong (V).

5 Cover the wire, including the prongs, with some Nile green tape. Wrap extra tape around the prongs so that they will later fit snugly in a medium posy pick.

6 Repeat steps 1–5 to make a second wire attachment piece the same way.

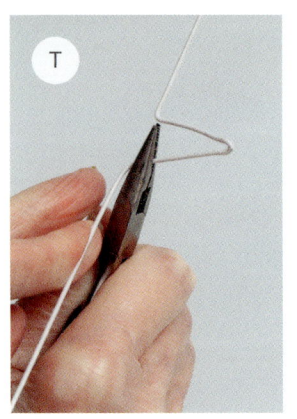

top tip

When making flowers it is always wise to make spares, especially daisies as the small petals are prone to breaking.

Assembling The Flowers

1 Gather together five daisies, one poppy of each colour, three leaves and three pieces of grass. Arrange the flowers and foliage into a 10cm – 12.5cm (4" – 5") tall posy.

2 Hold the arrangement against the 10cm (4") cake so that it extends about 7.5cm (3") above it and then trim the stems level with the base of the cake. Bind the cut stems together with Nile green tape 5cm (2") up from their base.

3 Arrange the remaining flowers and foliage into a second posy about 12.5cm – 15cm (5" – 6") tall. Hold the arrangement against the 15cm (6") cake so it extends about 10cm (4") above it. Trim the stems level with the bottom of the cake. Bind the cut stems 5cm (2") up from their base.

Attaching The Flowers

1 Hold one of the wire attachment pieces against the back of one of the posies, with the short part of the wire at the bottom and level with the ends of the stalks. Bind the section between the two prongs to the posy with Nile green tape. Trim the longer part of the wire so that it mingles in with the stalks if needed. Repeat to secure the second posy to the second wire attachment.

2 To start attaching the flowers to the cakes, position the 15cm (6") tier with the join at the back. Hold the taller posy against the cake tier, 3.5cm (1³⁄₈") to the right of the centre with the end of the stalks level with the bottom of the cake. Gently press it against the cake to mark their positions.

3 Insert two medium posy picks at the marked points and then insert the pronged sections into the picks.

4 Fix some yellow ribbon tightly around the middle of the cake, running over the stalks of the posy, and secure at the back with a little stiff royal icing. The ribbon can be held in place with a sterilised stainless steel pin while the icing dries, but be sure to remove the pin once the icing has set.

5 Repeat steps 2–4 to attach the remaining posy and ribbon to the 10cm (4") cake, but this time insert the posy 3.5cm (1³⁄₈") to the left of the centre.

top tip

When putting items into posy picks, inserting a little piece of sugarpaste or royal icing in the pick is an option to stop the wires wobbling.

Assembling The Cake

1 Attach the 15cm (6") cake centrally on top of the covered double height drum, with the flowers about 3.5cm (1³⁄₈") to the right of the centre and with the ribbon joins at the back. Dowel the cake, spacing them evenly within a central 10cm (4") square, and attach the hexagonal cake (see technique on page 41). Ensure it is centred and that a flat panel is at the front.

2 Dowel the hexagonal tier with three trimmed cake dowels in a central 10cm (4") circle and secure the 10cm (4") cake centrally on top. Make sure the flowers are positioned about 3.5cm (1³⁄₈") to the left of the centre.

GOLDEN
anniversary

Celebrate a milestone with this elegant 50th wedding anniversary cake, featuring a gorgeous gold leaf tier and stunning sugar flower arrangement.

YOU WILL NEED

Edibles

Round, filled sponge cakes covered with ganache/buttercream with a sharp edge finish, secured on cake boards of the same size (see page 29), 10cm (4") deep: 10cm (4") and 15cm (6") wide

Round, filled sponge cake covered with ganache/buttercream with a sharp edge finish, secured on a cake board of the same size (see page 29), 15cm (6") deep: 12.5cm (5") wide

SK Fairtrade Sugarpaste: 2kg (4lb 6½oz) Bridal White

SK Professional Instant Mix Royal Icing: 100g (3½oz) White

SK Edible Leaf Transfer Sheets, Book of 25: Gold

SK Designer Metallic Lustre Dust: Classic Gold

Clear alcohol, e.g. vodka or gin

SK Sugar Florist Paste (SFP): 160g (5½oz) White

SK Essentials Edible Glue

White vegetable fat

Equipment

Round cake drums: 20.5cm (8") and 23cm (9")

1.5cm (½") width satin ribbon: 1.45m (1yd 21") Bridal White

Round cake boards: 10cm (4"), 12.5cm (5") and 15cm (6")

Dusting brush

SK High-Quality Paintbrush: no. 10

Floral wires: 18-, 24-, 26- and 28-gauge white

Tweezers

White matt round head stamens: 45 micro

SK Multi Flower Cutter Set 1A, Round Petal/Leaf: nos. 2–4

Modelling tools: metal ball and veining

Dimple foam drying tray

Cocktail stick

Food-grade cupped former

Half-width floral tape: white

2cm (¾") polystyrene balls: 2

CelStick: 6mm (¼")

FMM Rose Calyx Cutter: 4.5cm (1¾")

PME Modelling Tool: Tapered Cones 5/6 Star

FMM Rose Leaf Cutters: 2.5cm (1") and 3.1cm (1¼")

SK-GI Silicone Veiner Rose - Tea: Medium Leaf

Posy picks: various sizes

SEE PAGES 11–15 FOR ESSENTIAL EDIBLES AND EQUIPMENT

Covering The Cake Drums

1　Roll out 250g (8³/₄oz) of Bridal White sugarpaste and cover the 20.5cm (8") cake drum. Next, cover the 23cm (9") drum using 295g (10¹/₂oz) of Bridal White sugarpaste (see technique on page 32). Set both drums aside to firm overnight.

2　Fix the Bridal White ribbon around the edge of each cake drum (see technique on page 32).

3　To stack the drums, spread a little royal icing in the middle of the 23cm (9") drum. Place the 20.5cm (8") drum centrally on top, lining up the ribbon joins at the back. Set aside for later.

Covering The Cakes

1　You will be using the panelling method to cover the cakes. For the top tier, roll out 75g (2⁵/₈oz) of Bridal White sugarpaste and cut out a 12.5cm (5") disc. Place the disc on top of the 10cm (4") cake and trim away the excess (see technique on page 32).

2　For the middle tier, repeat step 1 to cover the top of the 12.5cm (5") wide cake using 105g (3³/₄oz) of Bridal White sugarpaste and cutting out a 15cm (6") disc. Repeat step 1 again to cover the top of the 15cm (6") wide cake, this time using 135g (4³/₄oz) of Bridal White sugarpaste and cutting out an 18cm (7") disc.

3　To cover the sides, start with the 10cm (4") wide cake. Roll out 310g (11oz) of Bridal White sugarpaste and cut out a 34cm x 11.5cm (13³/₈" x 4¹/₂") panel. Roll up the panel and wrap it around the cake (see technique on page 32). Pinch off small bits of sugarpaste at a time from the overlapping top to create a jagged edge. Try to keep the pinches irregular in width but of a similar depth.

4　Repeat step 3 to cover the side of the 12.5cm (5") wide cake with a

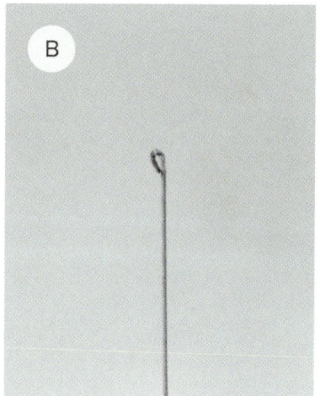
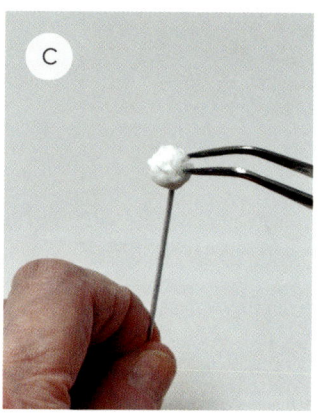

jagged edge. This time, roll out 480g (1lb 1oz) of Bridal White sugarpaste and cut out a 42cm x 16.5cm (16¹/₂" x 6¹/₂") rectangle.

5   Repeat step 3 again for the 15cm (6") wide cake with a jagged edge. This time, roll out 430g (15¹/₄oz) of Bridal White sugarpaste and cut out a 50cm x 11.5cm (19³/₄" x 4¹/₂") rectangle. Set the cakes aside to dry overnight.

Attaching The Gold Leaf

1   Use a pastry brush and a little cooled, boiled water to dampen a section on the bottom half of the middle tier, slightly larger than a gold leaf sheet.

2   Trim the overlapping transfer paper away from one side of a gold leaf sheet.

3   Holding the edges of the transfer sheet carefully, apply the gold leaf to the cake. Make sure the cut side is flush with the bottom. Gently press it into place and carefully peel away the transfer sheet.

top tips

Gold leaf is very light and fragile so make sure there is no breeze blowing though the room when using it.

top tip

Save any little bits of loose gold leaf to cover up gaps or scratches on the cake. You can also use the leftovers for the filler flower centres.

4   Lightly brush over the gold leaf with a dusting brush to ensure it is well adhered.

5   Following steps 1–4, dampen a similar area next to the first piece of gold leaf and apply a second sheet in the same way, taking care to just overlap the first sheet. Repeat until the bottom half of the tier is covered.

6   Repeat steps 1–5 to attach gold leaf around the top half of the tier in the same way until it is covered entirely.

Finishing The Torn Edges

1   Mix a little Classic Gold lustre dust with some clear alcohol to make a gold paint.

2   Load a no. 10 paintbrush with the gold paint and dab most of it off on a piece of kitchen paper. Now gently brush the jagged top edges of the 10cm (4") and 15cm (6") wide cakes with the gold paint (A).

Assembling The Cake

1   Attach the 15cm (6") wide cake centrally on top of the double height drum. Dowel the 15cm (6") wide cake, spacing them evenly within a central 12.5cm (5") circle, and attach the 12.5cm (5") wide cake centrally on top. Dowel the 12.5cm (5") tier, positioning them within a central 10cm (4") circle, and then fix the 10cm (4") wide cake on top (see technique on page 41).

Making The Rose Centres

1   Cut a 10cm (4") piece of 18-gauge white floral wire for the flower's centre. Use a pair of pliers to bend a small closed hook in one end of the wire (B).

2   Push the hook into a 1cm (³/₈") ball of White SFP. Pinch the top with a pair of tweezers to texture it (C), then set it aside to harden.

3   Repeat steps 1–2 to create two other rose centres in total.

4   Lightly moisten one rose centre with cooled, boiled water and apply a small piece of gold leaf.

5   Bend 15 micro white matt round stamens in half and position them so they are sitting just above the gold rose centre and distributed evenly around it. Once positioned, bind the stamens

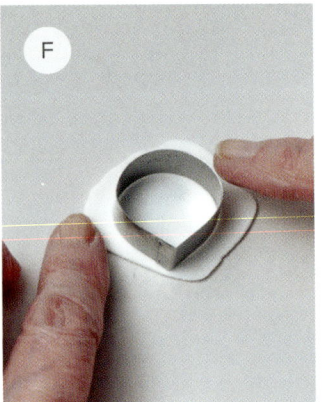

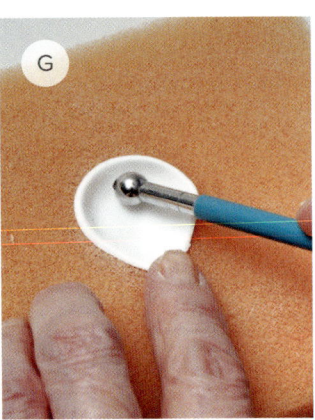

to the stem with half-width white floral tape (D). To finish, lightly dust over the stamens with some Classic Gold lustre dust (E).

6 Repeat steps 4–5 to finish making the other two centres.

Making The Rose Petals

1 Thinly roll a small piece of White SFP over one of the grooves on a non-stick board. Cut out a petal using a 3cm (1¹/₈") round petal cutter, making sure the thicker ridge of paste runs through the centre (F).

2 Transfer the petal to a soft foam pad and run the small end of a metal ball tool around the edge to make a lip (G). Next, roll the large end of the metal ball tool in the centre to cup the petal and draw it towards the pointed end.

3 Cut an 8cm (3¹/₈") length of 28-gauge white floral wire, dip one end in edible glue and wipe off the excess. Hold the pointed end of the petal between your finger and thumb and insert the wire about 1cm (³/₈") up into the ridge (H).

4 Repeat steps 1–3 to make 11 more 3cm (1¹/₈") petals the same way. Repeat steps 1–3 again to make a further 15 petals, this time using the 3.5cm (1³/₈") round petal cutter. Leave the petals to dry overnight on a dimple foam drying tray.

5 Over a groove on the non-stick board, use a 4.5cm (1³/₄") round petal cutter to cut out a rose petal from a small piece of thinly rolled White SFP. Use the large end of the metal ball tool to lightly cup the petal, before inserting an 8cm (3¹/₈") length of 28-gauge white floral wire as in step 3.

6 Gently curl back the top left and top right sections of the petal around a cocktail stick (I).

7 Repeat steps 5–6 to make nine more 4.5cm (1³/₄") rose petals. Leave the petals in cupped formers to dry overnight.

Assembling The Roses

1 Bind four small petals to each flower centre with white floral tape, making sure that they are butted up against the base of the centre and evenly spaced apart (J).

2 Bind five medium petals to each flower centre with white floral tape, again making sure they are evenly spaced and butted up against the bases of the first set of smaller petals. To make the flower look more realistic, ensure the

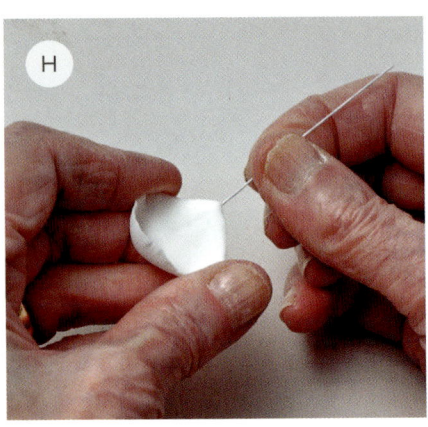

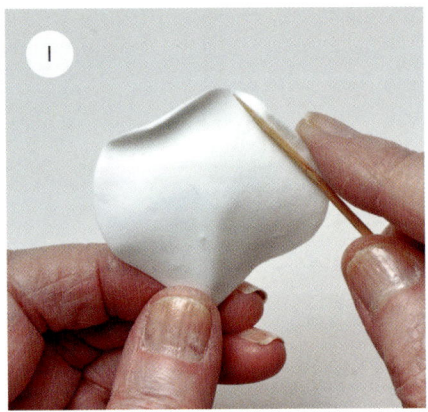

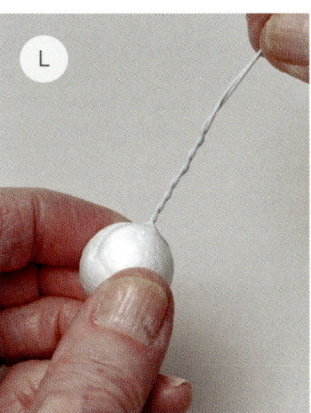

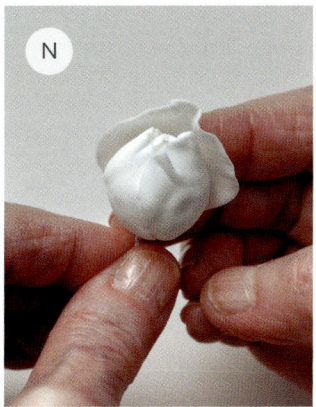

petal layers are not positioned directly over the top of one another; rather, have each layer situated over the join of the previous layer.

3   To finish, repeat the technique in step 2 to bind five large petals to two of the flowers.

Making The Rose Bud

1   Slide a 15cm (6") piece of 24-gauge wire through the centre of a 2cm (³/₄") polystyrene ball until the ball is halfway along its length (K). Bend the wires down and twist them together (L).

2   Thinly roll a small piece of White SFP over the flat side of the non-stick board and use a 3cm (1¹/₈") round petal cutter to cut out three rose petals. One at a time, thin and vein each petal on the foam pad using a veining tool.

3   One at a time, attach the petals to the polystyrene ball using edible glue. Position them so they overlap each other and cover the top of the ball (M).

4   Repeat step 2 to make three more petals of the same size. Glue them to the bud so they also overlap each other but are positioned higher and less closed than the first three petals (N).

5   Slightly flatten a 5g (<¹/₄oz) ball of White SFP. Using a small CelStick, roll outwards from the centre of the SFP in all directions but leave a 5mm (¹/₄") wide mound in the middle to create a Mexican hat shape (O).

6   Place the SFP on the flat side of the non-stick board with the tall mound facing upwards. Use a 4.5cm (1³/₄") Rose Calyx cutter to cut out a calyx (P), ensuring the mound is in the centre.

7   Transfer the calyx to the foam pad and use the small end of the metal ball tool to thin and slightly lengthen each segment of the calyx (Q).

8   Turn the calyx over and lightly brush it with some edible glue, stopping a little short of the points of the calyx.

9   Slide the wired bud down through the centre of the calyx and wrap the segments up around it, bending the tips slightly backwards (R). Gently taper the underside of the calyx to the wire using your fingers.

10   To finish, bind the exposed wire with white floral tape. Tape directly underneath the calyx and down to the bottom of the wire until fully covered.

11   Repeat steps 1–10 to make a second rose bud. Set both buds aside until assembly.

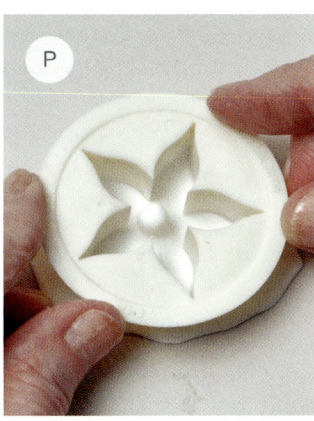

Making The Filler Flowers

1 Cut a 7.5cm (3") piece of 28-gauge white floral wire and make a small hook in one end.

2 Push the hook into a 4mm ($^3/_{16}$") ball of White SFP. Moisten the ball with cooled, boiled water and cover it with a small piece of gold leaf (S). Set the flower centre aside to dry.

3 Roll a 1cm ($^3/_8$") diameter ball of White SFP into a cone shape and flatten the top (T). Push a Tapered Cones 5/6 Star tool into the flat top of the SFP cone to indent (U).

4 Use a pair of small scissors to cut along the tool marks, dividing the cone into five petals (V).

5 Pinch the individual segments flat, then pinch in the corner points to round them off and create the petal shapes (W).

6 Place the flower on the foam pad and use the small end of the metal ball tool to thin and cup each individual petal (X).

7 Feed the wired centre down through the middle of the flower and pull it through until the ball is nestled in the paste (Y).

8 Repeat steps 1–7 to make 22 flowers in total. Leave them all to dry overnight. Once the flowers are dry, bind them into four sprays of five flowers with white floral tape. Leave the two remaining flowers unbound for later use.

Making The Leaves

1 Roll a small piece of White SFP to a 1mm (<$^1/_{16}$") thickness over one of the grooves on the non-stick board.

Cut out a leaf using a 2.5cm (1") Rose Leaf cutter, ensuring the thicker ridge of paste runs through the centre. Keep your offcuts.

2 Cut a 6.5cm (2$^1/_2$") length of 26-gauge white floral wire, dip one end in edible glue and wipe off the excess. Holding the leaf between your finger and thumb, insert the wire about 1cm ($^3/_8$") up into the groove.

3 Place the leaf on the foam pad and thin the edges with the small end of the metal ball tool. Firmly press the leaf between the two halves of the Tea Rose Leaf veiner. Remove from the veiner and use your fingers to give the leaf a little movement. Set it aside to dry.

4 Repeat steps 1–3 to make five more leaves using the 2.5cm (1") Rose Leaf cutter. Then repeat steps 1–3 again to make a further 20 leaves, this time using a 3.1cm (1$^1/_4$") Rose Leaf cutter. Set all the leaves aside to dry overnight.

5 Once dry, lightly smear two small leaves and seven large leaves with a small amount of white vegetable fat. Next, brush the leaves one at a time with a little Classic Gold lustre dust (Z). Keep the other leaves white in colour.

Making A Filler Branch

1 Roll a small piece of White SFP to a 1mm (<$^1/_{16}$") thickness over one of the grooves on the non-stick board. Use a craft knife or a cutting wheel to hand cut a leaf shape that is 1cm ($^3/_8$") wide and long, ensuring the groove is in the centre of the leaf when cutting.

2 Wire the leaf as in step 2 of Making The Leaves, before placing on the foam pad and thinning the edges with the small end of the metal ball tool.

3 Repeat steps 1–2 to make a second leaf the same size. Repeat steps 1–2 again, this time making three leaves that are 1.5cm ($^1/_2$") wide and long.

4 Bind the five leaves and the two remaining filler flowers together with some white floral tape, alternating between pairs of leaves and flowers (AA).

Assembling The Leaves

1 Cut seven 12.5cm – 15cm (5" – 6") lengths of 26-gauge white floral wire.

2 Bind the white leaves to four of the cut wires and the gold leaves to three of the cut wires. Stagger the leaves about 2.5cm (1") apart and only use the small leaves as the top leaf on any branch.

Attaching The Flowers

1 Insert each wired element into posy picks, fixing them inside the picks with a little sugarpaste or royal icing.

2 Insert one of the large roses into the front left of the middle tier so that it sits level with the top of the bottom tier. Insert the smaller rose to the right of the first rose so it overlaps the bottom tier. Add the remaining large rose above the smaller rose.

3 Position the rose buds either side of the three roses. Add two sprays of filler flowers below the roses and one each to the left and right.

4 Attach the filler branch above the roses centrally on the cake. Finally, insert the branches of leaves. Add the white leaves so they overlap the middle gold tier and add the gold leaves so they overlap the bottom white tier.

A SIGN OF
summertime

This strawberry and cream cake is the perfect summertime dessert. Featuring sugarpaste panelling and fun ruffle techniques, the showstopper is topped off with some seasonal ranunculus and strawberry sugar flowers.

YOU WILL NEED

Edibles

Round, filled sponge cake covered with ganache/buttercream with a sharp edge finish, secured on a cake board of the same size (see page 29), 10cm (4") deep: 10cm (4") wide

Round, filled sponge cake covered with ganache/buttercream with a sharp edge finish, secured on a cake board of the same size (see page 29), 12.5cm (5") deep: 15cm (6") wide

SK Professional Paste Food Colours: Leaf Green, Poinsettia (Xmas Red) and Sunflower

SK Fairtrade Sugarpaste: 450g (1lb) Bridal White and 1kg (2lb 3^1/$_4$oz) Palm Green

SK Sugar Florist Paste (SFP): 250g (8^3/$_4$oz) White

SK Essentials Edible Glue

SK Professional Dust Food Colours: Leaf Green and Vine

SK Designer Paste Food Colour: Olive

SK Essentials Confectioners' Glaze

SK Professional Instant Mix Royal Icing: 100g (3^1/$_2$oz) White

Equipment

Round cake drum: 23cm (9")

1.5cm (^{1}/$_2$") width satin ribbon: 76cm (30") white

Round cake boards: 10cm (4") and 15cm (6")

Templates: page 228

Sterilised pins: 2

Food-grade card

FMM Multi Ribbon Cutter

Water brush pen

Safety razor blade

Circle cutter: 12.5cm (5")

CelPin: medium

Cutting wheel

Modelling tools: dresden, medium ball, rounded cone, scribing needle and veining

2cm (^{3}/$_4$") polystyrene balls: 2

Floral wires: 24-, 26- and 28-gauge Nile green, and 18-, 20- and 26-gauge white

Floral tape: half-width and quarter-width Nile green

JEM Easy Rose Cutters: 5cm (2") and 6cm (2^3/$_8$")

Wilton Fondant Shaping Foam Set

Flat paintbrush

Orchard Products Calyx Cutter: 1.9cm (^{3}/$_4$")

Fine Cut Rose Leaf Cutters: 2.2cm (^{7}/$_8$") and 3cm (1^1/$_8$")

SK-GI Silicone Strawberry Veiner: Large Leaf

Dimple foam drying tray

FMM Rose Leaf Cutters: 2.6cm (1") and 3.4cm (1^3/$_8$")

Posy picks: various sizes

SEE PAGES 11–15 FOR ESSENTIAL EDIBLES AND EQUIPMENT

Covering The Cake Drum

1   Use a cocktail stick to gradually add a little Sunflower paste food colour to 1kg (2lb 3^1/$_4$oz) of Palm Green sugarpaste until you reach a grass green colour. This sugarpaste will be used at different stages throughout the project so make sure to keep all your leftover pieces.

2   Roll out 295g (10^1/$_2$oz) of the grass green sugarpaste and cover the 23cm (9") cake drum (see technique on page 32). Set the drum aside to firm overnight.

3   Fix the Bridal White ribbon around the edge of the drum (see technique on page 32).

Covering The Cakes

1   You will be using the panelling method to cover the cakes. For the top tier, roll out 75g (2^5/$_8$oz) of Bridal White sugarpaste and cut out a 12.5cm (5") disc. Place the disc on top of the 10cm (4") cake and trim away the excess (see technique on page 32). For the bottom tier, repeat to cover the top of the 15cm (6") cake with an 18cm (7") disc using 135g (4^3/$_4$oz) of the grass green sugarpaste mixture.

2   To cover the sides, start with the 10cm (4") cake. Roll out 310g (11oz) of Bridal White sugarpaste and cut out a 34cm x 11.5cm (13^3/$_8$" x 4^1/$_2$") panel. Roll

up the panel and wrap it around the cake (see technique on page 32).

3   Repeat step 2 to cover the side of the 15cm (6") cake. This time, roll out 495g (1lb 1$\frac{1}{2}$oz) of the grass green sugarpaste and cut out a 50cm x 14cm (19$\frac{3}{4}$" x 5$\frac{1}{2}$") rectangle. Set both cakes aside to dry overnight.

Adding The Lines

1   Transfer the round spacing template onto a piece of food-safe paper, cut it out and place it centrally on top of the 15cm (6") cake. Position it so that when looking down on the cake one of the single marked lines is about 2mm ($\frac{1}{16}$") to the right of the sugarpaste join if you are right-handed, or 2mm ($\frac{1}{16}$") to the left of it if you are left-handed. This is so the join will be covered by a strip. Fix the template in place with two sterilised pins so that it cannot rotate.

2   Transfer the rectangular guide template to a piece of food-safe card and cut it out. Fold it at the dotted line, making sure that the fold is perfectly perpendicular to the long edge.

3   Roll out 8g ($\frac{1}{2}$oz) of White SFP to a 1mm (<$\frac{1}{16}$") thickness and use a ribbon cutter to cut out a 5mm x 15cm ($\frac{1}{4}$" x 6") strip. Cut 12 strips in total.

4   Rest the guide template on the cake. If you are right-handed, its right edge should be up against one of the lines. If you are left-handed, its left edge should be up against one of the lines.

5   Use a water brush pen to wet a 5mm ($\frac{1}{4}$") strip down the line side of the guide with some cooled, boiled water (A).

6   Take a White SFP strip and place it up against the cake, positioning it flush with the base and using the guide template to keep it straight (B). Press it

into place and trim it flush with the top of the cake using a safety razor blade.

7   Repeat steps 4–6 for each remaining line on the spacing template. Work anti-clockwise if you are right-handed and clockwise if you are left-handed. When finished, remove the sterilised pins and the template from the cake.

Adding The Green Circle

1   Roll out 100g (3$\frac{1}{2}$oz) of the green grass sugarpaste and cut out a 12.5cm (5") disc using the circle cutter. Leave the disc to firm up for an hour to make it easier to handle.

2   Lightly wet the centre of the top of the 15cm (6") cake using cooled, boiled water. Make sure the wet area is a little smaller than the 12.5cm (5") disc.

3   Place the disc centrally on top of the cake (where you have wet it) and press it into place with a smoother (C).

Making The Ruffles

1   Roll 40g (1$\frac{1}{2}$oz) of Bridal White sugarpaste into a 10cm x 1cm (4" x $\frac{3}{8}$") sausage shape.

2   Roll the sausage flat until it is about 1mm (<$\frac{1}{16}$") thick and then pick small bits of paste off one of the long edges. Continue rolling over the paste, applying more pressure towards the torn edge until that edge is wafer thin (D).

3   Use a cutting wheel or sharp knife to trim the untorn edge of the sugarpaste to a straight line. Try to make the width of the cut strip no more than 4cm (1$\frac{1}{2}$") wide at its widest point.

4   Wet a 2.5cm (1") band around the 10cm (4") cake with some cooled, boiled water, approximately 1cm ($\frac{3}{8}$") down from the top. Apply a ruffle strip to the wet area of the cake so the torn edge

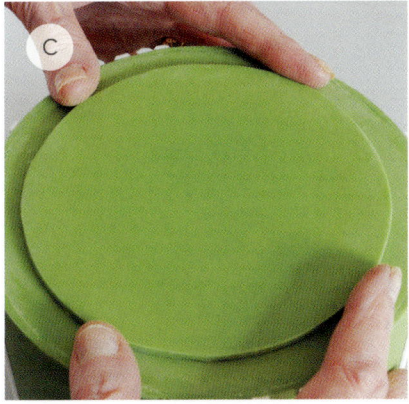

extends just over the top of the cake. Once it is attached, curl back the torn edge of the ruffle (E).

5 Repeat steps 1–4 to continue adding ruffles to the cake, gradually working your way down to the bottom (F). Try to be irregular when adding them – they do not need to be in neat layers, and it's okay if the ends do not match up or even if they overlap.

6 Once all the ruffles have been attached, use a dresden tool to make any adjustments required. Leave the cake to dry overnight.

Assembling The Cake

1 Attach the 15cm (6") cake centrally on top of the covered drum. Dowel the 15cm (6") cake, spacing them evenly within a central 10cm (4") circle. Attach the 10cm (4") ruffled cake centrally on top (see technique on page 41).

Making The Ranunculuses

1 Use a scribe tool to poke a hole through the centre of a 2cm (³/₄") polystyrene ball.

2 Slide a 12.5cm (5") length of 26-gauge white floral wire though the hole in the ball, making sure there is an equal amount of wire either side.

3 Use pliers to bend a small hook in one end of a 10cm (4") length of 20-gauge white wire. Insert the hooked end of the wire into the centre of the polystyrene ball, perpendicular to the first wire, to make a T-shape (G).

4 Bend the thinner wire down towards the thicker wire and twist the two ends around it (H). Cover the wire stem with some half-width Nile green floral tape (I).

5 Colour a pea-sized piece of White SFP a light green shade using a little Leaf Green paste food colour. Divide the green SFP in two, roll one piece into a ball and then roll it flat into a 1.5cm (¹/₂") circle. Cover and keep the other SFP piece for the second flower.

6 Attach the green circle to the top of the ball using a little edible glue (J). Mark a 5mm (¹/₄") and a 1cm (³/₈") circle centrally in the paste – a pen lid and a straw are about the right size (K).

7 Thinly roll out 5g (<¹/₄oz) of White SFP and use a 5cm (2") Rose cutter to cut out a set of petals. Vein and thin each individual petal on a non-stick board using a veining tool, making them as thin as you can (L). Turn the petals over

and lightly cup the centre of each petal segment on a soft foam pad using a medium ball tool (M).

8   Place the petals – still veined side down – centrally on a thin, firm foam pad with a hole in the centre. Lightly brush the petals halfway up with edible glue (N).

9   Slide the wired ball through the middle of the petal set and through the hole in the pad until the ball rests in the centre (O). Lift each individual petal and attach it to the flower centre, keeping the tops pulled back enough to allow some of the green disc to show (P).

top tip

If you do not have a pad with a hole in, a piece of card of craft foam will do just as well.

Remove from the foam pad and carefully set aside.

10   Repeat step 7 to cut out and texture a second set of petals using the 5cm (2") Rose cutter. Then run the small end of a rounded cone tool just under the outer edge of each petal segment to give it some extra shape (Q).

11   Place the petals centrally on the foam pad with a hole in the centre. Lightly brush the bottom half of each petal segment with some edible glue in a U-shape, and also lightly brush the centre of the petal set.

12   Take the flower stem you previously set aside and slide the wire down through the middle of the petal set until it rests in the centre. Lift each individual petal and attach them to the flower one at a time, being careful not to lose the cupped shape. Keep the

tops of the petals slightly away from the previous set (R). Remove from the foam pad and carefully set aside.

13   Repeat steps 10–12 to make and attach two more sets of 5cm (2") petals. This time, slightly stretch the petals using a ball tool before veining, thinning and shaping them.

14   Repeat step 10 to cut out and texture two sets of petals using the 6cm (2³/₈") Rose cutter.

15   One set at a time, lightly brush the bottom half of each petal segment with edible glue in a shallow U-shape. Attach each petal set using the foam pad with a hole in the centre, but this time let the petals fall slightly further away than with the previous sets.

16   Open or adjust any petals if required using a dresden tool (S).

Remove from the foam pad and carefully set aside in an upright position to dry.

17   To make the second ranunculus flower, first repeat steps 1–12. Next, repeat steps 14–16 to add only one set of 6cm (2³/₈") petals, but do not let them fall as far away as with the same-sized petals on the previous flower. Leave this ranunculus flower to dry on its side so it will sit properly on the top of the cake.

18   Once both flowers are dry, dust the tops of the centre petals with a little Leaf Green dust food colour.

Making The Strawberry Flowers

1   Roll a 1cm (³/₈") diameter ball of White SFP into a cone shape and flatten the top. Push a rounded cone tool into the flat top of the cone.

2   Use a pair of small scissors to divide the cone into five petals, making each cut about 3mm (¹/₈") deep (T).

3   Pinch the individual segments flat and then pinch in the corner points to round them off and create the petal shapes (U).

4   Place the flower on a foam pad and use a medium ball tool to thin and cup each petal.

5   Cut a 7.5cm (3") piece of 28-gauge Nile green floral wire and make a small hook in one end.

6   Feed the wire down through the middle of the flower and pull it through until it is nestled in the SFP.

7   Colour a small piece of White SFP a light yellow shade with a little Sunflower paste food colour. Take the yellow SFP and roll out a small ball the size of a round head pin. Dab a spot of

edible glue in the centre of the flower and attach the light yellow ball (V).

8   Repeat steps 1–7 to make five flowers in total. Leave them to dry overnight.

Making The Strawberries

1   Colour 120g (4¹/₄oz) of White SFP a bright red shade using some Poinsettia (Xmas Red) paste food colour.

2   Colour 25g (>³/₄oz) of White SFP green using a mixture of Olive paste food colour and a little Leaf Green dust. Most of this will be used to create the leaves later, so make sure you wrap up and keep any offcuts!

3   Roll 20g (³/₄oz) of the red SFP into a ball in your hand. Use your fingers to roll one end slightly thinner to achieve a strawberry shape.

4   Cut a 6cm (2³/₈") length of 26-gauge Nile green floral wire and make a small hook in one end. Dip the hook in edible glue, wipe off the excess and insert it centrally into the wide end of the strawberry.

5   Use a scribe tool to prick small indentations in the strawberry to represent the seeds (W).

6   Thinly roll out a small piece of the green SFP and use a 1.9cm (³/₄") calyx cutter to cut out a calyx. Place the calyx on the foam pad and thin it slightly with a ball tool.

7   Dab a little edible glue in the centre of the calyx and slide it up the wire, attaching it to the strawberry (X). Turn the calyx tips up using a dresden tool so they are flaring away from the strawberry.

8   Repeat steps 3–7 to make six strawberries in total. Leave them to dry overnight.

9   Dip the dried strawberries in Confectioners' Glaze and leave them to dry. Once dry, finely bind each wire with some quarter-width Nile green floral tape.

top tip

If you don't have any quarter-width tape, use a tape cutter and shredder to cut quarter-width pieces quickly and accurately from some half-width tape.

Making The Strawberry Leaves

1   Roll a small piece of the green SFP mixture from Making The Strawberries to a 1mm (<¹/₁₆") thickness over one of the grooves on the non-stick board. Cut out a leaf using a 3cm (1¹/₈") Rose Leaf cutter, positioning the thicker ridge in the centre of the cutter (Y).

2   Cut a 6.5cm (2¹/₂") length of 26-gauge white floral wire, dip one end in edible glue and wipe off the excess. Hold the ridge in the centre of the leaf between your finger and thumb and gently insert the wire about 1cm (³/₈") into it.

3   Place the leaf on the foam pad and thin the edges with a ball tool. Firmly press the thinned leaf between the two halves of a Strawberry Leaf veiner. Carefully remove the leaf and shape it with your fingers to add some movement.

4   Repeat steps 1–3 to make five more leaves using the 3cm (1¹/₈") Rose Leaf cutter. Next, repeat steps 1–3 again to make 15 leaves using a 2.2cm (⁷/₈") Rose Leaf cutter. Set all the leaves aside to dry overnight on a dimple foam drying tray.

5   Once dry, lightly dust the leaves all over with some Vine dust food

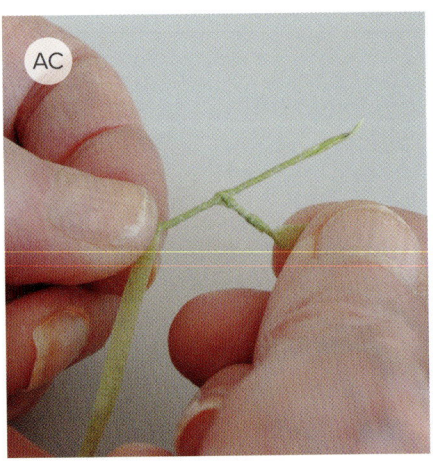

colour. Dust the centres with a little Leaf Green dust, blending out towards the edges (Z, see page 145). Once dusted, lightly steam the leaves to set the colour and allow them to dry.

6   Dip the finished leaves in Confectioners' Glaze and set them all aside to dry overnight.

Making The Filler Leaves

1   Follow steps 1–3 in Making The Strawberry Leaves to make two leaves using a 2.6cm (1") Rose Leaf cutter and five leaves using a 3.4cm (1³/₈") Rose Leaf cutter.

Assembling The Sprays

1   Cut six 7.5cm (3") lengths of 26-gauge Nile green floral wire. Bind a larger strawberry leaf to the end of each wire using quarter-width Nile green floral tape. Next, attach two smaller strawberry leaves opposite each other directly below the first leaf (AA). Continue this method to make six sprays of three leaves each.

2   Cut a 10cm (4") length of 26-gauge Nile green wire. Bind a spray of strawberry leaves to one end using some half-width floral tape. In no particular order, continue down the wire adding

the following: six strawberries, five strawberry flowers and three more strawberry leaf sprays. You can add extra single strawberry leaves if needed. Make sure to bind the strawberries so they hang 2.5cm – 4cm (1" – 1¹/₂") away from the wire (AB).

3   Cut a piece of 24-gauge Nile green floral wire in half. Also cut seven 2cm (³/₄") pieces of quarter-width Nile green floral tape to use for small branches.

4   Bind the first 2.5cm (1") of one end of a wire with some half-width Nile green tape. Fold one of the 2cm (³/₄") pieces of quarter-width tape around the wire just above where you taped down to and twist the ends together to make a small branch (AC). Bind a little further down the wire and add one of the smaller filler leaves. Continue working down, adding two more branches and two of the larger filler leaves as you go.

5   Repeat steps 3–4 to make a second branch, this time with four branches and four leaves: one small and three big.

Attaching The Sprays And Flowers

1   Cut two 5cm (2") lengths of 18-gauge white wire and cover them with half-width Nile green tape. Bend

each wire into a U-shaped pin. Insert each wired element into posy picks, fixing them inside the picks with a little leftover sugarpaste or royal icing.

2   Gently bend the spray of strawberries to give it a curve and pin it to the front edge of the top tier, pointing towards the left.

3   Insert the two filler branches just behind the strawberry spray. Have the one on the left curving up and the one on the right curving down.

4   Insert the first ranunculus flower behind the strawberry spray and to the right of the filler branch curving upwards. Position the ranunculus so it is facing upwards and towards the front right of the cake.

5   Trim the stem of the second ranunculus flower (which was left to dry on its side) to about 4cm (1¹/₂"). Fix it to the cake with a little royal icing, positioning it to the right of the first ranunculus flower and facing slightly more to the side than to the front.

6   Attach the final two sprays of strawberry leaves to the top of the cake at the back so they cover up the stems of the two ranunculuses.

FRESH
as a daisy

Fall in love with this crisp, contemporary orange arrangement of sugar flowers and seasonal berries, ideal for autumnal celebrations and showstopper occasions.

YOU WILL NEED

Edibles

Round, filled sponge cake covered with ganache/buttercream with a sharp edge finish, secured on a cake board of the same size (see page 29), 10cm (4") deep: 20.5cm (8") wide

Round, filled sponge cake covered with ganache/buttercream with a sharp edge finish, secured on a cake board of the same size (see page 29), 7.5cm (3") deep: 15cm (6") wide

SK Fairtrade Sugarpaste: 1.62kg (3lb 9^1/$_8$oz) Bridal White

SK Sugar Florist Paste (SFP): 160g (5^1/$_2$oz) White

SK Designer Paste Food Colour: Olive

SK Dust Food Colour: Orange

SK Professional Dust Food Colours: Bulrush (Dark Brown), Leaf Green, Sunflower and Vine

SK Pastelz Paste Food Colour: Cream

SK Neonz Paste Food Colours: Orange, Red and Yellow

SK Essentials Edible Glue

SK Professional Instant Mix Royal Icing: 100g (3^1/$_2$oz) White

PME Edible Glaze Spray

Equipment

Round cake boards: 15cm (6") and 20.5cm (8")

Round cake drum: 25.5cm (10")

1.5cm (^{1}/$_2$") width satin ribbon: 84cm (33") Bridal White

Floral wires: 24-, 26- and 28-gauge Nile green, and 18-, 20- and 26-gauge white

Tweezers

Yellow long head stamens: 75

Cream matt pointed head stamens: 50

Full-width floral tape: Nile green and brown

Fine Cut Iceland Poppy Petal Cutters: 4.5cm (1^3/$_4$") and 6cm (2^3/$_8$")

Circle cutters: 6mm (^{1}/$_4$"), 9mm (^{3}/$_8$") and 1.5cm (^{1}/$_2$")

SK Multi Flower Cutter Set 1A, Round Petal/Leaf: no. 2

Modelling tools: dresden, medium ball and veining

Dimple foam drying tray

Cupped formers

SK High-Quality Paintbrush: no. 4

Polystyrene balls: 2 x 2cm (^{3}/$_4$")

Safety razor blade

Five-petal cutters: 3cm (1^1/$_8$"), 4.5cm (1^3/$_4$"), 4.8cm (1^7/$_8$") and 5.9cm (2^3/$_8$")

Daisy centre mould: 1.1cm (^{7}/$_{16}$")

Daisy plunger cutters: 2cm (^{3}/$_4$") and 2.7cm (1^1/$_{16}$")

FMM Rose Leaf Cutters, Set of 3: 2.6cm (1"), 3.4cm (1^3/$_8$") and 4.3cm (1^3/$_4$")

Leaf cutter: 3cm (1^1/$_8$")

SK-GI Silicone Veiner Rose - Tea: Large Leaf

Posy picks: various sizes

SEE PAGES 11–15 FOR ESSENTIAL EDIBLES AND EQUIPMENT

Covering The Cake Drum

1   Roll out 350g (12^1/$_4$oz) of Bridal White sugarpaste and cover the 25.5cm (10") cake drum (see technique on page 32). Set the drum aside to firm overnight.

2   Fix the Bridal White ribbon around the edge of the drum (see technique on page 32).

Covering The Cakes

1   You will be using the panelling method to cover the cakes. For the top tier, roll out 135g (4^3/$_4$oz) of Bridal White sugarpaste and cut out an 18cm (7") disc. Place the disc on top of the 15cm (6") wide cake and trim away the excess (see technique on page 32). For the bottom tier, repeat to cover the top of the 20.5cm (8") cake with a 23cm (9") disc using 215g (7^3/$_4$oz) of Bridal White sugarpaste.

2   To cover the sides, start with the 15cm (6") cake. Roll out 370g (13oz) of Bridal White sugarpaste and cut out a 50cm x 9cm (19^3/$_4$" x 3^1/$_2$") panel. Roll up the panel and wrap it around the cake (see technique on page 32).

3   Repeat step 2 to cover the side of the 20.5cm (8") cake. This time, roll out 550g (1lb 3^1/$_2$oz) of Bridal White sugarpaste and cut out a 65cm x 11.5cm (25^1/$_2$" x 4^1/$_2$") panel. Set both cakes aside to dry overnight.

top tip

It's worth remembering that you can scale the size of the cake up or down to meet your requirements. Just keep the proportions roughly the same and adjust how much decoration you need.

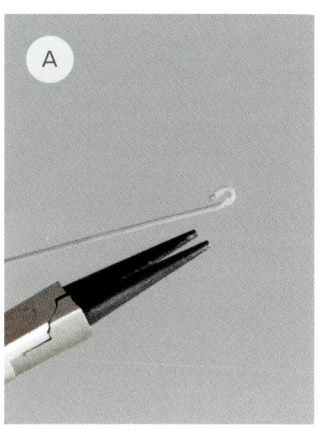

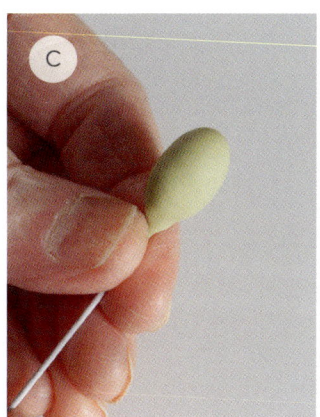

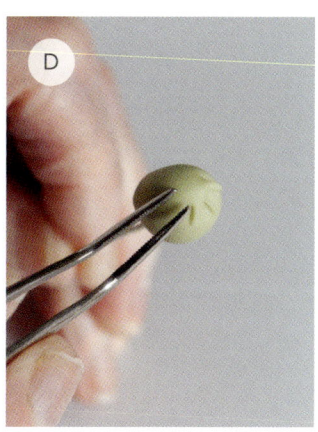

Making The Iceland Poppy Centre

1   Cut a 7.5cm (3") length of 18-gauge white floral wire and bend a small closed hook in one end with a pair of pliers (A).

2   Colour a 1.9cm ($^3/_4$") ball of White SFP a light green shade with Olive paste food colour and a little Leaf Green dust. You'll be using this green SFP later in the project, so make sure you keep it wrapped up as you work to prevent it from drying out.

3   Roll a 1.25cm ($^1/_2$") ball of the green SFP and shape it into a teardrop (B). Wrap up the remaining green SFP for later use.

4   Dip the hooked end of the wire in edible glue and wipe off the excess. Insert the hook into the thin end of the teardrop. Pinch the paste closed around the wire and pull away any excess (C).

5   Use a pair of tweezers to pinch out five or six spokes in the top of the ball. Set it aside to dry (D).

6   Take two bundles of yellow long head stamens and, without removing the tape, cut them each in half (E).

7   Position one half bundle against the dried centre so that the bottom of the stamen heads are just below the top of the paste. Bind the stamens to the wire with full-width Nile green tape (F).

8   Bind two more half bundles evenly spaced around the centre. Rough up the three sets so that they are nice and irregular.

9   As a finishing touch, use the no. 4 paintbrush to lightly dust the tips of the stamens with a mix of Orange and Sunflower dust food colours.

Making The Iceland Poppy Petals

1   Cut six 7.5cm (3") lengths of 26-gauge white floral wire. Colour 25g ($^7/_8$oz) of White SFP a cream shade using a little Cream pastel paste colour.

2   Roll a small piece of the cream SFP over a groove on a non-stick board to just over 1mm (<$^1/_{16}$") thick.

3   Turn the paste so it is ridge side up and cut out a petal using a 4.5cm (1$^3/_4$") Iceland Poppy Petal cutter, making sure the cutter is centred over the ridge (G).

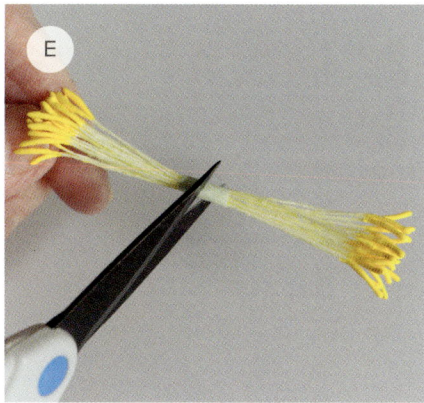

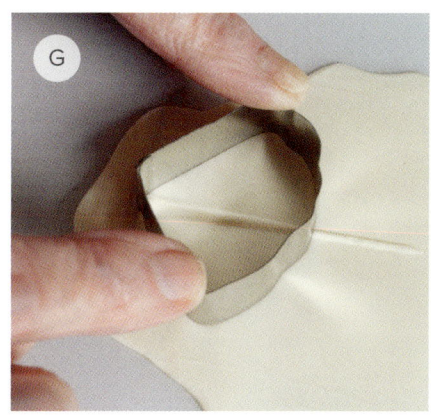

4 Dip one end of a cut wire in edible glue and wipe off the excess. Insert the wire 1cm ($^3/_8$") into the ridge at the base of the petal (H).

5 Place the petal on a foam pad and thin the edges with a medium ball tool (I).

6 Remove the petal from the foam pad and transfer to a flat surface. Use a veining tool to vein and frill the petal; keep the tip of the tool pointed towards the point of the petal and press down firmly on the veined end as you hold the other side and twist it back and forth (J). Work across the petal until it has widened to about one and a half times its original width.

7 Drag a dresden tool from the centre outwards at a few points on the petal to add some deeper ridges (K).

8 Carefully bend the wire within the petal to form a gentle curve inwards. To finish, style the petal with various folds and undulations (L). Place on a dimple foam drying tray to dry.

9 Repeat steps 2–8 to make two more petals. Don't worry about trying to shape the petals too much like each other.

10 Repeat steps 2–8 to make three larger petals using the 6cm ($2^3/_8$") Iceland Poppy Petal cutter, but with less

top tip

All sorts of things can be used as formers, from products designed for the task to egg boxes and shaped foil. Whilst sometimes a specific former is best, almost anything that has a cupped shape can be called into use. The most important thing is to take care how you shape the petals before leaving them to dry.

folds and undulations than the smaller petals. To finish, place the larger petals in cupped formers to dry (M).

11 Once the petals have dried, dust them with a mix of Orange and Sunflower dust food colours. Work from the base up, fading out by about halfway. Start lightly with the colour and build it up gradually – remember you can always add more but you can't take it away (N).

top tip

The dusting on the petals in this instance is to tie them in with the other flowers on the cake. You can carefully add more dust once the cake has been assembled if you feel it needs it.

Assembling The Iceland Poppy

1 One at a time, hold each petal at the point that the wire enters and bend the wire down by 45˚ on the smaller petals and by 60˚ on the larger petals.

2 Starting directly underneath a small petal, bind the petal to the flower centre using full-width Nile green tape (O). Continue to secure the other two small petals around the centre, making sure they are evenly spaced. Position all three petals so they are butted up against the non-taped base of the stamens.

3 Bind on the three larger petals using the Nile green tape; position them so they are butted up against the

top tip

If you can, I'd suggest making a couple extra of each petal. Because the shape is fairly organic, it can be useful to have some options to see which ones go together best.

first set of petals and so the gaps are offset in relation to the first set (P). Finish by binding right down to the end of the wire.

Making The Small Poppies

1 Repeat steps 1–5 from Making The Iceland Poppy Centre to make three centres, but this time use 20-gauge white wire and a 1cm ($^3/_8$") ball of green SFP for each centre.

2 Repeat steps 6–8 from Making The Iceland Poppy Centre, this time using 50 cream pointed head stamens dusted with some Sunflower dust.

3 Cut some 28-gauge Nile green wire into 12 pieces that are 7.5cm (3") in length.

4 Mix 16g ($^1/_2$oz) of White SFP with a combination of Orange and Red neon paste food colours to achieve a rich salmon (pinky-orange) shade.

5 Roll a small piece of the pinky-orange SFP mixture out to a 1mm ($<^1/_{16}$") thickness over a groove on the non-stick board.

6 Remove the paste from the board and turn it ridge side up. Cut out a petal using a 2.6cm (1") round petal cutter, making sure the cutter is centred over the ridge.

7 Dip one end of a cut wire in edible glue and wipe off the excess. Insert the glued end 1cm ($^3/_8$") into the ridge at the base of the petal.

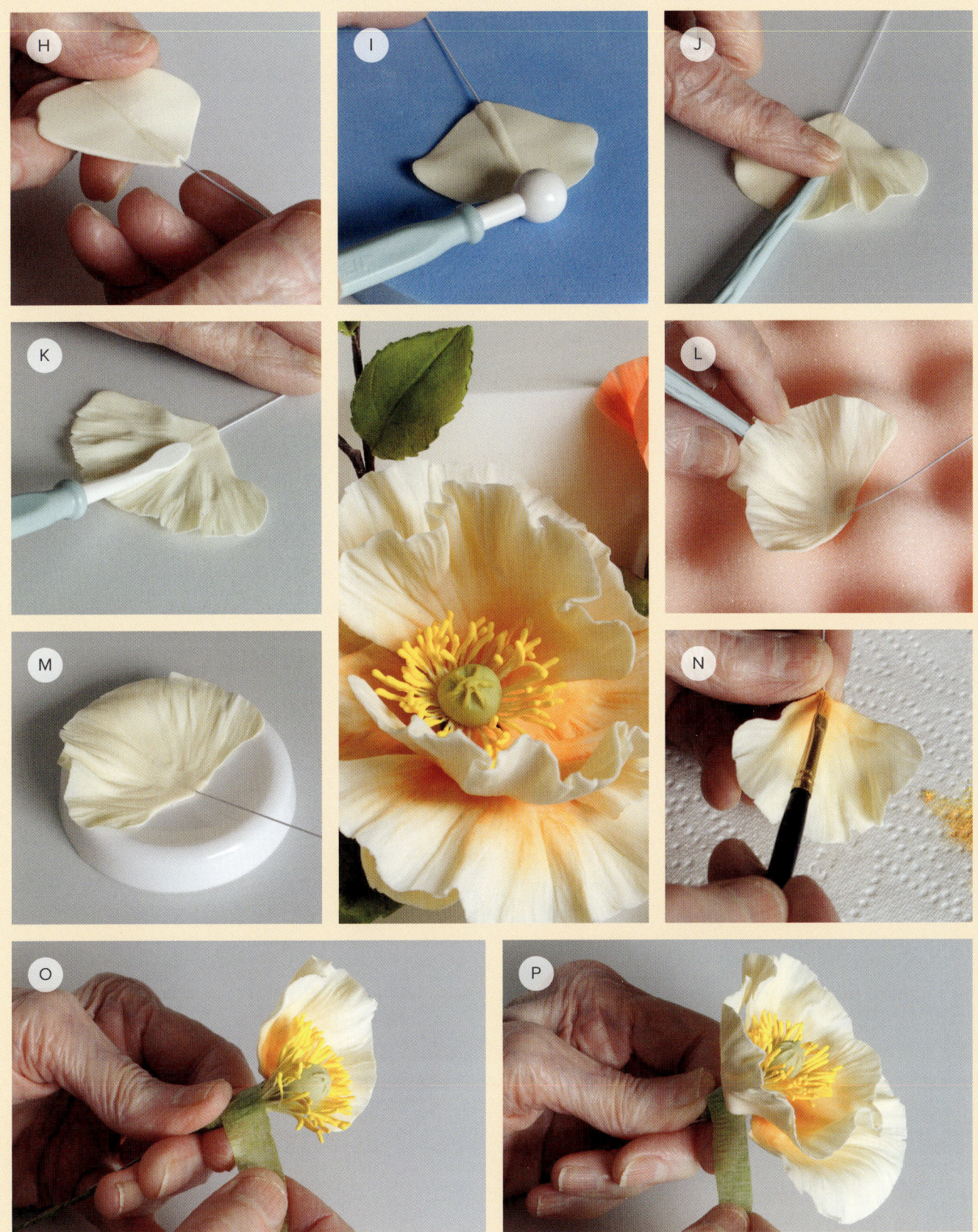

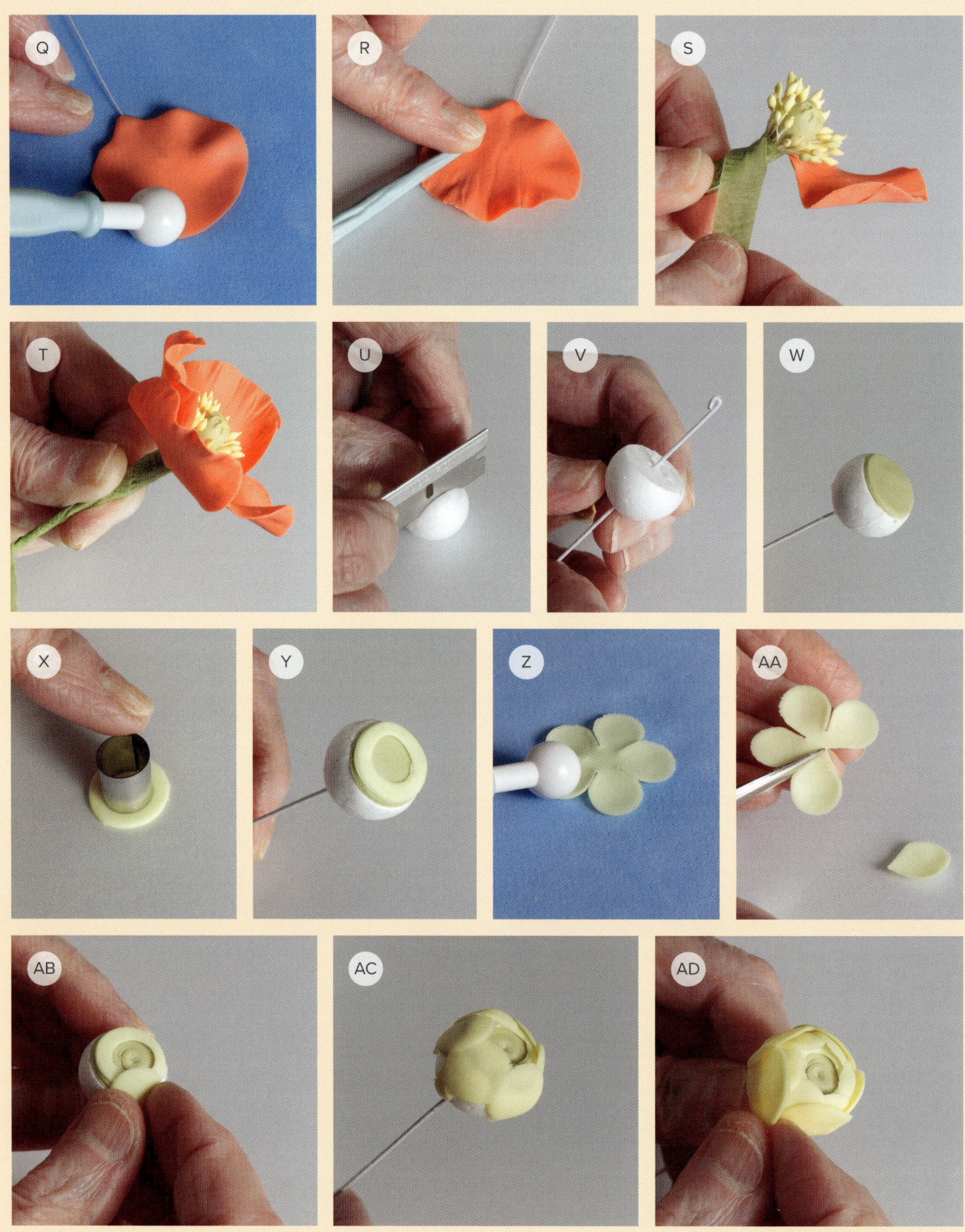

8 Place the petal on the foam pad and use the medium ball tool to stretch and thin the petal upwards and outwards (Q). Also lightly texture the petal with the veining tool, keeping the tip pointed towards the base of the petal (R). Place the petal on the dimple foam drying tray and leave to dry.

9 Repeat steps 5–8 to make 11 more petals.

10 One at a time, hold each of the 12 petals at the base where the wire enters and bend down by just under 90°.

11 Starting directly underneath a petal, bind it to a wired centre using full-width Nile green tape (S). Attach three more petal to the centre in the same way, spacing them evenly. Position each petal so its base sits level with the bottom of the green centre. After the last petal, bind right down to the end of the wire (T).

12 Repeat step 11 to attach the remaining petals to the other two flower centres: four petals per centre.

top tip

When taping petals to centres, you can pull down on an already attached petal's wire to tighten it if it's a bit high.

Making The Ranunculus Centres

1 Mix some Sunflower dust with 10g (¼oz) of White SFP to achieve a light yellow shade. Take just over half of the light yellow SFP and make it a slightly richer yellow using a little more Sunflower dust.

2 Use a razor blade to cut off one third of a 2cm (¾") polystyrene ball (U).

3 Cut a 7.5cm (3") length of 20-gauge white wire and bend a small closed hook in one end.

4 Slide the wire down through centre of the cut side of the ball, add a little bit of glue to the hook and pull it down until it sits flush with the ball (V).

5 Thinly roll out a piece of the green SFP you set aside earlier and cut out a disc using a 1.5cm (½") circle cutter.

6 Lightly brush the flat section of the polystyrene centre with edible glue and attach the green disc (W).

7 Thinly roll out a small piece of the light yellow SFP from step 1 and cut out another 1.5cm (½") disc. Once cut, use a 9mm (⅜") circle cutter to cut a hole in the centre of the yellow disc (X).

8 Lightly brush the underside of the pale yellow ring with glue and attach it to the green disc on the centre (Y).

9 Use a 6mm (¼") circle cutter to mark a circle in the green paste visible through the yellow disc. To finish, mark the very centre with the end of a paintbrush.

10 Roll out a piece of the light yellow SFP thinly and cut out a blossom using a 3cm (1⅛") five-petal cutter.

11 On the foam pad, thin and cup each individual petal with the medium ball tool (Z).

12 Use a pair of scissors to cut the blossom into five small petals (AA).

13 Lightly brush the inside of a small petal with glue and attach it to the flower centre so it just overlaps but does not fully cover the yellow ring (AB). Attach the remaining four petals the same way, making sure they are evenly

spaced around the centre. Tuck the edge of the last petal under the edge of the first so that each petal is overlapping the one next to it (AC).

14 Roll out a small piece of the richer yellow SFP to a 1mm (<1/16") thickness and cut out a blossom using a 4.5cm (1¾") five-petal cutter. Repeat step 11 to thin and cup the blossom.

15 Brush the centre of the blossom and the lower half of each individual petal with a little edible glue. Slide the blossom up the wire and bring the petals up so that their tops are level with the top of the first set but sit very slightly away (AD). As with the first set of petals, make sure each petal overlaps the next. Do not worry if the petals tear away from each other on the underside.

16 Finish by lightly dusting the middle of the flower centre with a combination of Leaf Green and Bulrush (Dark Brown) dust colours.

17 Repeat steps 2–16 to make a second ranunculus centre.

Making The Ranunculus Petals

1 Colour a 1.6cm (⅝") ball of White SFP a pale orange shade using a little Orange neon paste. Also colour a 2.5cm (1") ball of White SFP a bright orange shade using Orange neon paste.

2 Roll out the pale orange SFP to a 1mm (<1/16") thickness. Cut out a blossom using the 4.5cm (1¾") five-petal cutter.

3 Place the petal set on the foam pad and use the medium ball tool to thin and cup the individual petals.

4 Lightly brush the centre of the set and the bottom third of each petal

with a little glue. Take one of the flower centres and slide the wire down through the middle of the blossom, bringing it up to the main flower. Fold the petals up and position them so they sit at least 3mm (¹/₈") away from the petals already attached to the centre. As with those petals, make sure each one overlaps the next (AE).

5   Repeat steps 2–4 using a 4.8cm (1⁷/₈") five-petal cutter and the bright orange SFP, this time leaving the petals about 6mm (¹/₄") away from the previous set (AF).

6   Cut a second blossom from the bright orange SFP using the 4.8cm (1⁷/₈") five-petal cutter. Place the blossom on the foam pad and use the veining tool to thin and texture the individual petals. Also cup with the medium ball tool.

7   Brush the centre of the blossom and the lower quarter of each petal with glue. Slide the main wire through the middle of the blossom and slide it up to the flower centre. Press the glued portion of the paste in place but leave the petals fairly flared out.

8   Repeat step 6 to cut and texture a final bright orange blossom, this time using the 5.9cm (2³/₈") five-petal cutter. Repeat step 7 to attach the petals but slightly curl them back or wave the individual petals (AG).

9   Repeat steps 1–8 to make a yellow ranunculus flower using the remaining wired centre. For this you will need to make two shades of yellow SFP. Use the Yellow neon paste food colour to achieve these shades.

top tip

You can add more layers of petals to the ranunculus flowers if you like, just make the gaps between layers slightly smaller.

top tip

You can easily add a ranunculus bud. First, attach a small thin disc of yellow paste to the top of an uncut 2cm (³/₄") wired polystyrene ball.

Secondly, cut five individual thinned and cupped light orange petals from a 3cm (1¹/₈") five-petal blossom and interlock them on the top half of the ball, leaving just a little bit of the yellow disc showing through.

Finally, cut a light green set of petals using a 4.5cm (1³/₄") five-petal cutter, thin and cup them, and then wrap them up around the ball.

Making The Daisies

1   Colour a 1.5cm (¹/₂") ball of White SFP a yellow shade using Sunflower dust.

2   Cut some 26-gauge Nile green wire into 11 pieces that are 7.5cm (3") in length. Bend a small closed hook in one end of each cut wire.

3   Take a small pea-sized ball of the yellow SFP and push the hooked end of a cut wire up into it. To texture, press the ball into a daisy centre mould (AH).

top tip

You can stipple the flower centres with the end of a small paintbrush if you do not have a daisy centre mould.

4   Dust the daisy centre with some Sunflower dust and then set it aside to dry.

5   Repeat steps 3–4 to make three more daisy centres of the same size. Then repeat again to make seven small centres, half the width of the larger ones.

6   Roll out a small piece of White SFP to a 1mm (<$^1/_{16}$") thickness. Use a 2.7cm (1$^1/_{16}$") daisy plunger cutter to cut out a daisy.

7   Brush the underside of one of the larger daisy centres with a little glue. Slide the wire through the middle of the daisy petals and attach the centre to the flower (AI).

8   Repeat steps 6–7 to make three more large daisies and attach them to the remaining larger centres.

9   Repeat steps 6–7 again to make seven small daisies, this time using a 2cm ($^3/_4$") daisy plunger cutter and attaching them to the remaining centres.

10 Leave the 11 daisies to dry hanging upside down and/or stuck in a polystyrene cake dummy angled so that the petals are not falling back towards the wire.

11 Once the daisies are dry, bind them into two bunches using full-width Nile green tape: one bunch of five daisies and one bunch of six. Mix the sizes randomly on each bunch and arrange the flowers at varying heights. Don't begin taping directly underneath the flowers, rather start about halfway down each of the wires so you are able to rearrange and position the daises however you like.

Making The Berries

1   Cut six 7.5cm (3") lengths of 26-gauge Nile green wire and make a small closed hook in one end of each.

2   Mix together an equal amount of leftover paste from the small poppies and the orange ranunculus flowers.

3   One at a time, roll out six pea-sized balls from the SFP mixture and

slide a wire down through each ball until the hook nestles in the top (AJ).

4   Lightly dust the berries with some Orange dust. Steam to set the colour and allow to dry. Next, dip each berry in edible glaze and set aside to dry.

5   Once dry, bind the berries together with full-width Nile green tape. Arrange them in a loose bunch with varying heights, leaving a large area underneath each berry not taped so you can adjust their positions if needed.

Making The Leaves

1   Cut some 28-gauge Nile green wire into 35 pieces measuring 7.5cm (3") in length.

2   Mix 65g (2$^1/_4$oz) of White SFP with some Olive paste food colour to achieve a green shade.

3   Roll out a small piece of the green SFP to a 1mm (<$^1/_{16}$") thickness over a groove on the non-stick board. Cut out a leaf using a 4.3cm (1$^3/_4$") Rose Leaf cutter, making sure the cutter is positioned centrally over the ridge.

4   Dip the end of a wire in edible glue, wipe off the excess and insert the wire 1cm ($^3/_8$") into the ridge at the base of the leaf.

5   Place the wired leaf on the foam pad and thin the edges with the medium ball tool.

6   Place the leaf between the two halves of a Tea Rose Leaf veiner and press down firmly to texture (AK). Remove from the veiner and use your fingers to shape the leaf to give it some movement. Set aside to dry.

7   Repeat steps 3–6 to make 20 leaves in total. Make them in a variety of sizes using the 2.6cm (1"),

3.4cm (1³/₈") and 4.3cm (1³/₄") Rose Leaf cutters.

8   Repeat steps 3–6 again to make 15 simple leaves using a basic 3cm (1¹/₈") leaf cutter. This time, instead of texturing them with the veiner, simply mark a line down the centre of each leaf using the dresden tool.

9   Once the rose leaves are dry, brush their faces with some Vine dust. Next, mix some Leaf Green dust with a little Bulrush (Dark Brown) dust and apply to the centre of each leaf, fading out towards the edges. For the basic leaves, just dust them with a mixture of Leaf Green and Bulrush (Dark Brown) dusts.

10 Steam all the leaves to set the colour, set aside to dry and then spray them with some edible glaze. Set aside until assembly.

Making The Branches

1   Cut a 20.5cm (8") length of 24-gauge Nile green wire. Cover roughly the first 5cm (2") with full-width brown tape.

2   Bind on a rose leaf of any size, making sure the base of the leaf is sitting flush against the wire. Add two or three more leaves about 2.5cm (1") or so apart, varying which side of the branch they are secured on. Make sure you bind

right down to the end of the branch after the last leaf. Add a few bends to the branch to give it life.

3   Make three more branches with rose leaves and then three with the basic leaves. Make the branches in a variety of lengths, from 15cm – 20.5cm (6" – 8"). You should have several loose leaves remaining, which are to be used as fillers when the cake is assembled.

4   If you like, at this point you can add occasional little twigs to the branches. To do this, simply fold a short length of brown tape over the branch and then twist it between your fingers until you form a twig.

Assembling The Cake

1   Attach the 20.5cm (8") cake centrally on top of the covered drum. Dowel the cake, spacing them evenly within a central 15cm (6") circle. Attach the 15cm (6") cake on top (see technique on page 41). Position the top tier off centre, about 6mm (¹/₄") in from the back edge of the cake and with its seam at the back.

top tip

Add a plain 12.5cm x 7.5cm (5" x 3") top tier to make a chic three tier wedding cake. As with the second tier, position the third tier at the back of the tier below and dowel the second tier with four dowels.

Attaching The Arrangement

1   Insert each wired element into posy picks, fixing them inside the picks with a little leftover sugarpaste or royal icing.

2   The flowers will be attached to the top of the 20.5cm (8") cake so they sit in front of and against the top tier. Before you start, decide where the large Iceland poppy will go. Mark the position and then put the flower aside.

3   Attach the branches to the top of the 20.5cm (8") cake so they spread left, right and upwards. Make sure the point at which the Iceland poppy will be inserted is not blocked.

4   Add a spray of daisies on each side and the berries roughly in the centre. Next, attach the small poppies and the ranunculus flowers.

5   Use some of the loose leaves to fill any gaps that need it, or to cover exposed points where flowers or branches enter the cake.

6   Finally, attach the Iceland poppy to the cake and any other spare leaves if required.

66 Always leave yourself plenty of time. I always think of Hofstadter's Law, which essentially states that it always takes longer than you think, even when you take into account that it takes longer than you think. 99

A WALK IN
the woods

This wild blackberry and rose cake is truly a showstopper and great for all occasions. You could even swap out the blackberries for something more seasonal, like raspberries, dewberries or mulberries.

YOU WILL NEED

Edibles

Round, filled sponge cakes covered with ganache/buttercream with a sharp edge finish, secured on cake boards of the same size (see page 29), 10cm (4") deep: 10cm (4") and 15cm (6") wide

Round, filled sponge cake covered with ganache/buttercream with a sharp edge finish, secured on a cake board of the same size (see page 29), 12.5cm (5") deep: 12.5cm (5") wide

SK Fairtrade Sugarpaste: 920g (2lb $^1/_2$oz) Bridal White and 1.1kg (2lb 6$^3/_4$oz) Opera Violet

SK Professional Instant Mix Royal Icing: 100g (3$^1/_2$oz) White

SK Professional Dust Food Colours: Leaf Green, Thrift and Vine

SK Designer Pollen Style Grains: Pale Golden

SK Essentials Edible Glue

SK Edible Wafer Paper: 2 sheets, white

Glycerine

SK Professional Paste Food Colours: Blackberry (Black), Leaf Green, Poinsettia (Xmas Red), Rose, Thrift and Vine

SK Sugar Florist Paste (SFP): 230g (8$^1/_4$oz) White

SK Paste Food Colour: Brown

SK Essentials Confectioners' Glaze

PME Edible Glaze Spray

Cornflour

Equipment

Round cake drums: 20.5cm (8") and 23cm (9")

Round cake boards: 10cm (4"), 12.5cm (5") and 15cm (6")

1.5cm ($^1/_2$") width satin ribbon: 1.81m (2yd) Opera Violet

Bevel-edged ruler

Floral wires: 24- and 26-gauge Nile green, and 18- and 30-gauge white

White cotton

Full-width floral tape: brown, white and Nile green

Template: page 227

SK High-Quality Paintbrushes: nos. 4 and 10

SK-GI Silicone Veiner Cosmos: Medium

Cream matt pointed head stamen: 8 small

Cocktail sticks

Polystyrene balls: 6 x 2.5cm (1"), 5 x 3cm (1$^1/_8$"), 5 x 3.5cm (1$^3/_8$"), 4 x 4.5cm (1$^3/_4$") and 3 x 5.5cm (2$^1/_4$")

SK Multi Flower Cutter Set 1, Round Petal/Leaf: nos. 2–6

Cake dummy or polystyrene block

Modelling tools: dresden, rounded cone, medium ball and small ball

White matt pointed head stamen: 25 small

Orchard Products Calyx Cutter: 1.9cm ($^3/_4$")

CelStick: 6mm ($^1/_4$")

FMM Rose Leaf Cutters: 2.6cm (1"), 3.4cm (1$^3/_8$") and 4.3cm (1$^3/_4$")

SK-GI Silicone Veiner Rose - Tea: Large Leaf

Posy picks: various sizes

SEE PAGES 11–15 FOR ESSENTIAL EDIBLES AND EQUIPMENT

Covering The Cake Drums

1 Roll out 250g (8³/₄oz) of Opera Violet sugarpaste and cover the 20.5cm (8") cake drum. Next, cover the 23cm (9") drum using 300g (10¹/₂oz) of Opera Violet sugarpaste (see technique on page 32). Set both drums aside to firm overnight.

2 Fix the Opera Violet ribbon around the edge of each drum (see technique on page 32).

3 To stack the drums, spread a little royal icing in the centre of the 23cm (9") drum. Place the 20.5cm (8") drum centrally on top, lining up the ribbon joins at the back. Set aside for later.

Covering The Cakes

1 You will be using the panelling method to cover the cakes. For the top tier, roll out 75g (2⁵/₈oz) of Bridal White sugarpaste and cut out a 12.5cm (5") disc. Place the disc on top of the 10cm (4") wide cake and trim away the excess (see technique on page 32). For the bottom tier, repeat to cover the top of the 15cm (6") wide cake with an 18cm (7") disc using 135g (4³/₄oz) of Opera Violet sugarpaste.

2 To cover the sides, start with the 10cm (4") wide cake. Roll out 310g (11oz) of Bridal White sugarpaste and cut out a 34cm x 11.5cm (13³/₈" x 4¹/₂") panel. Roll up the panel and wrap it around the cake (see technique on page 32).

3 Repeat step 2 to cover the side of the 15cm (6") wide cake. This time, roll out 430g (15oz) of Opera Violet sugarpaste and cut out a 50cm x 11.5cm (19³/₄" x 4¹/₂") rectangle. Set both cakes aside to dry overnight.

4 Repeat step 1 to cover the top of the 12.5cm (5") wide cake. For this middle tier, use 105g (3³/₄oz) of Bridal White sugarpaste and cut out a 15cm (6") disc.

5 Repeat step 2 to cover the side of the 12.5cm (5") wide cake. This time, roll out 425g (14³/₄oz) of Bridal White sugarpaste and cut a 42cm x 14cm (16¹/₂" x 5¹/₂") rectangle.

6 To texture the middle tier, use the tapered edge of a ruler to mark the lines on the side of the cake. Holding the ruler roughly in a vertical position, press firmly and evenly into the sugarpaste to mark on the line. Place a piece of plastic or card on top of the cake when marking the lines to avoid making finger marks on the top. The pressure needs to be quite firm because the sugarpaste will spring back a little over time.

7 Move along the sugarpaste a little bit and press again to mark on another line – don't worry about the lines being perfectly vertical, as the marks need to be a little loose. Keep working around the cake, leaving random gaps varying from 2mm (¹/₁₆") to 1cm (³/₈") in between each line (A). Set the cake aside to dry overnight.

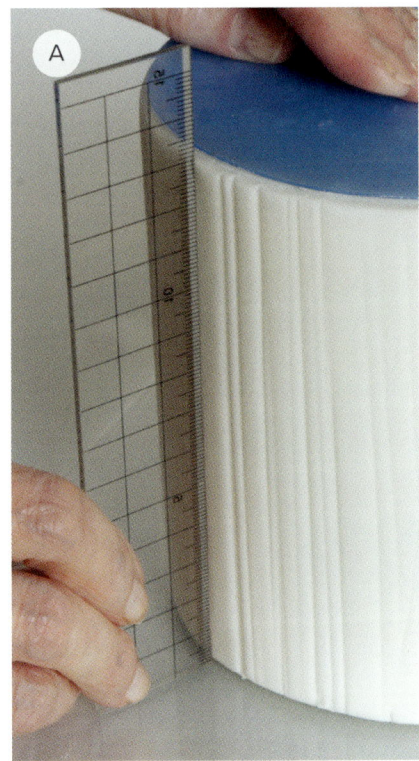

Assembling The Cake

1   Attach the 15cm (6") wide cake centrally on top of the covered double height drum. Dowel the cake, spacing them evenly within a central 12.5cm (5") circle, and attach the 12.5cm (5") wide cake centrally on top. Dowel the 12.5cm (5") wide tier, positioning them within a central 10cm (4") circle, then fix the 10cm (4") wide cake on top (see technique on page 41).

2   Fix the remaining Opera Violet ribbon around the base of the top tier and secure it at the back with a little stiff royal icing. The ribbon can be held in place with a sterilised stainless steel pin while the icing dries, but be sure to remove the pin when the icing has set.

Making The Cosmos Centres

1   Cut two lengths of 30-gauge white floral wire in half to give you four cut wires.

2   Hold your palm out and wind some white cotton around your fingers 50 times, then cut it from the reel. Remove the wound cotton loop from your fingers.

3   Slide one of the cut pieces of wire halfway through the loop of cotton, bend it in half and then twist the ends together to secure it around the cotton. Repeat this with the other piece of cut wire on the opposite side of the loop (B).

4   Twist the loop of cotton so that it forms a figure of eight with the wires at either end.

5   Fold the figure of eight in half to make one small loop (C). Cut through the top of the loop with a pair of scissors – this will give you two centres.

6   Bind the wires of each centre with some white floral tape. Start the

binding from about half way down the cotton and wrap around each wire until you reach the bottom (D).

7   Trim the tops off the ends of the cotton to make them all the same length. Do this for both centres.

8   Using a no. 10 paintbrush, dust both cotton centres with a little Thrift dust food colour.

9   Dip the no. 4 paintbrush into some edible glue and wipe off the excess. Paint some glue on the tips of the cotton. One at a time, take your centres and dip the glued cotton ends into some Pale Golden pollen style grains.

10   Repeat the steps 2–9 to make another two small centres, giving you four cosmos centres in total.

Making The Cosmos Petals

1   Transfer the cosmos petal template to a piece of card and cut it out.

2   Lay a piece of wafer paper flat on your work surface, making sure the rough side of the paper is facing upwards. Using a ruler, fold a strip about 3cm (1^1/$_8$") wide (E). Cut the sheet in line with the edge that has been folded over to give you a long folded piece of wafer paper, with the smooth side on the outside.

3   Trace copies of the cosmos petal onto the paper – you should get seven petals on one strip. Cut out the petals from the paper, being careful to cut just inside the lines and keep them in their pairs.

4   Repeat the method in steps 2–3 to make 36 pairs of petals in total.

5   Lightly brush the smooth side of one petal with a little cooled, boiled

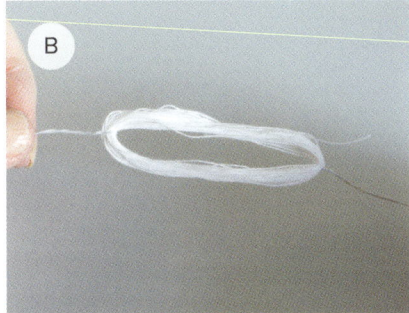

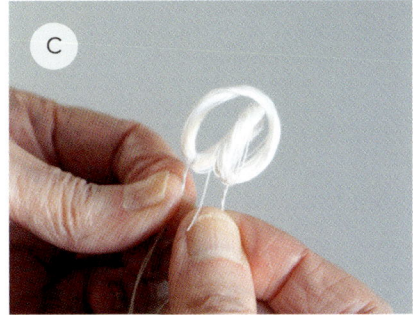

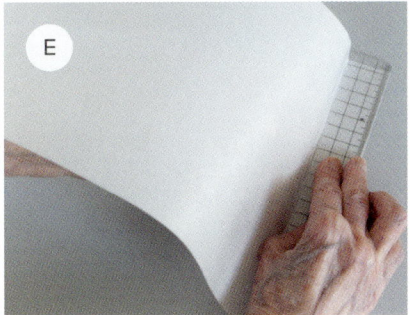

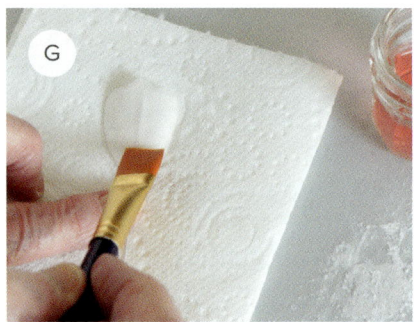

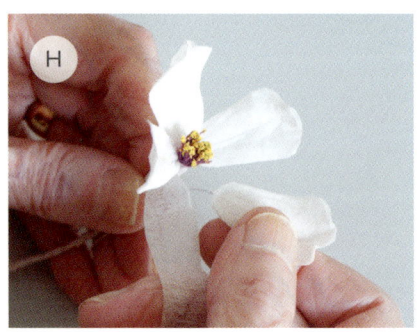

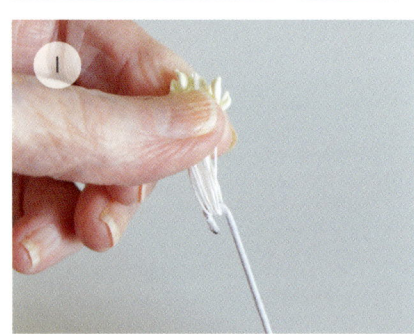

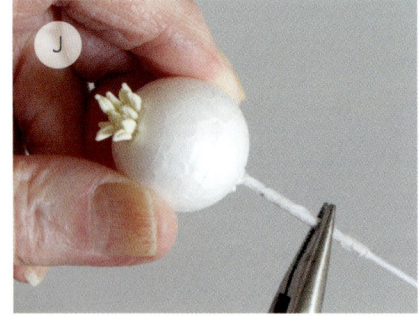

water. Position a 7cm (2³/₄") length of 30-gauge white floral wire along the centre of the petal so that it ends just below the top (F). Place the second petal of the pair rough side up directly on top of the first and press it down firmly to adhere. Leave the petal to dry. Repeat for the remaining 35 pairs of petals.

6 Once the petals are all dry, add a few drops of glycerine to some cooled, boiled water in a small jar and add a small drop of Rose paste food colour to make a weak pink solution. Brush the tinted water on a spare piece of wafer paper to test the colour – it should be a very pale pink. If it is too dark, dilute it; if it's too light, add a tiny bit more colour. Keep testing until the colour is correct.

7 Prepare a twice-folded piece of kitchen roll on which to wet the petals, as well as a small patch of cornflour to dry them.

8 Lay a wired petal on the kitchen roll and, using the no. 10 paintbrush, brush it with the pink water. Turn it over and brush the other side (G).

9 Press both sides of the petal into the cornflour and then run your fingers over it to take off the excess.

10 Press the petal in between the two parts of a medium Cosmos veiner. Remove it from the veiner and set it aside to dry.

11 Repeat steps 8–10 for the remaining petals and set them all aside to dry.

Assembling The Cosmos

1 Take nine petals and bend each wire down by 45°.

2 Position the first petal against one of the cosmos centres so that it is about 6mm (¼") below the top of the

stamens and bind it onto the wire with some white floral tape. Start directly below the petal and tape part of the way down. Don't tape all the way down, as you don't want the stem to become too thick.

3 Following the process in step 2, add three more petals at the same level as the first so they are even in height, making sure they are all evenly spaced around the centre (H). Vary the amount that you tape down the stem as you add the petals so that it tapers to the bottom and does not become too thick.

4 Attach a second layer of petals using some white floral tape. This time, attach five petals just below the first four petals. Make sure they are all evenly spaced.

5 To finish, cover the wire stem with some brown floral tape, starting from 1.25cm (½") below the petals and down to the bottom of the wire.

6 Repeat steps 1–5 to make three more assembled cosmos flowers.

Making The Rose Centre

1 Cut a piece of 18-gauge white floral wire into an 8.5cm (3³/₈") length. Bend a 5mm (¼") open hook in one end.

2 Bunch together eight small cream pointed head stamens and fold them all in half. Hook the hooked end of wire around the centre of the stamen bunch and use a pair of pliers to pinch it closed (I).

3 Bind the stamens together with some white floral tape, starting about 1cm (³/₈") below the tips and finishing around 2.5cm (1") down the wire.

4 Use a cocktail stick to make a hole all the way through the centre of

a 2.5cm (1") polystyrene ball. Once the hole is made, remove the stick.

5 Slide the wired stamen bunch down through the hole in the ball, pulling it through with pliers until just the tops of the stamens are protruding (J).

Making And Attaching The Rose Petals

1 Colour about 70g (2½oz) of White SFP a very pale pink shade using a tiny amount of Rose paste food colour. Make sure you keep the rest of the SFP wrapped up as you work to prevent it from drying out and going brittle.

Layer One

1 Roll a small piece of the pale pink SFP mixture out very thinly on a non-stick board and cut out a petal using a 3cm (1⅛") round petal cutter.

2 Move the petal to a foam pad and gently thin around the edges using a medium ball tool (K).

3 Use a pair of small scissors to cut a 1cm (⅜") slit from the pointed end of the petal towards the centre.

4 Insert a cocktail stick into a 2.5cm (1") polystyrene ball, making sure it doesn't come out through the other side.

5 Place the petal centrally on top of the polystyrene ball, with one cut part overlapping the other, and then lightly shape the petal over the ball with your fingers (L). Push the cocktail stick

into a piece of polystyrene or a cake dummy and leave to firm up.

6 Repeat steps 1–5 to make three more petals. Leave all four petals to firm for five minutes.

7 Brush one quarter of the rose centre with a little edible glue. Take one of the firm petals and attach it to the rose centre, making sure its overlapping part is at the bottom. Position it so that its top edge is roughly level with the top of the stamens (M).

8 Secure the remaining three petals in the same way as in step 7, so that each one overlaps the previous one. Finish the first layer by tucking the last petal under the first petal (N).

Layer Two

1 Repeat steps 1–5 from Layer One to make five more small petals. Leave them to firm up for five minutes.

2 Brush a V-shape of edible glue on the pointed lower half of a loose petal. Position the petal so its top is roughly level with the first set of petals attached to the centre. Ease the top of the petal slightly away from the first set of petals using the tip of a dresden tool. As with the first set of petals, make sure each petal overlaps the previous one. Repeat to attach the remaining loose petals to the centre (O).

Layer Three

1 Repeat steps 1–5 from Layer One to make five more petals, this time using a 3.7cm (1½") round petal cutter and shaping and drying them on 3cm (1⅛") polystyrene balls. Allow them to firm up for five minutes before assembling.

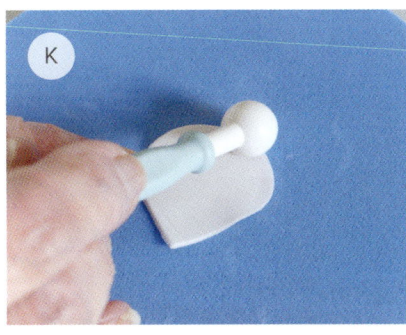

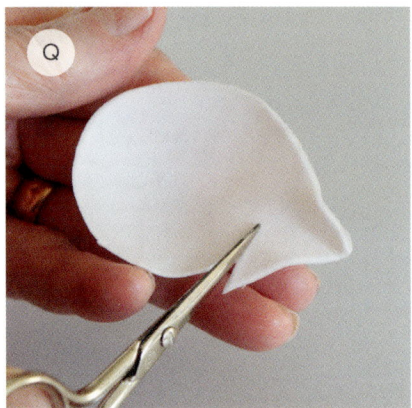

2   Brush a loose petal with a V-shape of edible glue on its pointed lower half. Position it just below the top of the second layer and with a bigger gap than there is between the first and second layers – pinch the bottom of the petal once applied to help this. Attach the remaining four petals in the same way, making sure that each overlaps the previous one.

Layer Four

1   Repeat steps 1–5 from Layer One to make five more petals, this time using a 4.7cm (1⁷⁄₈") round petal cutter and shaping them on 3.5cm (1³⁄₈") polystyrene balls. Allow them to firm up for 10 minutes this time.

2   Take a loose petal and brush a V-shape of glue on its pointed lower half. Position the petal so it's more flared out, about 1cm (³⁄₈") away from the third layer, and so the top is approximately 5mm (¹⁄₄") below the third layer (P). Repeat to attach the remaining four petals in the same way. By now, you should begin to see the appearance of an opening flower.

Layer Five

1   Repeat steps 1–2 from Layer One to make four petals using a 5.5cm (2¹⁄₄") round petal cutter. This time, do not cut a slit in the petals. Instead, place each petal on top of individual 4.5cm (1³⁄₄") polystyrene balls to shape and firm up. Let them rest for 10 minutes.

top tip

If you are having trouble with the petals staying in place, make a hook in the end of the wire and hang the rose upside down to set for half an hour.

top tip

You can add more or less petals on the outer few layers to give a fuller or looser look.

2   Once the petals have rested, take a pair of scissors and cut 1.25cm (¹⁄₂") off the pointed end of each one (Q).

3   Brush a little edible glue along the cut base of each loose petal and a little way up each side. Attach them one by one to the centre with their tops positioned approximately 1.25cm (¹⁄₂") away from and 1cm (³⁄₈") below the fourth layer (R).

Layer Six

1   Repeat step 1 from Layer Five to make three petals using a 6.3cm (2¹⁄₂") round petal cutter. Shape and firm up the petals on 5.5cm (2¹⁄₄") polystyrene balls for 15 minutes.

2   Once rested, take a pair of scissors and cut 1.25cm (¹⁄₂") off the pointed end of each petal.

3   Apply some edible glue to the cut bottom of each petal and a little bit up each side. Attach the petals one by one to the centre, positioning them so they are flared out to an almost horizontal angle. Set aside for later.

Making The Blackberry Blossom

1   Roll a 1.25cm (¹⁄₂") ball of White SFP into a 2.5cm (1") cone. With the pointed end facing upwards, flatten the wide end of the cone on your work surface.

2   Press a rounded cone tool into the flat end of the SFP cone to give you a cupped shape. Use a pair of scissors

to snip the cupped SFP into five equal sections.

3   Fold the five petals backwards and gently pinch the corners smooth with your fingers (S).

4   Place the blossom on its side on a foam pad and use a small ball tool to thin and cup each individual petal.

5   Bend a small closed hook in the end of a 7cm (2³/₄") length of Nile green 26-gauge floral wire.

6   Colour a pea-sized piece of White SFP a light green shade using some Leaf Green paste food colour. Take a small ball of the light green SFP mixture, about the size of a round headed pin, and push the hooked end of the wire into it. Work the lower half of the ball between your fingers to taper it to the wire.

7   Paint a little edible glue on the top of the SFP and dip it in some Pale Golden pollen grains.

8   Slide the wire down through the centre of the blossom until the top nestles in the centre (T).

9   Cut off the ends of some small matt white pointed head stamens to a length of 1.25cm (¹/₂"). Insert anything from four to six stamens around the flower centre. Do this by pushing them individually down and into the SFP (U).

10   Using a no. 4 paintbrush, dab a tiny bit of Brown paste food colour onto the heads of each stamen.

11   Repeat steps 1–10 to make five blackberry blossoms in total.

top tip

You can use these techniques to make general filler blossoms.

top tip

You can use this method to make raspberries too. Colour the paste a deep pinky red and elongate the shape slightly. Once finished, leave unglazed.

Making The Blackberries

1   Colour 50g (1³/₄oz) of White SFP a deep purple shade using a combination of Thrift, Blackberry (Black) and Poinsettia (Xmas Red) paste food colours. Start off with Thrift as the base, then add a little Blackberry (Black) paste to darken it, before finishing off with a little Poinsettia (Xmas Red) paste to richen the colour.

2   Colour a pea-sized piece of White SFP with some Blackberry (Black) paste, slightly less Thrift paste than in step 1 and a little bit of Poinsettia (Xmas Red) paste. You want to end up with a lighter purple colour.

3   Colour a 1.25cm (¹/₂") ball of White SFP a green shade using a little Leaf Green paste food colour.

4   Cut two pieces of 24-gauge Nile green floral wire into quarter lengths. You will end up with eight cut pieces, but you'll only be using seven of them. Bend a small open hook in one end of each cut wire.

5   Push the unhooked end of a cut wire through a 1.25cm (¹/₂") ball of the deep purple SFP mixture until the hooked end nestles in the top.

6   Pinch the SFP close to the wire underneath the ball. Use your fingers to pinch and close up the SFP over the hook at the top and slightly taper it (V).

7   Roll a 1.8cm (³/₄") ball of the dark purple SFP into a long rope, approximately 3mm (¹/₈") thick. Cut the

rope into 3mm (¹/₈") chunks and roll each one in the palm of your hand to make them into balls. Make around 60 balls in total (W).

8. Roll the lighter purple SFP into a 3mm (¹/₈") thick rope, cut it into 3mm (¹/₈") chunks and roll them each into small balls.

9. Brush the wired centre with a little edible glue. Start attaching the tiny dark purple balls to the berry, keeping them positioned snugly up against each other (X). Add one or two light purple balls to the centre randomly to give the blackberry a bit of character.

10. Very thinly roll out the light green SFP mixture and cut out a calyx with a 1.9cm (³/₄") calyx cutter.

11. Paint a little edible glue on the underside of the wired blackberry. Push the wire through the centre of the flat side of the calyx, slide it up to the blackberry and press it in place to adhere (Y). Use a dresden tool to tease the individual sepals back slightly.

12. Repeat steps 5–11 to make six more blackberries in total. Leave the blackberries to dry overnight, then dip them in Confectioners' Glaze and set them aside to dry again.

Making The Leaves

1. Cut some 26-gauge Nile green floral wire into 7cm (2³/₄") lengths. You will need 20 lengths of cut wire in total.

2. Colour 50g (1³/₄oz) of White SFP a green shade using a mixture of Leaf Green and Vine paste food colours.

top tip

This is one of several techniques for making leaves. See the other projects in the book for different methods!

3. Roll a 1.5cm (¹/₂") ball of the green SFP mixture into a cone shape, about 2.5cm (1") long and tapering at one end.

4. Insert a cut piece of wire about 1cm (³/₈") into the tapered end of the SFP, then pinch it all over so it's approximately 3mm (¹/₈") thick.

5. Lay the SFP on a non-stick board and use a small CelStick to thin it. Do this by rolling outwards left and right from the centre, leaving it thicker in the middle where the wire is. Finish by making sure the top is rolled out thinly too.

6. Cut out a large leaf using a 4.3cm (1³/₄") Rose Leaf cutter, making sure the cutter is positioned centrally over the wire (Z).

7. Transfer the leaf to the foam pad and thin its edges using a medium ball tool.

8. Press the leaf in between the two parts of the Tea Rose Leaf veiner and press down firmly to texture. Remove and shape the edges of the leaf with your fingers to give it some life. Set it aside to dry.

9. Repeat steps 3–8 to make five large leaves in total.

10. Repeat steps 3–8 to make 10 medium leaves, this time using a 3.4cm (1³/₈") Rose Leaf cutter.

11. Repeat steps 3–8 to make five small leaves using a 2.6cm (1") Rose Leaf cutter.

12. Once the leaves are dry, brush them all over with some Vine dust food colour. Next, colour just the centre of the leaves with a little Leaf Green dust.

13. Steam the dusted leaves to fix the colour and set them aside

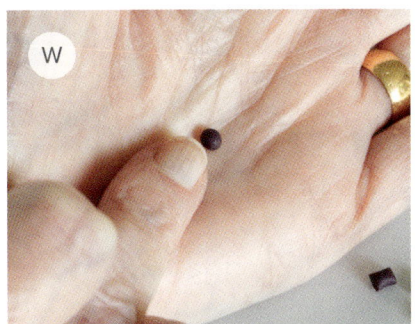

to dry. Once dry, spray the leaves with edible glaze and set aside to dry again.

Assembling The Leaves And Berries

1   To make a branch, take a 25.5cm (10") length of 24-gauge Nile green floral wire and start covering it with some brown floral tape. As you work your way down the wire, every now and again make a loop of tape around 2.5cm (1") long and twist it together in between your fingers to make a twig. Bind two or three leaves to the main branch as you go as well, using a mixture of leaf sizes. Do this for the top half of the wire only; cover the lower half of the wire without twigs or leaves (AA). Repeat to make two more branches the same way.

top tip

Give the branch some curves by gently bending the wire to give it some life.

2   Bind two cosmos, two blackberry blossoms, two blackberries and five randomly sized leaves to the bottom half of one of the branches with brown floral tape. This will be the posy for the top tier.

3   Bind a cosmos, a blackberry blossom, a blackberry and three randomly sized leaves together with brown tape to make a small individual spray with a stem around 7.5cm (3") long. This should not be attached to a branch. This will be to the right of the main posy on the bottom tier.

4   Bind three remaining leaves together in a small spray using some Nile green floral tape. Start by taping down the length of one leaf wire. About 1.5cm ($^1/_2$") down the wire, attach a second leaf and continue taping down. After another 1.5cm ($^1/_2$") down the wire, attach a third leaf on the opposite side of the previous one. Continue taping down until you get to the bottom of the wire (AB). Any remaining leaves can be used to fill in gaps as you see fit.

5   Bind the leaf spray, the remaining blackberry blossoms, blackberries, branches and cosmos together with some brown floral tape to make the main posy for the bottom tier (AC).

Attaching The Posies And Rose

1   Cut three 10cm (4") lengths of 18-gauge white floral wire and cover each piece with brown tape.

2   Bend each wire into long 1cm ($^3/_8$") wide U-shaped pins.

3   Take the posy for the top tier and, with the stem pointing to the left, arrange it on the cake so that the branch points upwards, two leaves point left, the cosmos point forward, and the blackberry blossoms, blackberries and remaining leaves point to the right. Do not attach it to the cake at this stage.

4   Once you're happy with the position, use a wire pin to attach the posy by its stem into a posy pick in the top of the second tier. The flowers should be positioned about halfway between the front and left of the top tier.

5   Insert the small posy into a posy pick and pin it at the top of the bottom tier, with its stem pointing to the left and the cosmos just forward of the right-hand side of the middle tier.

6   Hold the large posy against the top of the bottom tier with the stem pointing to the right. Arrange the cosmos, blackberry blossoms, blackberries and leaves so there is a gap left between it and the first posy for the rose to go into. Insert it into a posy pick and pin it at the top of the bottom tier.

7   Bend the rose slightly forward on its wire and insert it into a posy pick. Secure it at the bottom tier between the two posies and arrange the cosmos petals around it.

top tip

Remember to remove any inedible items, like wires and posy picks, from the cake before serving.

66 Look out for inspiration everywhere. Anything small or large can be the spark of a design: a button, a vase, a painting, a building; light, shape, colour and texture. 99

FABULOUS
fondant frills

Ruffles are a classic cake decoration that always come back around. While they are simple to make, they offer a bold statement. This tiered cake in particular is impressive but rather straightforward, with a combination of ruffles and stripes, topped off with a crisp sugar arrangement.

YOU WILL NEED

Edibles

Round, filled sponge cake covered with ganache/buttercream with a sharp edge finish, secured on a cake board of the same size (see page 29), 12.5cm (5") deep: 10cm (4") wide

Round, filled sponge cake covered with ganache/buttercream with a sharp edge finish, secured on a cake board of the same size (see page 29), 15cm (6") deep: 12.5cm (5") wide

Round, filled sponge cake covered with ganache/buttercream with a sharp edge finish, secured on a cake board of the same size (see page 29), 7.5cm (3") deep: 15cm (6") wide

SK Fairtrade Sugarpaste: 2.22kg (4lb 14³/₈oz) Bridal White

SK Sugar Florist Paste (SFP): 400g (14oz) White

SK Professional Dust Food Colours: Bulrush (Dark Brown), Sunflower and Vine

SK Professional Paste Food Colour: Olive

SK Essentials Edible Glue

SK Professional Instant Mix Royal Icing: 100g (3¹/₂oz) White

SEE PAGES 11–15 FOR ESSENTIAL EDIBLES AND EQUIPMENT

Equipment

Round cake boards: 10cm (4"), 12.5cm (5") and 15cm (6")

Round cake drums: 20.5cm (8") and 23cm (9")

1.5cm (¹/₂") satin ribbon: 1.45m (1yd 21") Bridal White

3mm (¹/₈") width satin ribbon: 2.5m (2yd 26") green

Template: page 228

JEM Strip Cutter: no. 2

Water brush pen

Safety razor blade

Round cutter: 6cm (2³/₈")

Modelling tools: dresden, small mall, medium ball and veining

SK High-Quality Paintbrush: no. 4

Non-toxic glue stick

Polystyrene balls: 4 x 3cm (1¹/₈")

Floral wires: 24- and 30-gauge Nile green, and 18-, 22- and 30-gauge white

JEM Easy Rose Cutter: 10cm (4")

SK Multi Flower Cutter Set 1, Round Petal/Leaf: nos. 3–5

Cupped formers

Tweezers

Floral tape: full-width and half-width Nile green

Blossom Sugar Art Mould & Cutter Single Set: Small Hydrangea

CK Products Flower Formers: 2cm (³/₄")

Cream round head stamens: 36 small

PME Modelling Tool: Taper Cones 5/6 Star

FMM Rose Leaf Cutters, Set of 3: 2.6cm (1"), 3.4cm (1³/₈") and 4.3cm (1³/₄")

SK-GI Silicone Veiner Rose - Tea: Large Leaf

Posy picks: various sizes

Covering The Cake Drums

1   Roll out 250g (8³/₄oz) of Bridal White sugarpaste and cover the 20.5cm (8") cake drum. Next, cover the 23cm (9") drum using 300g (10¹/₂oz) of Bridal White paste (see technique on page 32). Set both drums aside to firm overnight.

2   Fix some Bridal White ribbon around the edge of each drum (see technique on page 32).

3   To stack the drums, spread a little royal icing in the centre of the 23cm (9") drum. Place the 20.5cm (8") drum centrally on top, lining up the ribbon joins at the back. Set aside for later.

Covering The Cakes

1   You will be using the panelling method to cover the cakes. For the top tier, roll out 75g (2⁵/₈oz) of Bridal White sugarpaste and cut out a 12.5cm (5") disc. Place the disc centrally on top of the 10cm (4") wide cake and trim away the excess (see technique on page 32).

2   For the middle tier, repeat step 1 to cover the top of the 12.5cm (5") wide cake using 105g (3³/₄oz) of Bridal White sugarpaste and cutting out a 15cm (6") disc. Repeat step 1 again to cover the top of the 15cm (6") wide cake, this time using 135g (4³/₄oz) of Bridal White paste and cutting out a 15cm (6") disc.

3   To cover the sides, start with the 10cm (4") wide cake. Roll out 355g (12¹/₂oz) of Bridal White sugarpaste and cut out a 34cm x 14cm (13³/₈" x 5¹/₂") panel. Roll up the panel and wrap it around the side of the cake (see technique on page 32).

4   Repeat step 3 to cover the side of the 12.5cm (5") wide cake. This time, roll out 480g (1lb 1oz) of Bridal White sugarpaste and cut out a 42cm x 16.5cm (16¹/₂" x 6¹/₂") panel.

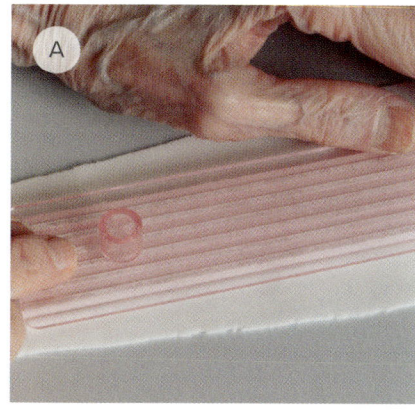

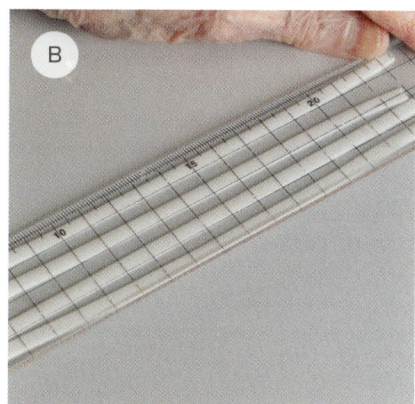

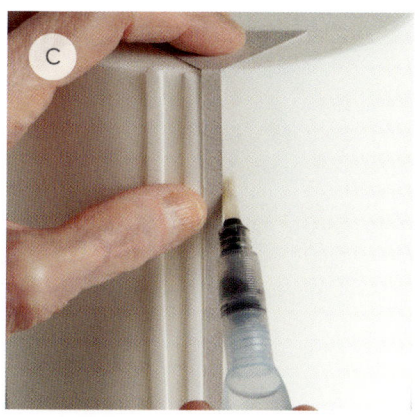

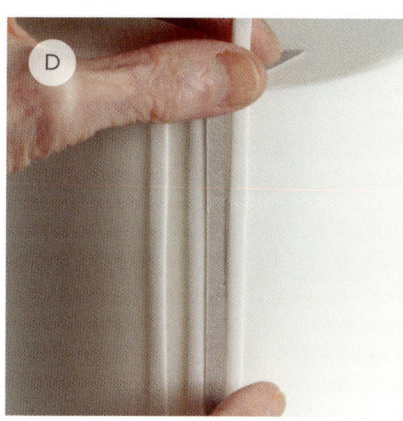

5 Repeat step 3 again to cover the side of the 15cm (6") wide cake. This time, roll out 370g (13oz) of Bridal White sugarpaste and cut out a 50cm x 9cm (19³/₄" x 3¹/₂") panel. Once all three cakes are covered, leave them to dry overnight.

Adding The Stripes

1 Trace the spacer template onto a piece of food-grade card and cut it out. Bend the template at the dotted line.

top tip

Because you are working with white on white, it can help to make the spacer out of non-white card.

2 Knead together 30g (1oz) of Bridal White sugarpaste and 30g (1oz) of White SFP.

3 Roll out 15g (¹/₂oz) of the white paste to a thickness of about 1mm (<¹/₁₆") and big enough for the strip cutter. Cut out a set of strips (A) before returning the offcuts to the white paste and wrapping it up to prevent it from drying out.

4 The strips can be slightly concave on their underside, so press them flat with a ruler so they will attach to the cake more easily (B).

5 Trim one end of each strip so that it is squared off.

6 Repeat steps 3–5 using the remaining white paste to cut at least 42 strips in total.

7 Rest the spacer template on the back of the 12.5cm (5") wide cake. Using a little cooled, boiled water and a water brush pen, wet a 5mm (¹/₄") area next to the spacer.

8 Carefully press a strip into place using the spacer guide to keep it straight. Make sure you have the squared off end at the bottom.

9 Use a safety razor blade to neatly trim the strip level with the top of the cake.

10 Move the spacer to the other side of the strip just applied, ensuring it is positioned flush up against it.

11 Use the water brush pen to wet a 5mm (¹/₄") area next to the spacer. Attach another strip to the cake and trim the top.

12 Repeat steps 10–11 working around the cake until you get about 3cm (1¹/₈") away from the first strip (C, D). The stripes and gaps are unlikely to fit an exact number of times around the cake, so space the last couple of strips by eye, only using the spacer to help keep them straight.

13 Repeat steps 2–12 for the 10cm (4") wide tier, this time using 20g (³/₄oz) of Bridal White sugarpaste mixed with 20g (³/₄oz) of White SFP and cutting at least 34 strips. Trim 2.5cm (1") off the end of the spacer template so that it fits the height of the cake.

Adding The Ruffles

1 Knead together 100g (3¹/₂oz) of Bridal White sugarpaste and 100g (3¹/₂oz) of White SFP. This 50:50 mixture will give you a paste soft enough to work with but firm enough to hold a shape.

2 Roll out a large marble-sized piece of the white paste to a thickness of just over 1mm (<¹/₁₆").

3 Cut out a circle using a 6cm (2³/₈") round cutter (E, see page 183). Keep and wrap up the offcuts for later use.

top tip

Very pale soft green ruffles would also work well on this cake.

4   Cut the circle in half with a sharp knife. One half at a time, use a veining tool to thin and frill along the curved edge of each semicircle to create a ruffle (F).

5   Set the two semicircles aside to firm up a bit. Ensure the semicircles are nicely ruffled up, not spread out too much and that the base of each is left straight.

6   Repeat steps 2–5 to make 20 ruffles in total, enough for about two layers.

7   Brush the lower half of the back of a ruffle with a little edible glue and the no. 4 paintbrush. Attach the ruffle to the 15cm (6") wide tier, positioned so its curved top is sat approximately 1cm (³/₈") above the top of the cake.

8   Attach another ruffle next to the first one, overlapping it by about 1cm (³/₈") (G). Carry on adding ruffles around the cake in the same way until you get back to the beginning.

top tip

If you find that your ruffles are falling backwards, you can turn your cake upside down while you attach them. Alternatively, you could change the paste ratio to one part sugarpaste to three parts SFP to make them firmer.

9   Add a second layer of ruffles approximately 1cm (³/₈") below the first layer and offset by half a ruffle's width.

10   Repeat steps 2–5 to make another 20 ruffles, then repeat steps 7–9 to attach another two layers of ruffles to the cake. Keep making and adding ruffles until you reach the bottom of the cake. On the final row of ruffles, trim the base of each ruffle as required to maintain the spacing.

Making The Roses

1   Cut four 10cm (4") lengths of 18-gauge white floral wire.

2   Working one at a time, apply some non-toxic glue to one end of the wires. Insert the glued end of each wire into a 3cm (1¹/₈") polystyrene ball to make four centres. Leave to dry.

3   Roll out 15g (¹/₂oz) of White SFP to a thickness of about 1mm (<¹/₁₆").

4   Cut out a set of petals using a 10cm (4") Easy Rose cutter (H). Wrap up the offcuts for later.

5   Place the blossom on a foam pad and thin the edges of each individual petal with a medium ball tool (I).

6   Brush the centre of the blossom with a little edible glue. Slide the wire of one rose centre down through the middle of the blossom until the paste is flush with the polystyrene ball (J). Press the glued section of the petals onto the base of the ball.

7   Brush the outer edges of one of the petals with a little glue. Fold the petal up around the flower centre and, on the top of the ball, bring the edges together to leave a peak (K).

8   Brush the outer edges of a petal on the opposite side of the first petal. Fold the petal so that it goes either side of the peak you just made and leave it standing slightly away from the peak (L).

9   Brush the outer edges of the three remaining petals. Fold them up so that they wrap around the two petals already glued and so each of the three petals overlap the next (M). Leave these about 3mm (¹/₈") away from the first two petals.

10   Roll out a 1.8cm (³/₄") ball of White SFP to a thickness of about 1mm (<¹/₁₆").

11   Cut out a rose petal using a 4.2cm (1⁵/₈") round petal cutter (N). Wrap up the offcuts for later use.

12   Place the petal on the foam pad and use the medium ball tool to thin the edges (O).

13   Remove the petal from the pad and transfer to a non-stick board. Use the veining tool to thin and texture the curved edge of the petal, making sure to keep the tool pointed towards the pointed end of the petal (P).

top tip

For added character, lightly dust the very edges of the petals with a little pale green dust.

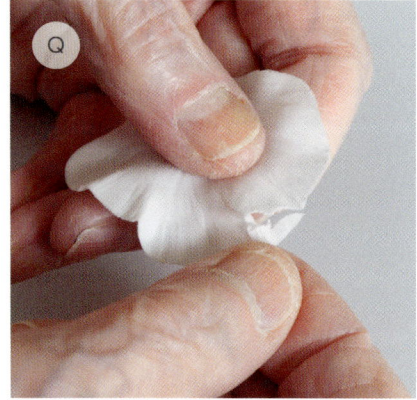

14 Very carefully tear little bits from the edge of the petal to give it a slightly ragged edge (Q).

15 Repeat steps 10–14 to make two more petals of the same size. Leave the three petals to firm up in cupped formers to give them a curve. Leave them for five minutes so they firm up a bit but are still malleable.

16 Repeat steps 10–14 to make three larger rose petals using a 5.1cm (2") round petal cutter. Leave these larger petals to firm up in cupped formers for five minutes, this time with the top edge curled over the side.

17 Lightly brush the lower half of one of the smaller petals with edible glue. Attach the petal to a flower centre so that it extends about 5mm (¹⁄₄") above the existing petals and stands roughly 1.2cm (¹⁄₂") away from them (R).

18 Repeat step 17 to attach the remaining two small petals, spacing them evenly and making sure each one overlaps the next.

19 Curl the top part of the three small petals backwards with your fingers. You can vary how much but they look best when they are not uniform (S).

20 Lightly brush the lower quarter of a large petal. Attach the petal to the underside of the flower so that it flares outwards and sits a little over halfway up the flower (T).

21 Repeat step 20 to attach the remaining two large petals, making sure that each one overlaps the next.

22 Repeat steps 3–21 to make three more roses using the remaining wired centres.

Making The Rose Leaves

1. Colour 25g (⁷⁄₈oz) of White SFP a fresh green shade using a little Olive paste food colour.

2. Roll out a small piece of the green SFP over a groove on the non-stick board to a thickness of about 1mm (<¹⁄₁₆").

3. Remove the paste from the board, lay it ridge side up and cut out a leaf using a 4.3cm (1³⁄₄") Rose Leaf cutter, making sure that the cutter is centred over the ridge.

4. Cut a 7.5cm (3") length of 30-gauge Nile green floral wire.

5. Dip one end of the wire in edible glue and wipe off the excess. Insert the wire 1cm (³⁄₈") into the ridge at the base of the leaf.

6. Place the leaf on the foam pad and use the medium ball tool to thin the edges.

7. Press the leaf firmly between the two halves of a Tea Rose Leaf veiner. Remove from the veiner and use your fingers to shape the leaf to give it some movement. Set aside to dry.

8. Repeat steps 2–7 to make at least 12 rose leaves using a combination of 2.6cm (1"), 3.4cm (1³⁄₈") and 4.3cm (1³⁄₄") Rose Leaf cutters.

9. Once the leaves are dry, dust their faces with some Vine dust. Also dust the bottom centre and just on the edges with a little Bulrush (Dark Brown) dust.

top tip

If you don't have the right size cutter, use the next smallest cutter, roll the paste a bit thicker and stretch it out.

Making The Rose Leaf Branches

1. Take a 20.5cm (8") length of 24-gauge Nile green wire and, using half-width Nile green tape, bind down roughly the first 4cm (1¹⁄₂") of the wire.

2. Bind on a small rose leaf with its base butted up against the wire.

3. Continue taping down the wire, adding another two or three leaves as you go, about 2.5cm (1") apart and increasing in size. Finish by binding down to the end of the wire.

4. Repeat steps 1–3 to make a second rose leaf branch. Add some bends to the branches to give them movement. Leave the remaining leaves loose to use as fillers.

Making The Lisianthus Centres

1. Mix a little Sunflower dust into a 1.3cm (¹⁄₂") ball of White SFP to achieve a yellow shade. Divide the paste into six equal balls and wrap them up individually until you are ready to use them.

2. Cut six pieces of 22-gauge white floral wire into 9cm (3¹⁄₂") lengths.

3. Bend 1.5cm (¹⁄₂") at one end of each wire by 90˚. Next, bend 1cm (³⁄₈") of each wire back the way it came by 180˚ to leave a T-shape at the end (U). Use pliers to pinch the folded end flat.

4. Take one ball of the yellow SFP and shape it into a sausage, very slightly longer than the width of the T-shape at the end of a wire.

5. Brush a little edible glue on the wired T-shape, press into the yellow sausage and then pinch the paste around it to adhere (V).

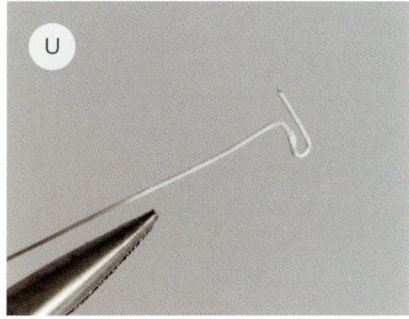

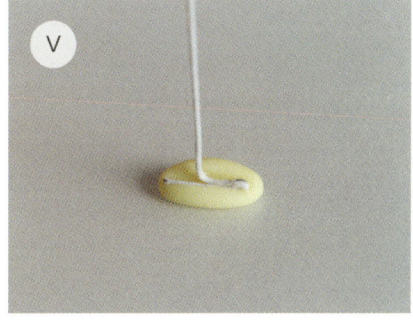

6 Pinch the middle of the paste with a pair of tweezers to create a sort of bone shape (W). Dust over the yellow paste with a little Sunflower dust.

7 Bend three small cream round headed stamens in half to give you six stamens. Dust each stamen head with a little Sunflower dust.

8 Bind about 1cm ($^3/_8$") down the main wire below the yellow paste with half-width Nile green floral tape, and then bind on the six stamens (three pairs) (X). Make sure the stamens are evenly spaced, with the heads positioned a little higher than the yellow centre. Continue taping right down to the end of the wire.

9 Repeat steps 4–8 to make six centres in total using the remaining cut wires.

Making The Lisianthus Flowers

1 Roll a 1.5cm ($^1/_2$") ball of White SFP out to a thickness of approximately 1mm ($<^1/_{16}$").

2 Cut out a petal using a 3.3cm (1$^1/_4$") round petal cutter. Transfer the petal to the foam pad and thin the edges with the medium ball tool.

3 Repeat steps 1–2 to make four more petals.

4 With the pointed end facing towards you, lightly brush the lower right half of one petal with some edible glue.

5 Place a new petal on top of the glued area so that the points of the two petals line up. Ensure the new petal only covers the right half of the first petal (Y).

6 Brush the lower right half of the petal just added with a little glue and repeat step 5 to add another petal.

7 Repeat step 6 to add the remaining two petals, leaving you with a fan of five petals (Z).

8 Dust the very centre of the petal fan with some Vine dust food colour (AA).

9 Apply edible glue to the bottom 1cm ($^3/_8$") of the petal fan, as well as to the lower right half of the last petal added.

10 Lay a flower centre in the middle of the first petal so that it comes about halfway up the petal (AB).

11 Roll up the petals around the centre from left to right, finishing by attaching the glued portion of the last petal to the outside of the first petal (AC).

12 Flare out the unglued parts of the petals and curl back the tops slightly using your fingers.

13 Bind from the base of the flower right down to the end of the wire with half-width Nile green tape.

14 Repeat steps 1–13 to make six flowers in total using the remaining centres. For variety, after step 2 you can use a veining stick to texture and lightly frill some of the flowers. You could also make some flowers more closed than others.

top tip

You can make a lisianthus bud by attaching a thin 2.5cm (1") White SFP cone to a wire, wrapping two overlapping petals closed around it and colouring the lower half with some Vine dust.

Making The Jasmines

1 Take a 1cm ($^3/_8$") ball of White SFP and shape it into a teardrop.

2 Push the five-divider end of a Taper Cones 5/6 Star tool firmly into the middle of the wide end of the teardrop (AD).

3 Snip the paste with scissors in line with the marked divisions to make an opened blossom. Pinch the five petal sections flat and each end into a point (AE).

4 Transfer the flower to the foam pad and rest it on its side. Use a small ball tool to thin and pull out each individual petal (AF). Lift the flower and pinch the ends of each petal again to give them a more defined point (AG).

5 Cut a 7.5cm (3") length of 30-gauge Nile green floral wire and bend a small open hook in one end.

6 Slide the wire down through the middle of the flower until the hook nestles in the centre of the paste (AH). Make sure to keep it straight so the wire comes out through the tapered end of the paste.

7 Repeat steps 1–6 to make at least 18 flowers in total. Be sure to slightly vary the size of the ball that you start with, that way you'll end up with a variety of sizes which will look more natural.

8 Gather the flowers together in four bunches of three or four and arrange them at varying heights. Bind the bottom 2.5cm (1") of the stems together with half-width Nile green tape. Leave the remaining flowers loose to use as fillers.

Making The Hydrangeas

1   Roll out a small marble-sized piece of White SFP very thinly and cut a flower using a 2.5cm (1") Small Hydrangea cutter.

2   Press the flower firmly between the two halves of a Small Hydrangea veiner to texture (AI).

3   Leave the flower to firm up a bit in small 2cm (³/₄") cupped formers or in the pits of a dimple foam drying tray (AJ).

4   Repeat steps 1–3 to make at least 18 hydrangeas. Try to vary the shapes in which you leave the flowers.

5   Cut a 7.5cm (3") length of 30-gauge white floral wire and make a small closed hook in one end.

6   Slide the wire down through the middle of a flower until it nestles in the centre of the paste (AK).

7   Take a 4mm (³/₁₆") ball of White SFP and shape it into a cone.

8   Brush the flat end of the cone with a little edible glue. Slide the wire down through the flat end and attach the cone to the underside of the flower (AL).

9   Repeat steps 5–8 to wire each flower.

10   Gather the flowers together in four bunches of three or four and arrange them at varying heights. Bind the bottom 2.5cm (1") of the stems together. Leave the remaining flowers loose to use as fillers.

Making The Bare Branches

1   Bind down the entire length of a 20.5cm (8") piece of 24-gauge Nile green wire with half-width Nile green floral tape.

2   Cut a 5cm (2") length of half-width Nile green tape. Fold the tape in half around the wire about 5cm (2") down from the end. Press the two halves together and twist them to make a branch.

3   Repeat step 2 to carry on adding branches every 1cm – 3cm (³/₈" – 1¹/₈") down the top half of the wire. Vary the lengths of the finished branches, from about 1cm – 3cm (³/₈" – 1¹/₈").

4   Use shorter pieces of tape to add small branches to some of the existing branches.

5   Repeat steps 1–4 to make at least 10 branches in total.

Assembling The Cake

1   Attach the 15cm (6") wide cake centrally on the double height drum, making sure the centre back part of the cake is in line with the ribbon join on the drum. Dowel the cake, spacing them evenly within a 12.5cm (5") circle, and secure the 12.5cm (5") wide cake centrally on top with its seam at the back (see technique on page 41).

2   Dowel the 12.5cm (5") wide cake, positioning them within a central 10cm (4") circle, and then fix the 10cm (4") wide cake on top.

top tip

The number of items instructed to make here is enough to complete the cake, but it is never a bad idea to make more pieces than you think that you need. Doing this will give you options when putting things together and act as a safety net if there are any breakages.

3   Wrap some 3mm (¹/₈") green ribbon around the bottom of each tier and tie it with a bow at the back, taking care to make sure the ribbon is not twisted at any point.

Attaching The Arrangement

1   Make several hooped pins by covering 6cm (2³/₈") lengths of 18-gauge white floral wire with some half-width Nile green tape and bending them into U-shapes.

2   Use posy picks to attach every wired element to the cake. The elements can either be inserted into posy picks or pinned into posy picks depending on what is most suitable.

3   Start by attaching some of the branches to the top tier, positioning them so they extend to the sides and front.

4   Secure some of the hydrangeas and jasmines on top of the top tier, leaving space for the lisianthus flowers and roses.

5   Add the first rose and lisianthus to the top tier, followed by some more branches surrounding the flowers.

6   Continue adding the remaining floral components and building up the shape. Use spare leaves, hydrangeas and jasmines to fill spaces or give balance where needed.

top tip

When attaching the flowers and leaves etc. to your cakes, always try to hide the workings by careful positioning and with filler flowers and leaves.

HELLO
autumn

Get in the mood for autumn with this gorgeous cake. Featuring seasonal conkers, fir cones and rose hips paired with a beautiful yellow bloom, this cake will be sure to rack up praise.

YOU WILL NEED

Edibles

Round, filled sponge cakes covered with ganache/buttercream with a sharp edge finish, secured on cake boards of the same size (see page 29), 15cm (6") deep: 10cm (4") and 12.5cm (5") wide

SK Fairtrade Sugarpaste: 750g (1lb 10^1/$_2$oz) Bridal White and 750g (1lb 10^1/$_2$oz) Coco Brown

SK Sugar Florist Paste (SFP): 145g (5oz) White

SK Designer Paste Food Colour: Olive

SK Neonz Paste Food Colours: Orange, Red and Yellow

SK Essentials Edible Glue

SK Dust Food Colour: Orange

SK Paste Food Colours: Cream and Brown

PME Edible Glaze Spray

SK Professional Dust Food Colours: Chestnut (Soft Beige), Leaf Green, Poppy and Vine

SK Professional Instant Mix Royal Icing: 100g (3^1/$_2$oz) White

Equipment

Round cake drum: 20.5cm (8")

1.5cm (^{1}/$_2$") width satin ribbon: 68cm (26^3/$_4$") Coco Brown

Round cake boards: 10cm (4") and 12.5cm (5")

FMM Multi Ribbon Cutter

Safety razor blade

Template: page 227

Food-grade card

Water brush pen

Floral wires: 24- and 26-gauge dark green, 24- and 26-gauge Nile green, and 18-, 22-, 24-, 26- and 28-gauge white

Tweezers

Cream matt pointed head stamen: 16–20 small

Floral tape: full-width brown, dark green and Nile green, and quarter-width brown and Nile green

SK Multi Flower Cutter Set 1A, Round Petal/Leaf: nos. 3–4

Modelling tools: dresden and medium ball

Dimple foam drying tray

SK High-Quality Paintbrush: no. 4

Polystyrene balls: 3 x 2cm (^{3}/$_4$")

Circle cutters: 2cm (^{3}/$_4$") and 3cm (1^1/$_8$")

Orchard Products Six-Petal Cutters: 1.4cm (^{1}/$_2$") and 1.9cm (^{3}/$_4$")

Fine Cut Horse Chestnut Leaf Cutters: 4.9cm (2"), 5.9cm (2^3/$_8$") and 6.5cm (2^1/$_2$")

SK-GI Silicone Veiner Chestnut (Castanea): Medium Leaf

FMM Maple Leaf Cutters: 3cm (1^1/$_8$") and 5.5cm (2^1/$_4$")

SK-GI Silicone Veiner Maple – Silver: Small Leaf

FMM Rose Leaf Cutters, Set of 3: 2.6cm (1"), 3.4cm (1^3/$_8$") and 4.3cm (1^3/$_4$")

SK-GI Silicone Veiner Rose - Tea: Large Leaf

Posy picks: various sizes

SEE PAGES 11–15 FOR ESSENTIAL EDIBLES AND EQUIPMENT

Covering The Cake Drum

1   Knead 750g (1lb 10¹/₂oz) of Coco Brown sugarpaste into 750g (1lb 10¹/₂oz) of Bridal White sugarpaste to make a light brown shade. You'll use this brown paste throughout the project, so make sure you keep all your offcuts and wrap it up to prevent the paste from drying out.

2   Roll out 250g (8³/₄oz) of the brown sugarpaste and cover the 20.5cm (8") cake drum (see technique on page 32). Set the drum aside to firm overnight.

3   Fix the Coco Brown ribbon around the edge of the cake drum (see technique on page 32).

Covering The Cakes

1   You will be using the panelling method to cover the cakes. For the top tier, roll out 75g (2⁵/₈oz) of the brown sugarpaste you made earlier and cut out a 12.5cm (5") disc. Place the disc on top of the 10cm (4") cake and trim away the excess (see technique on page 32). For the bottom tier, repeat to cover the top of the 12.5cm (5") cake with a 15cm (6") disc using 105g (3³/₄oz) of the brown sugarpaste.

2   To cover the sides, start with the 10cm (4") cake. Roll out 400g (14oz) of the brown sugarpaste and cut out a 34cm x 16.5cm (13³/₈" x 6¹/₂") panel. Roll up the panel and wrap it around the cake (see technique on page 32).

3   Repeat step 2 to cover the side of the 12.5cm (5") cake. This time, roll out 480g (1lb 1oz) of brown sugarpaste and cut a 42cm x 16.5cm (16¹/₂" x 6¹/₂") panel. Set both cakes aside to dry overnight.

Adding The Lines

1. When making and attaching the strips, start with the 12.5cm (5") wide cake. Roll out 135g (4³/₄oz) of the brown sugarpaste into a wide strip, at least 18cm (7") deep and about 2mm (¹/₁₆") thick. Use a ribbon cutter to cut out at least 21 strips, which are all 1.1cm (⁷/₁₆") wide. Wrap up the unused paste for later.

top tip

Cut some strips from thick card, such as mount board, to use as spacers when rolling out the strips.

2. Trim one end of each strip square using a sharp knife or a razor blade. Set the strips aside, making sure that they are straight and allow them to firm up for at least an hour. This will make them easier to handle.

top tip

If you are finding the sugarpaste too soft when cutting out the strips, you can add a little CMC to firm it up.

3. Trace the spacing template onto a piece of food-grade card and cut it out. Fold the template at the dotted line, taking care that the short section lines up perfectly with the long section to ensure the fold is perpendicular.

4. Rest the short section of the spacer on top of the 12.5cm (5") cake at the back, so the long section sits flush down the side of the cake just to one side of the join.

5. Using a water brush pen, paint some cooled, boiled water in a 1cm (³/₈") strip next to the guide.

6. Take a strip of brown sugarpaste and, with the squared end at the bottom, press it into place next to the guide, ensuring it sits flush with the base of the cake. Trim the top of the strip level with the top of the cake.

7. Move the guide and place it flush up against the strip you just applied. Repeat steps 5–6 to add a second strip.

8. Repeat step 7 to continue adding strips all the way around the side of the cake (A, B).

top tip

The strips and spaces combination may not fit exactly around your cake. When you get to the last two or three strips, space them by eye to make any shortfall or excess space less obvious. This is a good reason for starting and finishing at the back.

9. Now make the strips for the top 10cm (4") wide cake tier. To do this, repeat step 1 using 55g (2oz) of the brown sugarpaste and cutting out 18 strips that are 1.1cm (⁷/₁₆") wide.

10. These brown strips now need to be cut in two, in varying proportions to make enough strips to go around the top tier. Use a razor blade to divide the strips randomly, between a third and half of their length. This will leave a selection of strips between one third and two thirds of their original length. Ensure that all the ends are trimmed square. Set the strips aside, making sure they are straight, and then leave them to firm up for at least an hour.

11. Rest the spacing template on top of the 10cm (4") cake at the back.

12. Choose a strip and note where it comes up to on the cake. Use a

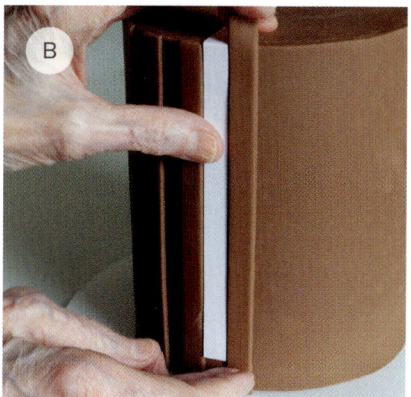

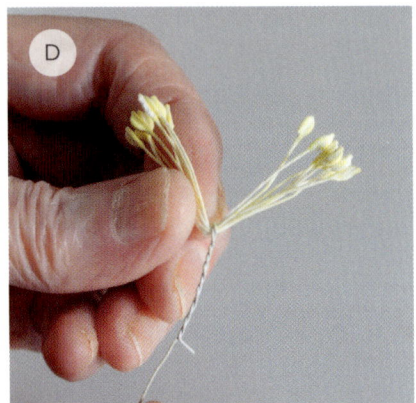

water brush pen to brush some cooled, boiled water in a 1cm (³/₈") strip next to the guide and up to the height of the chosen strip.

13 Take the chosen strip and press it into place next to the guide, positioning it flush with the base of the cake.

14 Move the guide and place it flush up against the strip just applied. Repeat steps 12–13 to add a second strip.

15 Repeat step 14 to continue adding strips all the way around the top tier. Make the heights of the strips random but try not to have too many of a similar height next to each other.

Making The Yellow Flower

1 Cut a 7.5cm (3") length of 18-gauge white floral wire and bend a small closed hook in one end.

2 Colour a 1cm (³/₈") ball of White SFP a pale green shade using a little Olive paste food colour.

3 Insert the hooked end of the wire into the green ball and pinch the paste closed around it to secure.

4 Use a pair of tweezers to pinch at least five evenly spaced ridges, like clock hands, around the top of the ball (C). Set the flower centre aside to dry.

5 Cut two 7.5cm (3") lengths of 28-gauge white floral wire.

6 Take 8–10 small cream pointed head stamens, fold 2.5cm (1") of a cut wire over the centre of the stamen lengths and twist the wire against itself to secure them together (D).

7 Fold the stamens up into a bunch. Bind the bottom 6mm (¹/₄") of the

stamens and down the length of the wire with quarter-width Nile green floral tape.

8 Repeat steps 6–7 to make a second stamen bunch using the remaining 7.5cm (3") cut wire.

9 Position a stamen bunch on either side of the wired flower centre so that the unbound part of the stamens is about 6mm (¹/₄") below the base of the SFP ball. Bind the stamens to the centre's wire with quarter-width Nile green floral tape (E). Arrange the stamen ends so they fan evenly around the centre.

10 Cut 10 pieces of 24-gauge white floral wire into 7.5cm (3") lengths. Colour 25g (>³/₄oz) of White SFP a yellow-orange shade using some Orange neon paste food colour.

11 Roll a small piece of the yellow-orange SFP out to about a 1mm (<¹/₁₆") thickness over one of the grooves on a non-stick board.

12 Cut out a petal using a 3.5cm (1³/₈") round petal cutter, being careful that the cutter is centred over the grooved channel. Using the pointed end of the cutter, cut out three nicks from the top edge of the petal (F).

13 Dip the end of one of the cut wires in edible glue and wipe off the excess. Hold the base of the petal between your finger and thumb and gently insert the glued end up into the ridged channel.

14 On a foam pad, thin and stretch out the edges of the petal with a medium ball tool.

top tip

Use a tape cutter to make yourself some quarter-width floral tape if you only have full-width tape.

15 Drag a dresden tool from the top edge of the petal towards the base, easing the pressure as you go. Do this across the width of the petal to give it texture and shape (G). Leave the petal to dry on a dimple foam drying tray.

16 Repeat steps 11–15 to make two more petals of the same size.

17 Repeat steps 11–15 again to make three petals, this time using a 4.3cm (1³/₄") round petal cutter.

18 Repeat steps 11–15 again to make four more petals using the 4.3cm (1³/₄") round petal cutter. This time, roll them slightly thicker and stretch them out a bit further than with the previous set to make them a little larger.

19 Tape about 2.5cm (1") down the length of the wire on each petal with quarter-width Nile green floral tape.

20 Dust the lower half of each petal with some Orange dust food colour and a no. 4 paintbrush (H).

21 Position one of the small petals against the flower centre so it is cupped around it. Once in place, bind it to the main wire with full-width Nile green tape (I).

22 Tape the remaining two small petals to the centre in the same way as in step 21, making sure they are evenly spaced around the ball.

23 Bend the wires on the three medium petals down by about 45°. Next, position one of the medium petals below the first three so that its centre is in line with an edge of one of

the small petals. Now bind it in place with full-width Nile green tape (J).

24 Tape the remaining two medium petals to the flower centre, ensuring they are evenly spaced below the first three petals.

25 Bend the wires on the four large petals down by about 90°. Bind the four petals to the flower with full-width Nile green tape, making sure they are all evenly spaced below the medium petals. Set the flower aside for later.

Making The Horse Chestnuts

1 To make the horse chestnuts (conkers), cut three 7.5cm (3") lengths of 22-gauge white floral wire.

2 Use a piece of the wire to poke a hole about halfway into a 2cm (³/₄") polystyrene ball. Remove the wire, dip one end in edible glue and reinsert it into the ball.

3 Repeat step 2 with two more polystyrene balls, leaving the glue on the wired balls to dry.

4 Colour a 1.5cm (¹/₂") ball of White SFP a deep brown shade using a little Brown paste food colour and a tiny bit of Red neon paste to richen it up.

5 Roll the brown SFP out to about a 1mm (<¹/₁₆") thickness. Cut out three discs using a 2cm (³/₄") circle cutter.

6 Using the no. 4 paintbrush, paint one side of a brown disc with a little edible glue. Stick the disc on the top of a

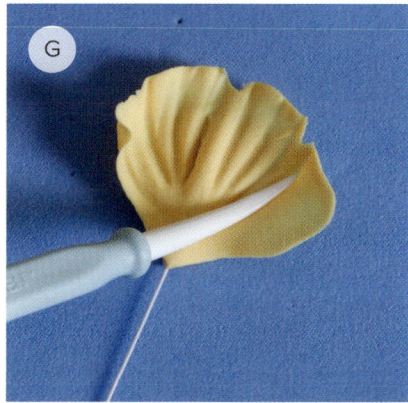

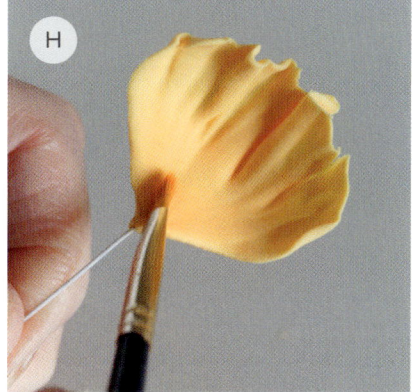

wired ball and flatten it down to secure (K). Repeat with the two remaining discs and wired balls. Leave the discs to dry.

7 Once dry, spray each disc with some edible glaze. Leave the glaze to dry before giving them a second coat.

8 Colour a 2.5cm (1") ball of White SFP a light green shade using some Olive paste food colour. Next, very slightly tint another 2.5cm (1") ball of White SFP with a tiny bit of Cream paste food colour.

9 Roll out one sixth of the light green SFP mixture to about a 1.5mm (<1/16") thickness and cut out a 3cm (1 1/8") circle from the SFP using the respective cutter. Keep all your offcuts. Use a small rolling pin to roll the circle in one direction to widen it to about 4cm (1 1/2").

10 Repeat step 9 to make another circle, this time using the light cream SFP mixture.

11 Brush one side of the light green circle with edible glue and stick the cream circle directly on top so they are in line with each other (L).

12 Use a razor blade to trim about 6mm (1/4") off one of the long sides of the combined pastes. Next, trim about 6mm (1/4") off the left and right edges of the paste (M).

13 Brush the cream-coloured side of the trimmed paste with a little edible glue. Wrap it around one half of a wired ball, making sure the long trimmed edge is at the top and that it just overlaps the brown disc (N). Shape the lower half of the paste to the polystyrene ball and pinch it in at the bottom.

14 Repeat steps 9–13 to cover the other half of the horse chestnut. To finish, use a pair of tweezers to pick

out some spikes on the light green outer paste (O). Set aside to dry.

15 Repeat steps 9–14 to make two more horse chestnuts.

16 Use the no. 4 paintbrush to lightly dust the green part of the horse chestnuts with Vine dust first and then with a little Leaf Green dust. Finish by dusting the spikes with a mixture of Leaf Green and Chestnut (Soft Beige) dusts (P).

17 Bind down the length of the stems of all three horse chestnuts with quarter-width Nile green floral tape.

18 Take two horse chestnuts and arrange them so one is positioned slightly above the other. Bind together the bottom 4cm (1 1/2") of the two stems with quarter-width Nile green floral tape. Leave the third conker loose.

Making The Fir Cones

1 Cut four pieces of 24-gauge Nile green floral wire into 7.5cm (3") lengths. Bend a small closed hook in one end of each piece.

2 Colour 15g (1/2oz) of White SFP a brown shade using a little Brown paste food colour.

3 Take a small pea-sized piece of the brown SFP and roll it into a rugby ball shape. Insert the hooked end of a cut wire into one of the tapered ends of the ball and pinch the paste closed around it.

4 Roll out a quarter of the remaining brown SFP to a thickness of about 1mm (<1/16"). Cut six small petal sets from the paste using a 1.4cm (1/2") Six-Petal cutter and three larger petal sets using a 1.9cm (3/4") Six-Petal cutter. Wrap up the unused paste for later.

5 Press the dresden tool down the inner part of the individual petals on each petal set, leaving them looking like tiny canoe hulls (Q).

6 Brush a bit of edible glue on the lower half of the wired ball. Take a small petal set, with its concave petal sides facing upwards, and insert the wire through the centre. Slide the petal piece up the wire (R) and gently close the individual petals around the centre.

7 Brush some glue on the underside of the petal set you just added. Slide a second small petal piece up the wire, concave side up again, and close it up a little around the previous piece.

8 Glue a third small petal piece below the first two, but do not close up the petals this time.

9 Next, glue and attach the three large petal sets one at a time, before attaching the final three small petal sets one by one (S).

10 Repeat steps 3–9 to make four fir cones in total.

11 Bind two fir cones to an 18cm (7") length of 24-gauge dark green floral wire using full-width brown floral tape. Position the cones so that their bases are butted up against the main wire and they are staggered on alternating sides, about 4cm (1 1/2") apart.

12 Add several twigs to the main wire by folding 4cm (1 1/2") pieces of full-width or quarter-width brown tape across the wire and twisting the resulting 2cm (3/4") piece against itself.

13 Repeat steps 11–12 to make a second branch using the remaining two fir cones.

14 Add little bits of fir below each cone by twisting short lengths

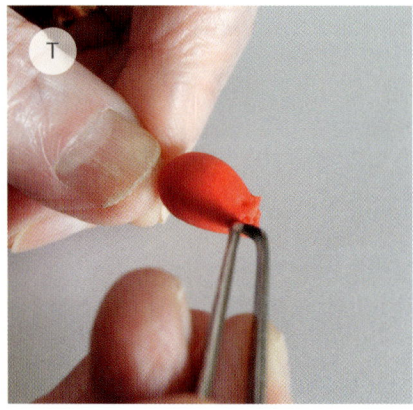

of full-width dark green tape into cords and then twisting two or three of them under each cone.

Making The Rose Hips

1   Cut five pieces of 26-gauge dark green wire into 7.5cm (3") lengths. Bend a small closed hook in one end of each piece.

2   Colour a 2cm (³/₄") ball of White SFP red using a little Red neon paste food colour. Divide the red SFP into five equal pieces.

3   Take one of the red SFP pieces and shape it into a ball. Roll the ball in your palm so that it elongates and gently tapers at one end like a teardrop.

4   Insert the unhooked end of a wire centrally into the tapered end of the SFP and thread it all the way down through the paste until the hooked end disappears.

5   Use a pair of tweezers to pinch a small frill around the top of the SFP where the wire entered (T).

6   Very lightly brush the pinched area with some Brown paste food colour and the no. 4 paintbrush (U).

7   Repeat steps 3–6 to make four more rose hips in total. Leave them all to dry.

8   Spray the five rose hips with edible glaze and set them aside to dry. Once dry, give them a second coat of glaze and allow them to dry once more.

9   Bind three rose hips to an 18cm (7") length of 24-gauge dark green wire using full-width brown tape. Position the rose hips so that their bases are about 1cm (³/₈") away from the main wire and they are staggered on alternating sides, approximately 2cm – 3cm (³/₄" – 1¹/₈") apart (V).

10   Repeat step 12 from Making The Fir Cones to add twigs to the wire.

11   Repeat steps 9–10 to attach the remaining two rose hips to a second wire.

Making The Horse Chestnut Leaves

1   Cut 10 7.5cm (3") lengths of 26-gauge Nile green floral wire. Colour 35g (1¹/₄oz) of White SFP a light green shade using a little Olive paste food colour.

2   Roll out a small piece of the light green SFP to a 1mm (<¹/₁₆") thickness over a groove on the non-stick board.

3   Position a 4.9cm (2") Horse Chestnut Leaf cutter centrally over the groove of the SFP and cut out a single leaf. Wrap up and keep your offcuts for later.

4   Dip one end of a cut wire in edible glue and wipe off the excess. Holding the base of the leaf between your finger and thumb, gently slide the wire about 1cm (³/₈") into the ridge.

5   Place the leaf between the two halves of a medium Chestnut Leaf veiner and press down firmly (W). Transfer the leaf to the foam pad and thin the edges using the medium ball tool. Set the leaf aside to dry. Leave it relatively flat; horse chestnut leaves don't have too much movement in them.

6   Repeat steps 2–5 to make nine more horse chestnut leaves: three more 4.9cm (2") leaves, four 5.9cm (2³/₈") leaves and two 6.5cm (2¹/₂") leaves using the respective Horse Chestnut Leaf cutters.

7   Use the no. 4 paintbrush to dust all over the face of each leaf with some Vine dust. Next, dust the inner part of each leaf with some Leaf Green dust. Lastly, lightly dust the very edge of each leaf with a little Chestnut (Soft Beige) dust (X). Once dusted, steam to set the colour. When dry, spray each leaf with edible glaze and allow to dry again.

8   Wrap some quarter-width Nile green tape about 2.5cm (1") down each wire length, starting immediately below each leaf.

9   Take one of the large leaves and bind a medium leaf to the side of it with quarter-width Nile green tape. Make sure the bases of the leaves are right next to each other.

10   On the opposite side, bind a second medium leaf next to the large centre leaf.

11   Finally, bind a small leaf below each medium leaf, again making sure that the bases of the leaves are butted up against each other.

12   Finish off by arranging the leaves into a flat fan – you want the small leaves to be roughly horizontal, the large leaf vertical and the medium leaves spaced evenly in between (Y).

13   Repeat steps 9–12 to make the second fan of horse chestnut leaves. Set aside for later.

Making The Japanese Maple Leaves

1   Cut six 7.5cm (3") lengths of 26-gauge white floral wire. Colour 16g ($^1/_2$oz) of White SFP a light yellow shade using some Yellow neon paste food colour.

2   Roll out a small piece of the light yellow SFP to a 1mm (<$^1/_{16}$") thickness over a groove on the non-stick board.

3   Cut out a leaf using a 5.5cm (2$^1/_4$") Maple Leaf cutter, making sure the cutter is placed centrally over the ridge. Wrap up the unused paste for later.

4   Thin the edges of the leaf on the foam pad using the ball tool.

5   Dip one end of a cut wire in edible glue and wipe off the excess. Hold the base of the leaf between your finger and thumb and gently slide the wire about 1cm ($^3/_8$") into the ridge (Z).

6   Place the leaf between the two halves of a small Maple Leaf veiner and press down firmly. Remove from the veiner and use your fingers to give the leaf a little movement. Set it aside to dry.

7   Repeat steps 2–6 to make five more maple leaves: two additional 5.5cm (2$^1/_4$") leaves and three 3cm (1$^1/_8$") leaves using the respective Maple Leaf cutters.

8   Use the no. 4 paintbrush to dust all but the edges of each leaf with some Orange dust. Dust the centre of each leaf with a little Poppy dust (AA).

9   Bind down the stem of each leaf with quarter-width brown floral tape, starting directly under the leaves.

10   Bind three maple leaves to an 18cm (7") length of 24-gauge dark green wire using full-width brown floral tape. Position the leaves so that their bases are about 1.5cm ($^1/_2$") away from the main wire and they are staggered on alternating sides, about 4cm (1$^1/_2$") apart. Use a mixture of sizes for this to make it look more realistic.

11   Repeat step 12 from Making The Fir Cones to add twigs to the wire.

12   Repeat steps 10–11 to make a second maple leaf branch. Set the branches aside.

Making The Beech Leaves

1   Cut 11 7.5cm (3") lengths of 26-gauge Nile green floral wire. Colour 15g (¹/₂oz) of White SFP a dark brown shade using some Brown paste food colour and a touch of Red neon paste. Also colour 6g (¹/₄oz) of White SFP green using Olive paste food colour.

2   Roll out a small piece of the dark brown SFP to a 1mm (<¹/₁₆") thickness over a groove on the non-stick board.

3   Position a 4.3cm (1³/₄") Rose Leaf cutter centrally over the groove and cut out a single leaf (AB). Keep and wrap up the offcuts. Transfer the leaf to the foam pad and thin the edges using the medium ball tool.

4   Dip one end of a cut wire in edible glue and wipe off the excess. Holding the base of the leaf, slide the wire about 1cm (³/₈") into the ridge.

5   Place the leaf between the two halves of a Tea Rose Leaf veiner and press down firmly. Remove from the veiner and shape the leaf with your fingers to give it some movement. Set aside to dry.

6   Repeat steps 2–5 to make seven more brown beech leaves. Make them in a selection of the following sizes using the respective Rose Leaf cutters: 2.6cm (1"), 3.4cm (1³/₈") and 4.3cm (1³/₄").

7   Using the green SFP, repeat steps 2–5 to make three green beech leaves in at least two different sizes using the Rose Leaf cutters.

8   Bind down the stem of each leaf with some quarter-width brown floral wire.

9   Repeat step 7 from Making The Horse Chestnut Leaves to dust the green leaves only. Once dusted, steam to set the colour. When dry, spray the leaves with edible glaze and leave to dry again.

10   Bind four brown leaves to an 18cm (7") length of 24-gauge dark green wire using full-width brown tape. Position the leaves so that their bases are butted up against the main wire and they are staggered on alternating sides, about 3cm (1¹/₈") apart. Start with a small leaf and then vary the leaf sizes as you go.

11   Repeat step 12 from Making The Fir Cones to add twigs to the wire.

12   Repeat steps 10–11 to make two shorter branches, each with two brown leaves.

13   Repeat step 10 again, this time to make a branch with the three green leaves.

Assembling The Cake

1   Attach the 12.5cm (5") cake centrally on top of the covered drum. Dowel the 12.5cm (5") cake, spacing them evenly within a central 10cm (4") circle. Attach the 10cm (4") cake centrally on top (see technique on page 41).

✿ top tip ✿

Make extra components to use as loose fillers anywhere on your cake that needs a bit of balance. This is good practice for all cakes; having extra pieces gives you flexibility and also means that you have cover for any breakages.

Attaching The Arrangement

1   Cut around six 7.5cm (3") lengths of 18-gauge white floral wire. Cover the length of each cut wire with some full-width brown floral tape.

2   Bend the wires into long 6mm (¹/₄") U-shaped pins.

3   Arrange the components around an area just to the right of the centre and on top of the bottom tier. Push the pins into posy picks to hold items that cannot be directly inserted into posy picks.

4   Attach the horse chestnuts and horse chestnut leaves so that one leaf spray and the single horse chestnut point right, and so the other spray and the pair of horse chestnuts point left and downwards.

5   Attach the maple leaf branches so that one branch goes up and one goes down. Do the same with the rose hip branches – have the rose hips on the left of the maples trailing upwards and the other branch bending down on the other side.

6   Attach the long brown beech branch so it climbs upwards on the cake. Secure the two short brown branches so that one points left and the other points right, making sure they are facing slightly upwards. Attach the green beech branch pointing upwards and to the left.

7   Attach the fir cone branches to the cake, with one pointing up and one pointing left.

8   Finally, insert the yellow flower into a posy pick in the centre of the foliage, covering all the pins and posy picks.

FROSTED
fantasy flowers

This beautiful wedding cake has a subtle wintry feel, with pearlescent flowers in soft shades of blue and pink. The textured top edges are really easy to create and add modern flair to this delicate design.

YOU WILL NEED

Edibles

Round, filled sponge cakes covered with ganache/buttercream with a sharp edge finish, secured on cake boards of the same size (see page 29), 10cm (4") deep: 10cm (4") and 15cm (6") wide

Round, filled sponge cake covered with ganache/buttercream with a sharp edge finish, secured on a cake board of the same size (see page 29), 15cm (6") deep: 12.5cm (5") wide

SK Fairtrade Sugarpaste: 1.9kg (4lb 3oz) Bridal White and 190g (6^3/$_4$oz) Vintage Pink

SK Sugar Florist Paste (SFP): 125g (4^3/$_8$oz) White

SK Professional Instant Mix Royal Icing: 100g (3^1/$_2$oz) White

SK Pastelz Dust Food Colour: Pale Blue

SK Professional Paste Food Colours: Hydrangea and Rose

SK Dust Food Colours: Extra White, Orange and Pearl

SK Professional Dust Food Colour: Rose

SK Essentials Edible Glue

Equipment

Round cake drums: 20.5cm (8") and 23cm (9")

Round cake boards: 10cm (4"), 12.5cm (5") and 15cm (6")

1.5cm (^{1}/$_2$") width satin ribbon: 1.45m (1yd 21") Bridal White

FMM Rose Leaf Cutters: 3.1cm (1^1/$_4$") and 4.2cm (1^5/$_8$")

Modelling tools: medium ball and veining

SK-GI Silicone Veiner Rose - Tea: Large Leaf

Cream round head pearl stamens: 56 small

Floral wires: 22-, 24-, 26- and 28-gauge white

Half-width floral tape: white

CelStick: 6mm (^{1}/$_4$")

SK Multi Flower Cutter Set 1A, Round Petal/Leaf: nos. 1–2

Framar Peony Petal Cutter: 5.5cm (2^1/$_4$")

PME Modelling Tool: Taper Cones 5/6 Star

Posy picks: various sizes

SEE PAGES 11–15 FOR ESSENTIAL EDIBLES AND EQUIPMENT

Covering The Cake Drums

1   Knead 190g (6³/₄oz) of Vintage Pink sugarpaste into 1.9kg (4lb 3oz) of Bridal White sugarpaste to make the pale pink colour for covering the cake and drums. Keep all your offcuts as you work.

2   Take 250g (8³/₄oz) of the pale pink sugarpaste and cover the 20.5cm (8") cake drum. Next, cover the 23cm (9") drum using 300g (10¹/₂oz) of the pale pink sugarpaste (see technique on page 32). Set both drums aside to firm overnight.

3   Fix the Bridal White ribbon around the edge of each cake drum (see technique on page 32).

4   To stack the drums, spread a little royal icing in the middle of the 23cm (9") drum. Place the 20.5cm (8") drum centrally on top, lining up the ribbon joins at the back. Set aside.

Covering The Cakes

1   Use the panelling method to cover the cakes. For the top tier, roll out 75g (2⁵/₈oz) of the pale pink sugarpaste you prepared earlier and cut out a 12.5cm (5") disc. Place the disc on top of the 10cm (4") wide cake and trim away the excess (see technique on page 32).

2   Repeat step 1 to cover the top of the 12.5cm (5") cake with a 15cm (6") disc using 105g (3³/₄oz) of the pale pink paste. Also cover the top of the 15cm (6") wide cake with a 18cm (7") disc using 135g (4³/₄oz) of pale pink paste.

3   To cover the sides, start with the 10cm (4") wide cake. Roll out 310g (11oz) of the pale pink paste and cut out a 34cm x 11.5cm (13³/₈" x 4¹/₂") panel. Roll up the panel and wrap it around the cake (see technique on page 32).

4   Repeat step 3 to cover the side of the 12.5cm (5") cake using 480g (1lb 1oz) of the pale pink paste and a 42cm x 16.5cm (16¹/₂" x 6¹/₂") panel. Repeat step 3 again to cover the side of the 15cm (6") wide cake, this time using 430g (15¹/₄oz) of the pale pink paste and a 50cm x 11.5cm (19³/₄" x 4¹/₂") panel.

5   Allow all the cakes to firm for one hour. Once the sugarpaste has firmed slightly, pinch off small bits of sugarpaste from the top of each panel to create a jagged edge (A). Try to keep the pinches irregular in width but of a similar depth. Set the cakes aside to firm overnight.

Finishing The Torn Edges

1   Make up 100g (3¹/₂oz) of royal icing to a fairly stiff peak consistency.

2   Use a no. 10 paintbrush to dab small amounts of icing along the top of the torn edges to create a frosty effect (B). Try to keep the icing mainly along the tops of the edges rather than down the sides. Lift the paintbrush up as you remove the brush to encourage peaks to develop along the top.

Assembling The Cake

1   Attach the 15cm (6") wide cake centrally on top of the covered double height drum. Dowel the 15cm (6") cake, spacing them evenly within a central 12.5cm (5") circle. Attach the 12.5cm (5") cake centrally on top. Dowel the 12.5cm (5") tier, positioning them within a central 10cm (4") circle, and fix the 10cm (4") wide cake on top (see technique on page 41).

Making The Leaves

1   Cut three lengths of 28-gauge white floral wire into quarter pieces. You'll end up with 12 cut wires.

2   Colour 20g (³/₄oz) of White SFP a very light blue shade using some Pale Blue pastel dust food colour. Roll a small piece of the pale blue SFP into a 5mm (¹/₄") ball and insert one cut wire into its centre. Work the paste down the wire until it covers around 2.5cm (1") at one end (C).

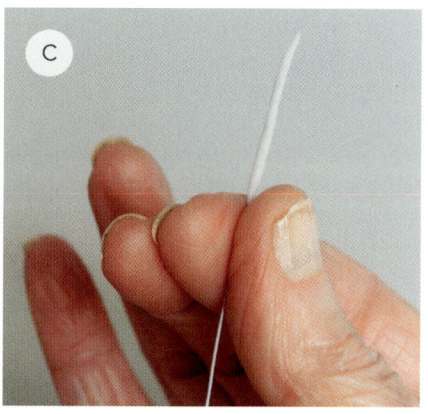

Making The Large Flower

1 Cut a 28-gauge white floral wire in half. Hold 30 cream round head pearl stamens and place one length of wire over the centre of the bunch. Twist the ends of the wire together to hold the stamens in place (G). Fold the ends of the stamens up and bind them together using white floral tape, continuing the tape approximately 5cm (2") down the wire stem (H).

top tip

If you wrap each of the wires on the petals with quarter-width white floral tape before putting them together it helps to keep them in place while assembling the flower.

2 Use a small amount of Rose dust to colour 50g (1$\frac{3}{4}$oz) of White SFP a very pale pink shade.

3 Roll out a small piece of the very pale pink SFP to a 2mm ($\frac{1}{16}$") thickness. Use a small CelStick or rolling pin to roll the left and right sides of the paste thinner, leaving a thicker ridge of paste in the centre for the wire (I).

4 Cut out a petal using a 2.7cm (1$\frac{1}{16}$") round petal cutter, making sure the thicker ridge of paste runs through the centre (J). Use the tip of the cutter to cut out two notches from the top of the petal (K). Place the petal on the foam pad and thin the edges with the medium ball tool.

5 Cut two lengths of 26-gauge white floral wire into fifths to give you 10 cut pieces. Dip the end of one piece in edible glue and wipe off the excess. Hold the petal between your finger and thumb and insert the wire into the central ridge, feeding it through until it runs approximately two thirds of the way along its length (L).

6 Place the wired petal on the foam pad and run a veining tool over the surface of the paste to texture (M). Lay the petal in a cupped former or the well of an artist's palette to firm (N).

7 Repeat steps 3–6 to make a total of four small petals using the cut wires.

8 Repeat step 3 to roll out a small amount of the very pale pink SFP with a thicker central ridge and cut out a petal using the 5.5cm (2$\frac{1}{4}$") Peony Petal cutter. Next, repeat steps 5–6 to wire (with the already cut pieces) and shape the petal, then leave it to firm in a former or palette.

9 Repeat step 8 to make a total of five large petals. Allow all the petals to firm overnight.

10 Once the petals are firm, hold each one between your finger and thumb at the point where the wire enters and bend the wires down by 90°.

11 Dust the base of each petal with a mixture of Rose and Extra White dusts, fading out towards the top and edges (O). Brush the front and back of each petal with Pearl dust.

12 Use white floral tape to fix the four smaller petals around the stamen centre one by one, positioning them so the bases of the petals are approximately 1.5cm ($\frac{1}{2}$") below the top of the stamens (P).

13 Tape the five larger petals in a single row around the smaller ones, spacing them evenly (Q).

top tip

When colouring SFP, especially for pale flowers, add colour to the paste in very small amounts, building it up gradually.

3 Roll out a small piece of the pale blue SFP into a thin sheet and cut out a leaf using a 4.2cm (1$\frac{5}{8}$") Rose Leaf cutter (D). Place the leaf on a foam pad and thin the edges with a ball tool (E).

4 Lightly moisten the paste on the wire and lay it across the centre of the leaf, running from the base to just short of the tip. Press the leaf between the two halves of a Tea Rose Leaf veiner, making sure the wire is on the underside of the leaf (F). Remove and shape the leaf to give it some movement.

5 Repeat steps 2–4 to make a total of seven 4.2cm (1$\frac{5}{8}$") rose leaves and five smaller leaves using the 3.1cm (1$\frac{1}{4}$") Rose Leaf cutter. Allow all the leaves to firm overnight.

6 Once the leaves are firm, brush them with some Pearl dust colour.

Making The Small Flower

1 Repeat step 1 from the Making The Large Flower instructions to make a centre for a smaller flower, this time using only 20 stamens.

2 Colour 25g (>³/₄oz) of White SFP a deep pink shade using some Rose paste food colour.

3 Repeat steps 3–6 from the Making The Large Flower instructions to create and wire three 2cm (³/₄") petals and five 2.7cm (1¹/₁₆") petals, this time not cutting notches from the top edges.

4 When the petals are firm, bend the wires on the three smaller petals down by 45° and the wires on the five larger petals by 90°.

5 Brush the back and front of each petal with Pearl dust.

6 Use white floral tape to fix the three smaller petals around the stamen centre one by one, spacing them evenly. Tape the five larger petals in a single row around the smaller ones.

Making The Filler Flowers

1 Colour 15g (¹/₂oz) of White SFP a salmon pink shade using a mixture of Rose paste food colour and Orange dust.

2 Roll a 1cm (³/₈") diameter ball of the salmon-coloured SFP into a cone and flatten the top. Push a Taper Cones 5/6 Star tool into the flat top of the cone to indent (R).

top tip

Filler flowers and berries are always useful to fill in gaps, as well as to provide contrast to larger elements.

3 Use a pair of small scissors to cut along the tool marks, dividing the cone into five petals (S).

4 Pinch the individual segments flat and then pinch in the corner points to round them off and create the petal shapes (T).

5 Place the flower on the foam pad and use the ball tool to thin and cup each petal (U).

6 Cut some 28-gauge white floral wire into 7.5cm (3") lengths and bend a small hook in one end of each – you want to end up with 12 cut pieces. Feed the straight end of a cut wire down through the middle of the flower and pull it through until the hook is nestled in the paste (V).

7 Cut a cream round head pearl stamen in half and trim the stem of each one to a 1cm (³/₈") length. Insert one stamen into the throat of the flower (W).

8 Using the remaining cut wires, repeat steps 2–7 to make 10 open filler flowers. Set them aside to firm.

9 Repeat steps 2–7 to make another filler flower, this time closing up the petals slightly.

10 Roll a small piece of the remaining salmon-coloured SFP into a teardrop. Insert the last cut wire into the narrow end and roll the paste down the wire to fix it in place. Set the unopened bud aside to firm.

11 Once firm, brush the flowers and buds with some Pearl dust.

12 Use white floral tape to bind the flowers together in a stem. Start with the bud, then the slightly closed flower, followed by eight open flowers. Leave two filler flowers loose to use later.

Making The Berries

1 Colour 8g (¹/₄oz) of SFP blue using Hydrangea paste food colour.

2 Roll a 1cm (³/₈") ball of the blue SFP and use the end of a paintbrush (or similar) to create a hole in the centre (X).

3 Cut some 26-gauge white floral wire into 7.5cm (3") lengths and bend a small hook in one end of each – you want to end up with seven cut pieces. Feed the unhooked end of a cut wire down through the middle of the berry and pull it through until the hook is nestled in the well (Y).

4 Repeat steps 2–3 to make seven blue berries and then set them aside to firm overnight.

5 Once firm, brush the berries with some Pearl dust.

6 Fix the berries into two sprays using white floral tape: one spray of three berries and one of four.

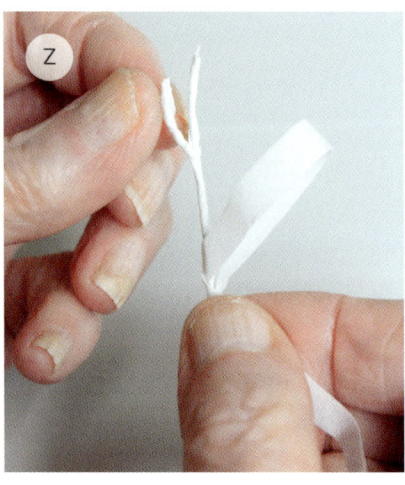

Making The Branches

1   Cut a 25.5cm (10") length of 24-gauge white floral wire and wrap 1.25cm ($^1/_2$") at one end of the wire with white floral tape. Leave a 1.25cm ($^1/_2$") loop of tape sticking out, then continue taping 1.25cm ($^1/_2$") down the wire (Z). Hold the loop and start twisting it from the wire outwards to form a small branch (AA).

2   Repeat the technique from step 1 to continue adding branches down the length of the wire. Vary the lengths of the branches but generally increase the sizes as you work along the wire. You can also create extra long loops, leaving you enough tape to add sub-branches.

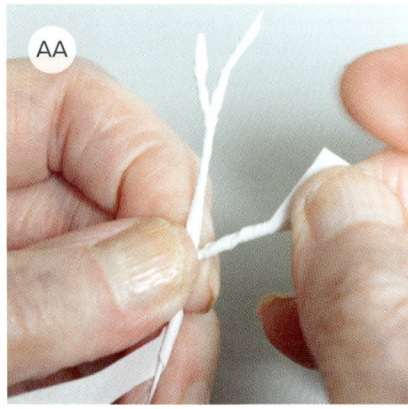

3   Repeat steps 1–2 to make a 20.5cm (8") long branch, taping in four leaves and the spray of four berries starting approximately halfway down the branch.

4   Repeat steps 1–2 to make a second 20.5cm (8") branch, taping in the spray of filler flowers and three leaves along its length.

5   Repeat steps 1–2 to make three 15cm (6") long branches: one with three leaves, one with two leaves and the two loose filler flowers, and one with two leaves and the remaining spray of berries.

6   Tape the ends of the two 20.5cm (8") branches together to create a 35cm (13$^3/_4$") long main branch with the berries at the top and the filler flowers at the bottom.

7   Tape the final 5cm (2") of the three 15cm (6") branches to the main branch so that, when folded out, they sit approximately one third of the way up the main branch. Bend the branch with the three leaves out to the left at 90˚ and the other two to the right at 45˚, with the branch with filler flowers pointing up and the branch with the berries pointing down.

Attaching The Branches And Flowers

1   Cut four 7.5cm (3") lengths of 20-gauge white floral wire. Bend the wires into U-shaped pins.

2   Pin the 25.5cm (10") branch into a posy pick and attach it to the front left of the middle tier so that its tip extends just over the top of the top tier.

3   Hold the assembled branches against the middle tier next to the 25.5cm (10") branch so that they mingle. Fix them in place using the pins and posy picks.

4   Insert the large flower into a posy pick, securing it in place with a little sugarpaste or royal icing. Push the pick into the side of the cake just above where the two branches on the right side join the main stem. Fix the smaller flower into a posy pick and attach it diagonally below and right of the large flower so it sits tightly against it.

top tip

When making branches, it can be useful to make them longer than you think you need and then trim them to length.

DECK
the halls

This festive holly and bark cake is the perfect piece for your table over the winter season. All the elements here are simple to make, yet super effective!

Edibles

Round, filled sponge cakes covered with ganache/buttercream with a sharp edge finish, secured on cake boards of the same size (see page 29), 12.5cm (5") deep: 10cm (4") and 12.5cm (5") wide

SK Fairtrade Sugarpaste: 835g (1lb 13^1/$_2$oz) Bridal White, 325g (11^1/$_4$oz) Coco Brown and 65g (2^1/$_4$oz) Tuxedo Black

SK Edible Wafer Paper: 2+ sheets, white

SK Sugar Florist Paste (SFP): 30g (1oz) White

SK Professional Paste Food Colours: Leaf Green and Poinsettia (Xmas Red)

SK Professional Dust Food Colours: Holly/Ivy (Dark Green) and Leaf Green

SK Designer Paste Food Colour: Olive

SK Essentials Confectioners' Glaze

SK Professional Instant Mix Royal Icing: 100g (3^1/$_2$oz) White

Equipment

Round cake drum: 20.5cm (8")

Round cake boards: 10cm (4") and 12.5cm (5")

Modelling tools: dresden, scribing needle and small ball

Floral wires: 26-gauge dark green, and 24- and 28-gauge Nile green

TinkerTech Holly Leaf Cutter: 3.5cm (1^3/$_8$")

Dusting brush

Half-width floral tape: Nile green

3mm (^{1}/$_8$") width satin ribbon: 51cm (20") Glamour Red

Red cotton

Posy pick: medium

SEE PAGES 11–15 FOR ESSENTIAL EDIBLES AND EQUIPMENT

Covering The Cake Drum

1   Roll out 300g (10¹/₂oz) of Bridal White sugarpaste to a 3mm (¹/₈") thickness. Lightly dampen the top and side of the 20.5cm (8") drum with cooled, boiled water. Lay the drum upside down in the centre of the sugarpaste and press it down firmly to adhere.

2   Bring the excess paste up the side and fold it over onto the drum, making sure to press the sugarpaste firmly against the side to secure (A). Neatly trim the excess paste away and level with the bottom (currently at the top) of the drum (B).

3   Turn the drum over so it is up the right way and smooth over it with a cake smoother. Set the covered drum aside to firm overnight.

Covering The Cakes

1   You will be using the panelling method to cover the cakes. For the top tier, roll out 75g (2⁵/₈oz) of Bridal White sugarpaste and cut out a 12.5cm (5") disc. Place the disc on top of the 10cm (4") cake and trim away the excess (see technique on page 32). For the bottom tier, repeat to cover the top of the 12.5cm (5") cake with a 15cm (6") disc using 105g (3³/₄oz) of Bridal White sugarpaste.

2   To cover the side of the 10cm (4") cake, roll out 355g (12¹/₂oz) of Bridal White sugarpaste and cut out a 34cm x 14cm (13³/₈" x 5¹/₂") panel. Roll up the panel and wrap it around the cake (see technique on page 32).

3   Drag the dresden tool part way down the side of the top tier to mark on lines. Start from the top, drag downwards and release the pressure just before you lift away to help it taper off (C). Vary the lengths of the strokes to

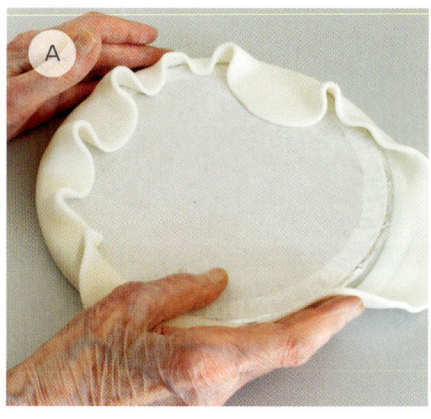

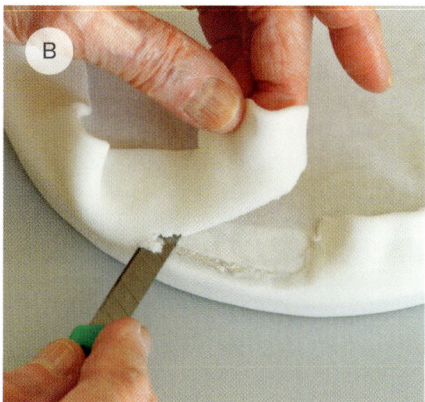

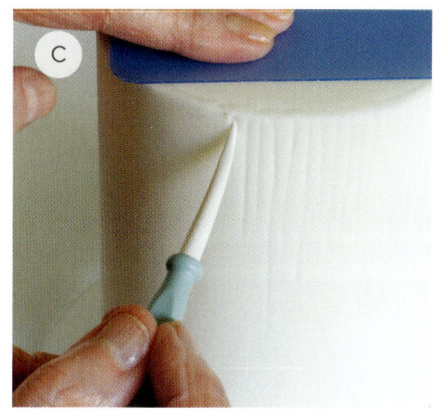

around half the way down the cake. The sugarpaste will gradually spring back a little so press quite firmly – if the lines are not distinct enough, don't be afraid to go over them a second time. Once finished, set both cakes aside until firm.

Making And Attaching The Bark

1   Knead 65g (2¹/₄oz) of Tuxedo Black sugarpaste into 325g (11¹/₄oz) of Coco Brown sugarpaste to make a dark brown shade.

2   Roll out 75g (2⁵/₈oz) of the dark brown sugarpaste to a 3mm (¹/₈") thickness and cut out a panel that is roughly 8cm x 15cm (3¹/₈" x 6") in size.

3   Tear a piece of wafer paper into quarters, approximately 10cm

x 15cm (4" x 6"). Tear away the long straight side of each piece to leave it about the width of the dark brown panel.

4   Brush the shiny side of a piece of the torn wafer paper with cooled, boiled water, but do not make it too wet (D). Lay the wet side of the paper down on the paste panel and press over it firmly to adhere. If there are any patches that did not get wet, dab on a little water and press again. Leave the panel for a minute for the paper and paste to bind together.

5   Use your fingers and thumbs to start easing the wafer paper apart. Do this by pressing down and pulling outwards, working on a small section at a time (E). Try to keep the tears random, working predominantly vertically but also horizontally and at angles. Aim to make the tears about 3mm (¹/₈") wide on average. The panel should

have stretched to about 10cm – 11cm (4" – 4³/₈") wide when finished.

6   Once all the tears have been completed, use the dresden tool to slightly press down in the gaps between the paste and the wafer paper. This will help to define its edges (F).

top tip

Gauging the correct wetness of the wafer paper can be tricky, so practice a few times with spare paper and paste before making the actual pieces for the cake.

7   Use a sharp knife to cut a straight base line along the bottom of the bark panel.

8   Repeat steps 2–7 to make three more bark panels in the same way.

top tip

Make two or three extra panels and pick your favourite four to go on the cake.

9   Choose which bark panel is to be at the front of the cake. Paint come cooled, boiled water over an area on the 12.5cm (5") wide cake that is the size of a panel. Attach the panel to the cake, keeping the straight edge base flush with the bottom of the cake.

10   Using a little water, attach a second panel to the cake to the left of the first. Butt it up against the first panel so that the uneven edges mesh together. Tear away or wet down any overlapping wafer paper that's not needed.

11   Repeat step 10 to attach a third panel, this time to the right of the first panel. Before attaching the final panel at the back, check that it is the correct width for the remaining gap. If it is too slim, stretch it a bit; if it is too wide, pinch off the excess.

12   Once all the panels have been attached, pinch off pieces from the top of the bark panels to leave a jagged edge that is about 1.5cm ($^1/_2$") over the top of the cake. This will emphasise the bark effect. Set the cake aside to dry overnight.

Making The Holly Leaves

1   Colour approximately 25g (>$^3/_4$oz) of White SFP green using a little Leaf Green and Olive paste food colours to make a light fresh green shade.

2   Cut 26 pieces of 28-gauge Nile green floral wire into 7cm (2$^3/_4$") lengths.

3   Take a large pea-sized ball of the light green paste and flatten one end to make it into a cone.

4   Insert a cut wire 1cm ($^3/_8$") into the pointed end of the paste, making sure to twist the wire as you push it in (G). Gently pinch the paste all over between your finger and thumb to flatten it.

5   Lay the wired paste on a non-stick board and run a small rolling pin out left and right from the centre until thin (H). Finish with one gentle roll along its length.

6   Cut out a leaf using the 3.5cm (1$^3/_8$") Holly Leaf cutter. Make sure that the point at which the wire enters the paste is at the base of the cutter and that the wire within the paste is centred inside the cutter (I). Neaten the paste where the wire enters if needed.

7   On a foam pad, use a small ball tool to thin the edges of the leaf (J). Lift the leaf off the pad and use your fingers to pinch the points sharp (K).

8   Use a scribe tool to mark veins on the leaf. Start by pressing a line down the middle of the leaf to make the central vein. Next, position the tool in line with a spike, angled towards the base and with its tip at the central vein, then gently press down. Repeat this technique for each spike (L).

9   Use your fingers to lightly fold each side of the leaf upwards

around the central vein and ease the tip back to give it some movement.

10   Repeat steps 3–9 to make at least 26 leaves in total. Set the leaves aside to dry overnight.

11   Dust all but the very tips of each leaf with some Leaf Green dust food colour. Also dust the centres of the leaves with a little Holly/Ivy (Dark Green) dust, making it slightly darker where the wire enters the leaf (M). Steam the leaves lightly to set the colour and allow them to dry for a few hours.

12   Dip the dried leaves in Confectioners' Glaze and set them aside to dry.

13   Starting at the base of the leaves, bind each individual stem with some half-width Nile green floral tape. Tape all the way down the wires and set aside for later.

Making The Berries

1   Colour 5g (<$^1/_4$oz) of White SFP a red shade using some Poinsettia (Xmas Red) paste food colour. Roll out at least 22 pea-sized balls from the red SFP, approximately 6mm ($^1/_4$").

2   Cut 22 lengths of 26-gauge dark green floral wire into 5cm (2") pieces and make a tiny hook in one end of each (N).

3   Push a wire all the way through a berry and pull it backwards back into the paste. The hook should nestle in the paste, leaving a small indentation (O). Reshape the berry if necessary. Repeat to wire all the berries and leave them to dry overnight.

4   Once dry, dip each berry in Confectioners' Glaze and set them aside to dry.

Making The Wreath Ring

1 Cover the entire length of a 24-gauge Nile green wire with half-width Nile green floral tape. Shape the wire into a loop and then partly open it out again.

top tip

Covering a floral wire with floral tape helps subsequent flowers and leaves better adhere to the wire.

Assembling The Leaves And Berries

1 Bind two holly leaves together with half-width Nile green tape, positioning one just below the other (P). Tape one, two or three berries below to sit at the base of the leaves (Q). Set aside.

2 Repeat step 1 until you have made 12 sprays, leaving a few spare leaves and berries in case they are needed later.

Assembling The Wreath

1 Take a holly leaf and berry spray and bind it to the curved wreath ring with half-width Nile green tape. Position it so the tips of the leaves are about 4cm (1¹/₂") from the end of the wire.

2 Continue adding sprays roughly 2.5cm (1") below the spray before, going until you are halfway along the wire (R).

3 Repeat steps 1–2 to add more sprays, this time to the other half of the wire. Attach the sprays until you join up with the sprays from the opposite side. Add any of the spare leaves and berries if required.

4 Bend the wire into a loop until the ends overlap. Bind the middle 6mm (¹/₄") of the overlap with half-width Nile green tape (S).

5 Bend the two unbound ends of the wire upwards to make two pins that are sticking up and away from the wreath (T).

6 Wind 28cm (11") of Glamour Red ribbon around a 5.5cm (2¹/₄") wide piece of card twice. Remove the card from the wound ribbon and tie a piece of red cotton around its middle to make a double bow. Trim the ends of the ribbon so they don't show.

7 Lay the wreath down with the leaves facing upwards and place the bow on it at the base of the pins.

8 Take a 23cm (9") length of Glamour Red ribbon and fold it in half. Slide the ribbon under the wreath so that the loop is inside it and the ends are between the pins.

9 Bring the ends of the ribbon up between the pins, over the bow and slide them through the loop (U). Pull the

top tip

Wet the loop end of the ribbon and the centre of the bow before tying it to help give it more purchase when pulled tight.

loop tight around the bow (V) and trim the tails so that one is slightly shorter than the other.

10 Bend the two pins down by a little over 90° so they are sticking out the back of the wreath (W).

11 Use the pins to fix the wreath into a medium posy pick at the front of the 10cm (4") cake, making sure it's almost level with the top but not so close that the pick bumps the top up.

Assembling The Cake

1 Attach the 12.5cm (5") wide cake centrally on top of the covered drum. Dowel the 12.5cm (5") cake, spacing them evenly within a central 10cm (4") circle. Attach the 10cm (4") cake on top slightly towards the back, making sure the wreath is positioned at the front (see technique on page 41).

Making The Snowballs

1 Roll the remaining Bridal White sugarpaste into roughly 25 balls. Vary the sizes between 1cm (³/₈") and 2cm (³/₄").

2 Arrange five or six of the snowballs in a pile on the drum at the front right of the cake. Use little dabs of royal icing to hold them in place. Add a further five or six snowballs on the drum to the left of the cake.

3 Finally, make a pile with the remaining snowballs in the centre of the left half of the top of the cake. Fix them in place with a little royal icing.

> 66 Don't be afraid to improvise and experiment; you never know when you might uncover a great new tool or technique or even start a brand new trend. 99

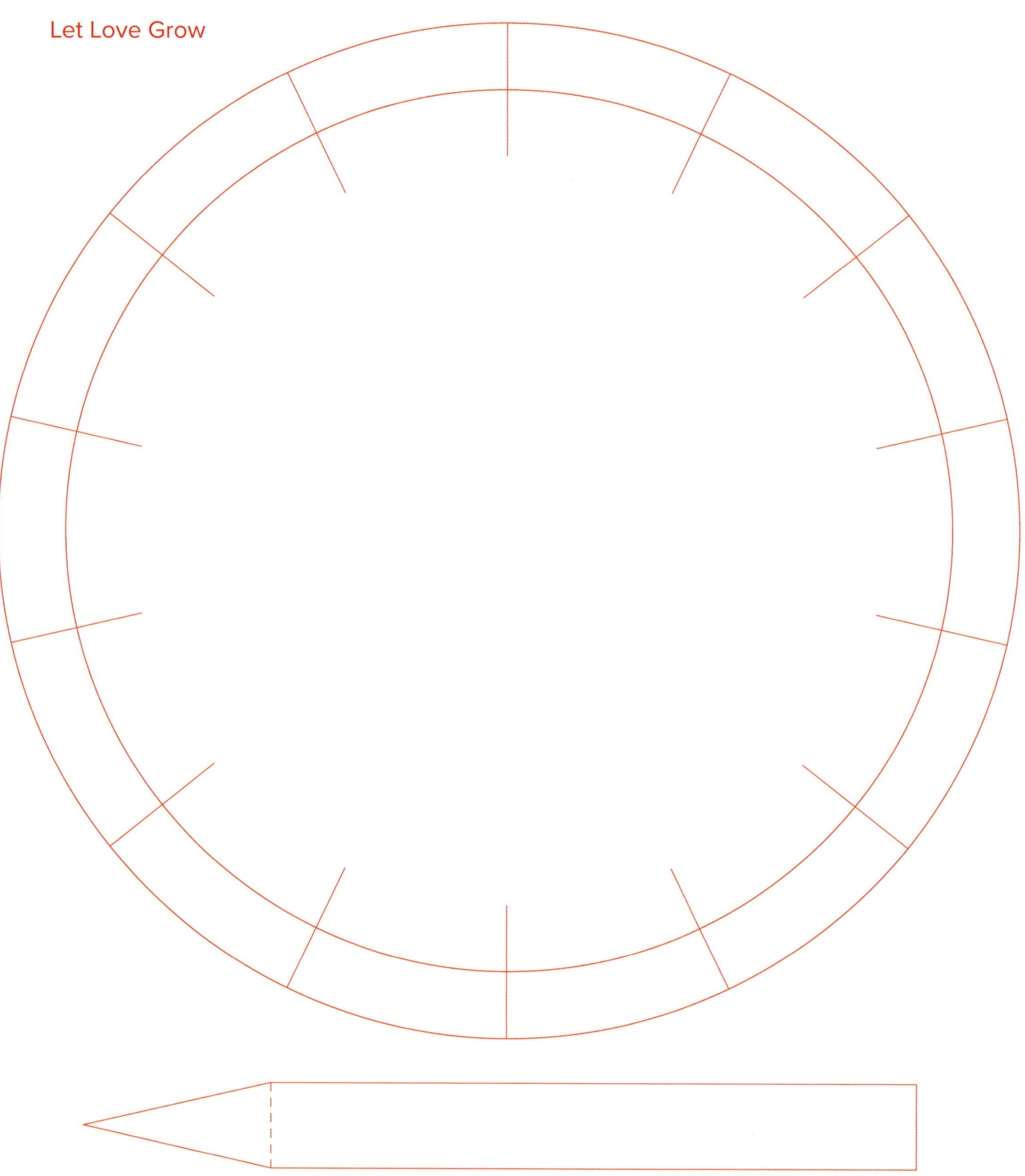

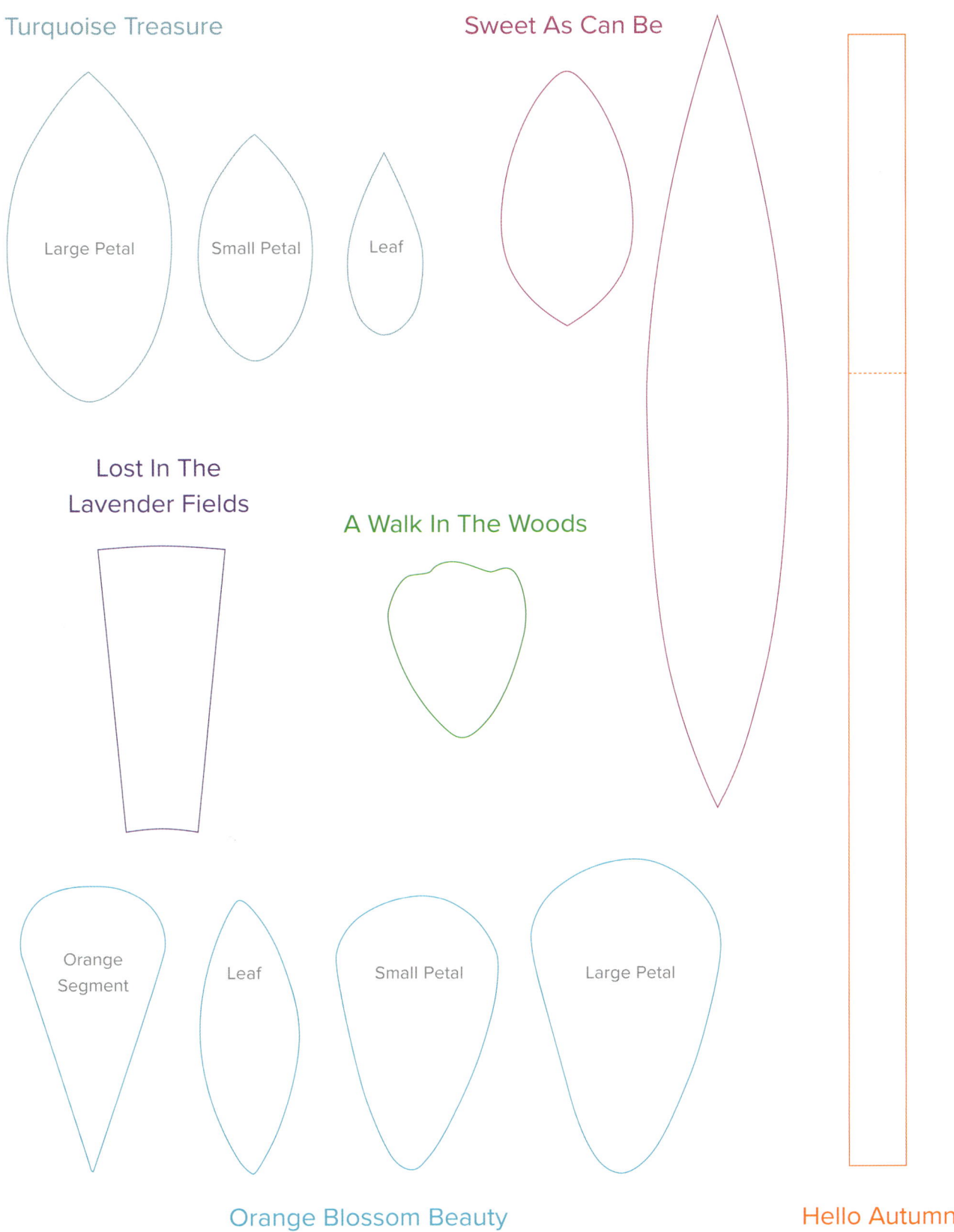

Turquoise Treasure

Large Petal

Small Petal

Leaf

Sweet As Can Be

Lost In The
Lavender Fields

A Walk In The Woods

Orange
Segment

Leaf

Small Petal

Large Petal

Orange Blossom Beauty

Hello Autumn

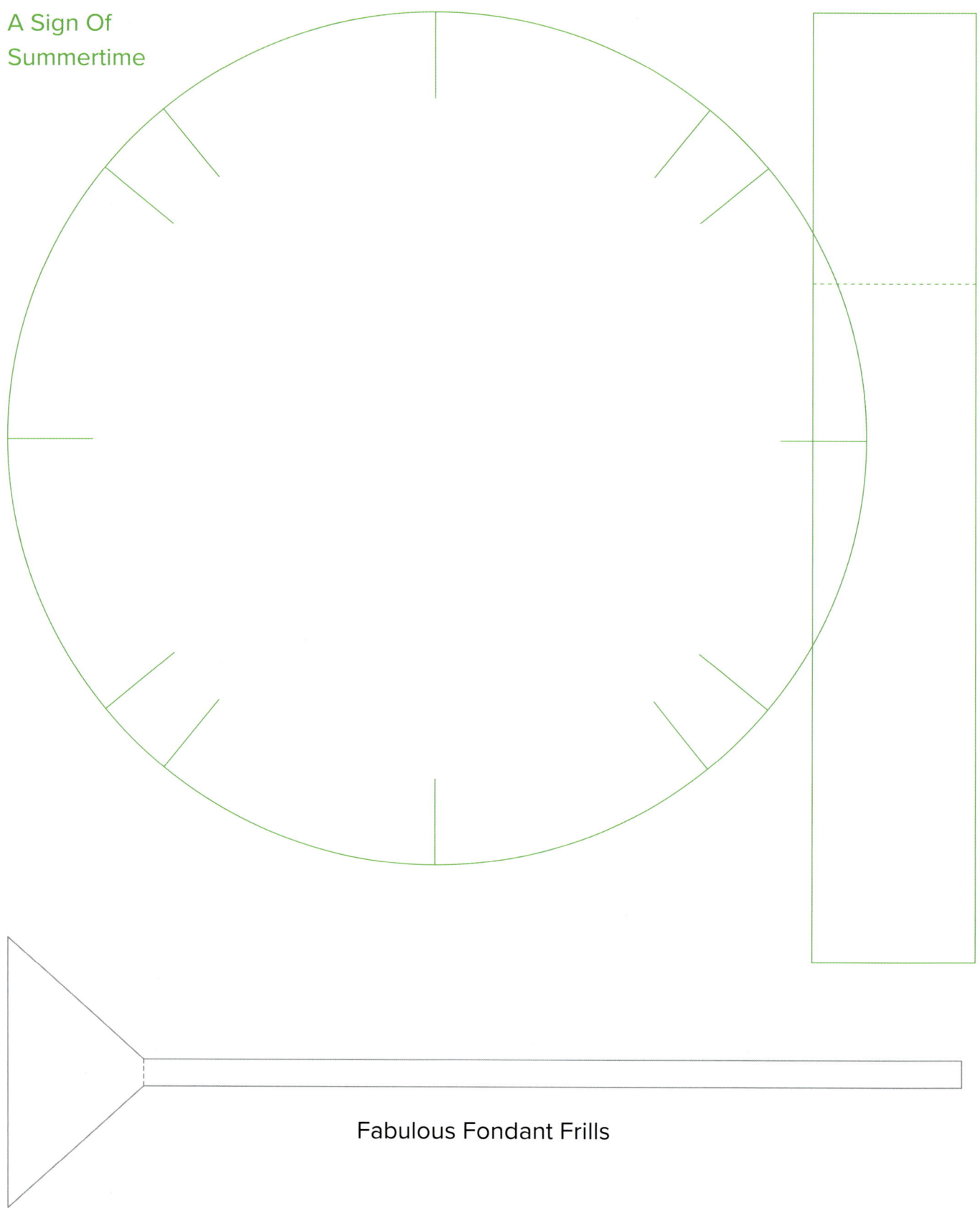

Fabulous Fondant Frills

CONVERSIONS

These conversions are approximate but the difference between an exact and an approximate conversion should not affect your cooking results. Try not to mix metric and imperial measures in one recipe; stick to one system or the other.

Oven Temperatures

Temperatures refer to conventional ovens. For fan-assisted ovens, reduce the temperature by 20°C.

°C	°F	GAS MARK
100	200	low
110	225	¼
120	250	½
140	275	1
150	300	2
160	325	3
180	350	4
190	375	5
200	400	6
220	425	7
230	450	8
250	475	9

Liquid Measurements

METRIC	IMPERIAL	US CUPS
30ml	1fl oz	$\frac{1}{8}$ cup
60ml	2fl oz	$\frac{1}{4}$ cup
90ml	3fl oz	$\frac{3}{8}$ cup
120ml	4fl oz	$\frac{1}{2}$ cup
140ml	5fl oz	$\frac{2}{3}$ cup
170ml	6fl oz	$\frac{3}{4}$ cup
200ml	7fl oz	$\frac{7}{8}$ cup
230ml	8fl oz	1 cup
260ml	9fl oz	$1\frac{1}{8}$ cups
290ml	10fl oz (½ pint)	$1\frac{1}{4}$ cups
500ml	17½fl oz	2 cups
600ml	20fl oz (1 pint)	$2\frac{1}{2}$ cups
1 litre	1¾ pints	4 cups

Dry Measurements

METRIC	IMPERIAL
15g	½oz
30g	1oz
60g	2oz
90g	3oz
115g	4oz (¼lb)
140g	5oz
170g	6oz
200g	7oz
225g	8oz (½lb)
255g	9oz
285g	10oz
310g	11oz
340g	12oz (¾lb)
370g	13oz
400g	14oz
425g	15oz
450g	16oz (1lb)
680g	24oz (1½lb)

Cake/Cake Board Sizes

METRIC	IMPERIAL
10cm	4"
12.5cm	5"
15cm	6"
18cm	7"
20.5cm	8"
23cm	9"
25.5cm	10"
28cm	11"
30.5cm	12"
33cm	13"
35.5cm	14"

SUPPLIERS

You can use this list of suppliers to stock up on all the respective equipment and ingredients you might need for the projects.

UK

Almond Art
www.almondart.com

Cake Cabinet
www.cakecabinet.co.uk

Cake Craft City
www.cakecraftcity.com

Cake Craft World
www.cakecraftworld.co.uk

The Cake Decorating Co.
www.thecakedecoratingcompany.co.uk

Cake Stuff
www.cake-stuff.com

Design A Cake
www.designacake.co.uk

Lakeland
www.lakeland.co.uk

Lawsons
www.lawsonshop.co.uk

Squires Kitchen
www.squires-shop.com

Sugarcrafters UK
www.sugarcrafters.com

Sugar 'n' Spice Cakes Ltd
www.sugarnspicecakes.co.uk

Things4craft
www.things4craft.co.uk

The Vanilla Valley
www.thevanillavalley.co.uk

Zoe's Fancy Cakes
www.zoesfancycakes.co.uk

EUROPE

Bagebixen Denmark
www.bagebixen.dk

Planète Gateau France
www.planete-gateau.com

MeinCupcake, CAKE MART GmbH
Germany
www.meincupcake.de

Sugarworld Greece
www.sugarworld.gr

M&P O Sullivan Ireland
www.mpos.ie

Stuff 4 Cakes Ireland
www.stuff4cakes.ie

The Cake Shop, Ellen's Creative Cakes
The Netherlands
www.ellenscreativecakes.nl

Kocham Lukier Poland
www.kochamlukier.pl

María Lunarillos Spain
www.marialunarillos.com